Making Sense of College Grades

*Why the Grading System
Does Not Work
and What Can Be
Done About It*

Ohmer Milton
Howard R. Pollio
James A. Eison

Foreword by Laura Bornholdt

Making Sense of College Grades

Jossey-Bass Publishers

San Francisco • London • 1986

MAKING SENSE OF COLLEGE GRADES
*Why the Grading System Does Not Work
and What Can Be Done About It*
  by Ohmer Milton, Howard R. Pollio, James A. Eison

Library of Congress Cataloging-in-Publication Data

Milton, Ohmer (1986)
    Making sense of college grades.

    (The Jossey-Bass higher education series)
    Bibliography: p.270
    Includes index.
    1. Grading and marking (Students)   2. College credits
I. Pollio, Howard R.   II. Eison, James A.
III. Series.   IV. Title.
LB2368.M57   1986   378'.16721   85-45910
ISBN 0-87589-687-1

Manufactured in the United States of America

The paper in this book meets the guidelines for
permanence and durability of the Committee on
Production Guidelines for Book Longevity of the
Council on Library Resources.

JACKET DESIGN BY WILLI BAUM

FIRST EDITION

Code 8616

The Jossey-Bass
Higher Education Series

Consulting Editor
Teaching and Learning

Kenneth E. Eble
University of Utah

Foreword

Who needs another book on grades and grading? Who should read it?

The answer is the same for both questions—any person who is in the business of giving grades and many others in related professions. Whatever your personal prejudices and whatever the ethos of your institution (from the professor who knows "I am above all *fair* as a grader" to the cynic who maintains "It is because all grades are meaningless that I give all my students A's," and from the institution that bases its graduation honors on a grade-point-average to the institution that has yet to give any student a grade), you are likely to find something fresh, illuminating, and probably jarring in these pages.

Professors Milton, Pollio, and Eison have found new ways of looking at questions that have plagued college and university faculty ever since the Yale professoriate first gave out grades in 1783 and thereby opened a Pandora's box. Do grades motivate the student to learn or do they discourage or even block student learning? Are grades good predictors and, if so, what do they predict? Is there such a thing as grade inflation or grade deflation? Do grades inspire competition among students or do they resolve it by identifying merit? Does the power of grades inspire cheating or is cheating like original sin—inherent in girl and boy, man and woman? Is grading on the curve a rational procedure or the antithesis of reason? Does any grading system have the potential of recognizing creativity?

With the possible exception of a fringe group of radicals (usually not persons of great influence on their campuses), most academics ultimately accept the academic convention that grades are meaningful because they see no practical alternative. The prospect of losing time and breaking lances in an old conflict attracts few comers. ("You can't win 'em all" is a sentiment not limited to students.) But Milton, Pollio, and Eison direct our attention to the fact that the academy in its grading system has developed conventions that often require individuals and institutions to suppress contradictory evidence and live with inconsistencies. The authors hit a group blind spot; they expose the myth of perfect objectivity.

One cannot dispute the fact that in certain situations grades have enormous significance for individuals. Grades can and do open or close gates of opportunity in American higher education and thereby determine entry to the most prized careers. Most faculty have evidence that grades inspire some students to think well of themselves (the authors gently remind us that most professors were successful "grade winners"), while they convince other students to lower their goals. The *Bakke* and *DeFunis* cases serve to remind us of the serious uses that are made of grades as well as of the challenge to them. Even as this book goes to press, consideration is being given to requiring "all passing grades" of every student receiving federal support. *Making Sense of College Grades* shows in sharp relief the complexities, the costs and risks, as well as the irrationalities of interpretations and applications of the American grading system.

After studying institutional histories, reviewing previous research, and analyzing an imaginative questionnaire distributed to a national sample of all the constituencies having an interest in grades (students, teachers, parents, and corporate recruiters), the authors reach clear and salient conclusions. The caveats they leave for the reader are these: Grades are relative to contexts, never independent of them. To reify grades and assume a cross-situational stability is to abuse both the student and the evaluative meaning of the procedure. Grades ought to refer more to the educational process and less to evaluative use by society.

The reader may be irritated or cheered by this book, but it will be hard to read it and not become aware of inadequacies in the preconceptions about grading that one held when first picking up *Making Sense of College Grades.*

Chicago, Illinois   Laura Bornholdt
October 10, 1985   *Special Assistant to the President*
                                              University of Chicago

Preface

Grades and many of the practices associated with them enjoy amazingly high status in most colleges and universities and throughout society; once a grade has been bestowed, it tends to be sacrosanct. The symbols A B C D F, and variations thereof, have become the primary focus of many students, faculty, and parents. And students should focus on grades, because often their professional and personal advancement depends solely on the grade-point-average number into which these letter symbols are cast. For these students, learning is distorted as grades become more crucial than learning itself; this state of affairs may characterize society's attitude, even if unwittingly.

The purpose of this book is to examine, in a scholarly fashion, what grades mean both for the society in which they are given and for the students to whom they are given. It is not a how-to book, nor does it represent one more attempt to shore up the great grade edifice sitting Kaaba-like at the center of higher education. Rather it seeks to examine some implications of the fact that grades are unidimensional symbols into which complex and multidimensional judgments are compressed and no one, least of all the college professor, appears willing to unpack the assumptions underlying the seemingly innocent letters running from A through F.

Above all, this book is based on our conviction that grades —especially in their relationship to classroom tests—are central to student learning because they determine very explicitly how and what students learn. It is based on our contention that grades are viewed by most people as peripheral to student learning and that the efforts to improve grading systems tend to be directed toward the rank-ordering and not the teaching and learning possibilities inherent in course tests and grades. Our position—the combined result of many years of observing and listening to students and colleagues, of carefully studying both the professional and general literature on teaching and grading, and of experimenting in our own classes with various testing and grading schemes—represents close to seventy-five years of experience in trying to help students learn. Our suggestions are not offered lightly.

In talks around the country, we have found it difficult to communicate the urgency of our convictions largely because most people have a mental block against the notion that grades have anything to do with learning per se. The more usual notion is that grades are just a fact of college life and if they have anything to do with the classroom it is principally to help decide who is the "best" student. Occasionally, grades may be viewed as incentives to studying or even as preparation for the competitive nature of "real" life. (We wonder, is higher education not real life?)

One major reason for the mental block against examining grades is that we do not understand the methods by which grades are given; this blindness is compounded because most of us think we do understand. A second reason for the block is the chasm of confusion between the evaluation of learning (have students learned those things they should have?) and the assignment of rank-ordering symbols for a national personnel selection enterprise. A third reason stems from the fact that grades are absorbed uncritically into all of our psyches during the school years, and millions of us have had sixteen or more years of such numbing exposure. Thus, a kind of set toward unexamined acceptance of grades perpetuates our unthinking use of them and encourages unwarranted meanings to be attributed to them.

We hope the thicket of dogma and the unexamined acceptance of grades as "just a fact of life" will be undercut by our presentation of several perspectives, including a historical one, a review of pertinent empirical and theoretical research, an analysis of the first national survey of attitudes toward grades, and an original set of observations and experiments regarding the various

effects exerted by grades on college students and their performance in the classroom.

The historical review, interesting in its own right and largely unassimilated by the contemporary professoriate, provides a
broad context within which to view what has been learned in some
200 years about what grades can and cannot do for student learning, motivation, and evaluation. We assembled considerable experimental research evidence that was scattered throughout a vast
literature and translated its somewhat specialized language into
more ordinary English. The National Grade Survey of faculty,
students, parents, and business people documents the magnitude
of many of the issues connected to grades and suggests some of
the needed changes in grading practices. Several questions in the
national survey have never before been asked formally; some are
common to the four groups and thus provide unique opportunities for cross-group comparisons. Finally, we report a series of
studies suggested by our concerns about the relationship of grades
to classroom listening and learning. We have made extensive use
of an intuitively meaningful, and experimentally measurable, distinction between grade orientations and learning orientations in
current American college students.

The importance of this book is now paramount because for
the first time in the history of the United States serious attention is
being given to improving *learning* by college and university students. This attention is illustrated by several recently released national reports; surely more are to come. While most of their
recommendations are sound and should be implemented, grades
and course tests have received scant mention. These are fundamental omissions. Although said in a different context, the words
of President Abraham Lincoln to Congress come to mind: "The
dogmas of the quiet past are inadequate to the stormy present. . . .
As our case is new, we must think anew, act anew."

There are two audiences for this book—those who give
grades and those who use them in making decisions about the lives
of college students and graduates. These audiences include undergraduate faculty, graduate and professional school faculty,
leaders in business and industry, parents, and financial aid policy
makers in government and philanthropic foundations. An indirect

audience, of course, is all of us who are interested in colleges and universities and the ways in which they promote student learning. We hope that all readers, especially those who made top grades as students, will employ a rigorous but nondefensive open-mindedness to these emotional matters.

Chapter One provides information about grades and grading practices throughout the history of this country; it is interesting and amusing and reveals that history does repeat itself. The chapter gives an overview of the literature on such continuing issues as grades and future achievement, GPAs, influences of grades on students, and deficiencies of classroom tests. Chapter Two extends the opening chapter by detailing the beginning of a theoretical analysis of factors and forces entering into a proper interpretation of the meaning of college grades. These factors include the socio-historical era, academic discipline, educational institution, instructor policies and idiosyncrasies, and student characteristics and values. Chapter Two is designed to assist grade givers—that is, faculty members—in becoming more aware of grade vagaries than many now are; it should assist grade receivers and users in becoming more aware of oft-hidden forces that play a significant role in determining grade meanings.

Chapter Three introduces the results of the National Grade Survey—an exploration of the attiudes toward grades of over six thousand people: faculty, students, parents, and business representatives. The results reveal a number of striking similarities in attitudes among the four groups as well as some striking discrepancies. This survey evolved from our ever-increasing concern about grades and their influences on the teaching/learning endeavor. On the one hand, we were struck by the extent to which grades dominated the pursuit of learning by many of our students and on the other, we were struck by the self-satisfied attitudes of faculty toward grades and their teaching. Parental reactions to good and bad grades earned by their offspring are most interesting. All groups agree on the importance of emphasizing the chief purpose of grades—to let students know how much and how well they have learned, not simply how well they have prepared for a test (sometimes at the expense of learning). The presentation of results from the national survey continues in Chapter Four, with emphasis on the attitudes of faculty and business people. There are several marked differences between these two groups, some surprises, and in a few instances, similarities in attitudes and beliefs. Some of the results are significant for individuals concerned with the personnel selection function of grades—both those individuals who favor and those who oppose such usage. Chapter Five concludes the National Grade Survey results; it focuses on responses of students and their *own* parents. This part of the survey is unique; it studies the origins of attitudes and beliefs about grades across three generations: students, their parents, and their parents' parents.

Chapter Six describes the development of a pencil-and-paper instrument designed to identify grade and learning orientations of college students. Research evidence is cited documenting important psychological differences between the grade-oriented (GO) and learning-oriented (LO) students. Some of these findings have special significance for business and industry. The title of Chapter Seven, "What Grade- and Learning-Oriented Students Think About and Do in College Classes," indicates its content; there are sometimes surprising differences between students' apparent attentiveness and what they report they are thinking about. The methodology designed to assess student awareness during the college lecture represents another novel feature of the book; it is included because lecturing is a predominant method of instruction and because grades and grading must be viewed within the broader context of listening/learning/teaching.

Chapter Eight offers research evidence supporting the use of Adaptation Level Theory in demonstrating that the meaning of a given grade is always a context-dependent phenomenon. College grades are the outcomes of judgments, and Adaptation Level Theory provides a rigorous quantitative procedure for specifying the factors that influence these judgments. It is clear from the use of this approach that the same grade is valued differently by different students. Many of the implications here are of profound importance for all organizations that provide financial aid to students.

Chapter Nine contains several recommendations for improving the grading game toward the ultimate goal of improving the quality of learning. Some of these recommendations are well-known but mental blocks and institutional inertia have blunted their use. Other recommendations may be controversial but are offered as ways of stirring serious and informed debate: "As our case is new, we must think anew, act anew." This chapter is directed, in the main, to those critical souls who advance knowledge in their disciplines; we hope they can direct themselves to the task of furthering the scope and effectiveness of learning by instituting proper changes in how grades are given, understood, and used.

The Appendixes contain a copy of the National Grade Survey questionnaire and complete data from respondents. They also contain some of the original research materials developed for use in connection with data and analyses presented in Chapter Seven.

We are grateful to the Lilly Endowment, Inc., and Learning Research Center (W. Lee Humphreys, director) of the University of Tennessee, Knoxville, for financial support during the National Grade Survey and subsequent studies. We deeply appreciate the time and energies of close to seven thousand people, many of whom completed the national survey questionnaires and some of whom served as subjects in the various experiments. To all of these individuals and our research assistants and associates (most especially our computer programmer, M. Donald Broach) we offer our sincere thanks.

Knoxville, Tennessee   Ohmer Milton
January 1986   Howard R. Pollio
                                                               James A. Eison

Contents

Contents

The Authors

Ohmer Milton is professor emeritus of psychology at the University of Tennessee, Knoxville, where he spent his entire academic career and helped establish the Learning Research Center, of which he was the first director. Milton received his A.B. degree from Berea College (1940), his M.A. degree from the University of Kentucky (1941), and his Ph.D. degree in psychology from the University of Michigan (1950). He continues to serve as a member of the editorial board of the *Journal of Higher Education,* as editorial advisor to the *National Forum,* and as consulting editor to the journal *College Teaching.*

Earlier in his career, Milton was executive secretary of the Tennessee Board of Examiners in Psychology and helped form the American Association of State Psychology Boards, where he served in several capacities for some fifteen years. He has published numerous journal articles, several chapters in books, and lectured at over 100 colleges and universities. His books include *Alternatives to the Traditional* (Jossey-Bass, 1972), *Behavior Disorders: Perspectives and Trends* (edited with Robert Wahler; J. B. Lippincott), and *On College Teaching* (Jossey-Bass, 1978).

Milton received a travel and study grant from the Ford Foundation in 1974–1975 (and investigated classroom tests) and the Distinguished Contribution to Education in Psychology Award from the American Psychological Foundation in 1974.

Howard R. Pollio is currently distinguished service professor in psychology at the University of Tennessee, Knoxville; he also holds a continuing appointment as senior research fellow in the university's Learning Research Center. He received his B.A. and M.A. degrees from Brooklyn College (1957, 1959) and his Ph.D. degree in psychology from the University of Michigan (1962). He has taught, conducted research, and studied at the University of London (1968), the University of Guelph (1972), and Cambridge University (1978). The majority of his career has been spent at the University of Tennessee, Knoxville.

Pollio has written on diverse issues such as the role of humor in social life, grades and grading, metaphor and metaphoric thinking in the arts and sciences, and the philosophical underpinnings of contemporary psychology, with special emphasis on the philosopher Merleau-Ponty. Pollio has published over seventy articles and book chapters encompassing these concerns and is the author or coauthor of five books, including *Behavior and Existence* (Brooks/Cole, 1982), *Psychology and the Poetics of Growth* (Lawrence Erlbaum, 1977), and *Psychology of Symbolic Activity* (Addison-Wesley, 1974).

Pollio is president of the Southeastern Psychological Association and a Phi Beta Kappa National Lecturer; he is the founding editor of *Metaphor and Symbolic Activity: A Quarterly Journal* and serves on the editorial boards of three other journals.

James A. Eison earned a B.A degree from the State University of New York, College at New Paltz (1972) and his Ph.D. degree in psychology from the University of Tennessee, Knoxville (1979). From 1976 to 1985, he taught at Roane State Community College and in 1985 became the founding director for the Center for Teaching and Learning at Southeast Missouri State University.

Eison received the Outstanding Teacher for 1978 to 1979 award given by the Roane State Community College Chapter of Gamma Beta Phi and won the 1980 Teaching Award for Community/Junior College Teachers of Psychology presented by Division Two of the American Psychological Association. He has served as a member of the American Psychological Association's Committee on Undergraduate Education and is currently a consulting editor for the journal *Teaching of Psychology*. In 1983 he established *NETWORK: The Newsletter for Teachers of Psychology at Two-Year Colleges*, published by the American Psychological Association. Eison developed the LOGO II Scale discussed in this volume.

Making Sense of College Grades

*Why the Grading System
Does Not Work
and What Can Be
Done About It*

Grades and Grading: A Tradition of Inconstant Standards

George Bernard Shaw once declared: "There is no harder scientific fact in the world than the fact that belief can be produced in practically unlimited quantity and intensity, without observation or reasoning, and even in defiance of both by the simple desire to believe." And so it is with the auras attached to those ubiquitous educational symbols A, B, C, D, and F. In an educated world, there are no better examples of beliefs that have been produced "without observation or reasoning" than those sustaining an abiding faith in the virtues and meaningfulness of college grades. This assertion will be documented by several lines of evidence; suffice it to say at this point that the academic achievement of many college students is distorted because of false beliefs about grades held by them and by their elders. Serious errors in certain public policies about higher education are made at both state and federal levels by undue reliance on the sanctity of grades. Legislation actually was introduced in 1982 to make student loans contingent on student grade-point-average (GPA). Grades are indeed serious business.

Conservatively, some 12 million students attend colleges and universities annually. If each student is enrolled in three courses, at the end of each term 36 million grades are assigned by faculty and then recorded for posterity. During an academic year, between 72 million and 108 million final marks will be dispensed. There is no way of calculating the numbers of grades that have been offered to an unsuspecting public since the origin of colleges

1

and universities in this country. By now untold millions of members of this public have had these mysterious symbols attached to their efforts; others have used these symbols to make conclusive decisions about those who hold these grades, whether these decisions were for admitting them to graduate school or for allowing them to enter into the world of business and commerce.

At present, society is quite occupied with grades, not because of an interest in education per se but rather because of a tendency to take a hard-nosed approach to what might collectively be termed the social welfare activities of the society. Within the context of higher education, this tendency frequently makes college grades or college grade-point-averages the single quantitative cipher on which the evaluating accountants base their decisions. Now, evaluation, quantification, and hard data are all appropriate social and research tools; what is not so appropriate is if significant qualitative data are overlooked in the zeal for quantification, or if quantitative metrics turn out to be flawed conceptually, empirically, or both. The evaluation of higher education, unfortunately, is too often undertaken in a mean-spirited way, and if we do not periodically examine the assumptions and the metrics by which we evaluate, then we have failed to protect ourselves from unwarranted attack and we have also failed our commitment to the very scholarship we espouse in our classrooms. Grades should be subject to vigorous and continuing scrutiny, not only because of their indiscriminate use by those outside the academy but, more significant, because of their uncritical use by those of us within it.

When we examine, even in a relatively abridged way, the history of grades in American higher education, certain facts stand out. Perhaps the most obvious of these facts is that superficial and cyclic alterations in grading practices surface every few years. When we examined the nature and content of these changes—and the arguments offered by faculty in support of them—we were a bit startled, and periodically amused, by many of the pronouncements made by some of our historical colleagues. When it comes to these tools of their trade, faculties of today often are as ahistorical as the ahistorical students they are so wont to criticize. The following condensed foray into the history of grades and grading practices will set the stage for this book.

College Grading Practices Prior to 1900

The grading practices and procedures of five early schools —Yale, Harvard, Mount Holyoke, William and Mary, and Michigan—have been reported in a little book by Smallwood (1935). Smallwood examined the original academic records of each of these institutions for all their years until 1900; we have extracted selectively from this work. It is instructive to note that knowledge about grading concepts has not advanced at all over the years, in marked contrast to the way knowledge in the various scholarly diciplines has advanced bit by bit throughout history.

Grades came into being in this country at Yale in 1783 and took the form of four descriptive adjectives: Optime, Second Optime, Inferiores, and Pejores. These categories were modifications of a much earlier English system of Rigorisi, Transibiles, and Gratiosi (or Honor Men, Pass Men, and Charity Passes) and a fourth—Unmentionables. Shortly after 1800, marking was on a scale of 4; 2 was average. In 1813 the lowest student average was 1.3 and the highest was 3.7. Note that here are the first grade-point-averages—those haloed statistics that continue to thrive.

A special rule was created for calculating the average of a student who had no previous standing for a term or more: "Multiply each term or examination average by the usual multiplier (3 or 4), and divide the sum of the products by the sum of the multipliers. To obtain the average for the whole College course: Multiply each annual average by the divisor used in obtaining it, and divide the sum of the products by the sum of the multipliers" (Smallwood, 1935, p. 67). No illustrations or interpretations of the derived averages were given. Too bad; they might have provided useful guidance for today. Currently GPAs are surely more precise and significant because they are calculated routinely to two decimal places; with computers, there is no telling how far they will go.

The University of Michigan also used descriptive terms when it was founded in 1838, and William and Mary sent reports such as the following to parents shortly after 1800:

The Society took into consideration the situation of different Classes, and the demeanors and improvement of each of the Students during the Course which has just terminated, Whereupon Resolved that a Communication to the following effect be transmitted to the Parent or Guardian of every young man at the Institution. [The names of students were listed in each category.]

No. 1. The first in their respective classes, orderly and attentive and have made the most flattering improvement.

No. 2. Orderly, correct and attentive and their improvement has been respectable.

No. 3. They have made very little improvement and as we apprehend from want of Diligence.

No. 4. They have learnt little or nothing and we believe on account of escapaid and Idleness [Smallwood, p. 44].

Harvard began using a 20-point scale in 1830. For a brief period Yale used a 9-point scale, but returned to a 4-point scale in 1832; that scale was utilized for fifty years. As early as 1837, mathematics and philosophy professors at Harvard marked on the basis of 100 points and grouped them into the following five categories: 100, 75 to 99, 51 to 75, 26 to 50, and 26 and below. This seems to be the origin of the current five groupings that were later to be labeled A, B, C, D, and F.

There was a great deal of criticism of numerical scales, and in 1850 the University of Michigan adopted a Pass/Fail system; a plus (+) sign, in fact, was the only mark utilized. While this may have been the first academic use of Pass/Fail, the scheme originated around 1200 B.C. on the shores of the River Jordan. A fugitive Ephramite, trying to cross one of the fords, was challenged by a Gileadite soldier with one test question: "Are you an Ephramite?" When the reply was "No," he was ordered to say "shibboleth." If the enemy said "sibboleth" the grade was Fail—conclusively (Judges 12: 5–6).

By 1860 Michigan had modified its scheme and added

"conditioned." By 1864 the freshman class was marked on a scale of 100; apparently 50 was the minimum mark for +. By 1867, P appeared along with an occasional C (conditioned) or A (absent). By 1866 Yale required an average of 2.30 (on a scale of 4) for graduation; twenty-four years earlier it had been 2.00. (This is called "raising standards" and is a never-ending faculty sport—with due disregard for the composition and magnitude of the numbers.) From 1850 to around 1900, several scales were devised and altered. There were six divisions at Harvard in 1877 and three in 1895— Passed with Distinction, Passed, Failed, *and* modifications via + and − signs.

Near the end of the nineteenth century, many faculty members apparently marked first on a scale of 100 and then converted numerical scores to letter symbols. The first record of a grade of B was at Harvard in 1883. Variations in cut-off scores for failure at different schools look like football scores presented on the evening news.

> Mount Holyoke—75
> Michigan—50
> Harvard—26

We assume more uniform standards today, although actual differences from school to school may be just as significant if not as immediately apparent. (See Chapter Two.)

The following observations, made at Harvard around 100 years ago during faculty discussions about the symbols A B C D F, are remarkably similar in tone and content to those one can hear on any campus today: "Some frankly admitted that it was impossible to get within 5 or 10 percent of absolute exactness; others were so delicately constituted that they could distinguish between fractions of one percent. One instructor . . . sometimes assigned marks *less than zero*" (italics in the original, Smallwood, p. 53). Almost from the beginning, the primary purpose of marks or grades has been that of *ranking* college students; grades as motivators or as devices to promote learning were mentioned only once for the period reviewed. The early uses of ranks included determining class positions and honors, commencement parts, special awards, and so on. (By contrast, the present primary use of grades is for personnel selection for graduate and professional schools and for business and industry—see Chapter Three.) More about selection purposes later on.

As is true today, little was recorded about the composition of a given grade or about the relation of tests to grades and to learning. Around 1700 there were two types of exams: disputations and declamations. Some of the early colleges maintained external examining committees; Dartmouth and the University of Georgia used them in the early 1800s and the examining sessions were open to the public. President Charles William Eliot declared in his inaugural address at Harvard: "It would be a great gain if all subsequent college examinations could be as impartially conducted by competent examiners brought from without the college. . . . The change in the manner of earning the University degrees ought, by right, to have brought into being an examining body distinct from the teaching body" (Smallwood, p. 22). This suggestion may have stimulated creation of the external examiner program at Swarthmore around 1920 and inspired President Robert Hutchins to institute separation of teaching and testing at the University of Chicago in the early 1930s. (The program was abolished some twenty-five years later.)

By the late 1800s there were more and more written examinations—these were introduced at Yale in 1830—each of which was prepared by the course instructor. Not long after written tests were introduced, faculties became upset about students cramming and blamed it on the tests. There was also some concern about examinations causing loss of valuable teaching time. (Sound familiar? We will return to tests, too.)

Throughout the period reviewed, a grade was assigned not only on the basis of scholarship or academic achievement, but it also included delinquency demerits. In 1870 Harvard issued a firm statement against the practice: "Voted, that the deductions from the scale of scholarship for absence, tardiness and misconduct, as well as those which accompany the various admonitions shall be discontinued; but the numbers representing such deductions and other similar numerical marks of censure, which Faculty may establish shall be regularly entered in the Dean's office, and shall form a separate scale of demerit" (Smallwood, p. 74). Was anyone listening to this declaration that conduct and scholarship cannot logically be judged together? Apparently not, because today, over 100 years later, on most campuses grades are altered for such conduct as cutting classes, being late with papers, cheating, and so on. And the composition of the modified grade is not explained on a student's transcript: An A is an A is an A.

Recent Practices in College Grading

By the turn of the century the A-B-C-D-F scheme was gaining acceptance, and shortly thereafter grading on the curve came into being. According to Cureton (1971), a most influential figure in this development was Max Meyer (1908) of the University of Missouri. A professor at the University of Missouri had failed an entire class and the governing board of the institution overruled him; this set Meyer to investigating grading practices, which he found to be in complete disarray throughout the school. There was no uniformity; students who were eager to win honors, for example, were advised openly to elect their work under certain instructors and to avoid others. Meyer was careful to point out that conditions were probably as bad elsewhere but had not been investigated. He declared: "Education is just beginning to realize that it is not merely an art, but an applied science" (p. 246).

Basing his arguments on certain assumptions of probability theory, Meyer proposed that students in the top 3 percent should be ranked excellent, the next 22 percent labeled superior, the middle 50 percent judged medium, the next 22 percent designated inferior, and the bottom 3 percent labeled failures. These labels went into official records as A through F respectively.

Not long after Meyer's paper appeared in *Science* (prestigious then as now), Starch and Elliott (1912, 1913a, 1913b) published their three classic papers. These investigators demonstrated that the marking of test papers in English, mathematics, and history tended to be highly variable in the use of the 100-point scale. A given paper was marked differently by two different teachers and even differently by the same teacher on separate occasions. A similar study was conducted in England a few years later with history, Latin, French, English, and chemistry examinations; results were essentially the same (Hartog and Rhodes, 1935). Even today people tend to get upset about this finding, particularly in the field of mathematics because "mathematics is so exact." There is at least one very simple explanation. One teacher demands accuracy and pays little attention to method of solution; another teacher is concerned about method and not accuracy. Scores on the papers will differ. Letter grades will differ and so, too, will evaluations of the student's knowledge of mathematics.

Seemingly, grading on the curve caught on during the period of World War I—we can only speculate as to why. Meyer's paper is couched in scientific and mathematical terms; these words were probably more impressive then than now, and such trappings must have been most appealing in contrast to the blatant biases of teachers that Starch and Elliott and others had exposed. Furthermore, an era of "objectivity" in testing began around 1915 (multiple-choice, true/false); it must have been comforting to know that this testing could be augmented by "scientific" grading.

All sorts of curve arrangements for grading have been utilized by individual faculty members in the intervening years. Yet in a sample of 400 schools by the American College Testing Program (1966) during the mid-sixties, distributions of final course grades were found to be essentially the same throughout the range of institutions, from those admitting all applicants to those admitting only top students. Some twenty years later, a smaller but comparable survey (Chickering, 1983) of five schools revealed highly similar grade distributions despite marked differences in their reported admission policies. Effects such as these have been found within a given course. For example: "In one university, the decision was made to section engineering students in calculus on the basis of previous grades. One professor, not knowing this, was assigned a group of students in integral calculus who had received A's in all preceeding mathematics courses. . . . On the first examination, he ended up with the usual distribution of grades from A to F. The reaction of the students forced him to reconsider. . . . The grades at the end of the term showed 40 percent A's, 50 percent B's, and 10 percent C's. Knowing the caliber of his students, the professor still could not bring himself to report a distribution of grades in which almost every student would be given an A" (Dressel, 1961, p. 244).

As Quann (1984) recently pointed out from the perspective of several national surveys, the five-letter grading system prevailed through the first half of this century; it is currently used in slightly over 90 percent of colleges and universities. (That percentage includes schools that have letters with pluses and minuses, letters with pluses only, and letters with minuses only.) Perhaps the grading front was relatively quiet over the period from 1910 to 1960 because colleges and universities were preoccupied with other matters. From 1930 to at least 1941—the Depression years— the issue was money; from 1948 to around 1965, ever-expanding enrollments were the concern.

The next flurry of concern about grading occurred in the mid-sixties following the student upheavals at the University of California, Berkeley, and elsewhere; Pass/Fail (P/F) schemes were introduced and these then spread. These alternative systems, which took many forms, such as Pass/No Credit (P/NC), were designed to encourage students to take courses that would broaden their views without jeopardizing their GPAs; for example, an art major might take a course in physics or a physics major might take a course in art.

One of the most intriguing developments in Pass/Fail grading occurred at the California Institute of Technology (Strong, 1967) where all freshman courses were graded on a P/F basis. During the first year of the policy the faculty was elated because learning improved in many ways; faculty members made such comments as "They're reading books again." In each successive freshman class, however, the learning improvements declined. It was concluded finally that benefits of the Pass/Fail system accrued more from the act of change than from the system.

A survey (Hewitt, 1967) of twenty-two selected colleges and universities revealed that eight of these schools had a P/F alternative for certain courses. In all eight of the schools a grade of Pass did not affect the student's GPA; in four of them, a grade of F was entered and thus served to lower the overall GPA. Later studies of Pass/Fail grading indicated that only a small percentage of students availed themselves of this alternative and that their work in such courses often was slighted to provide more time for coursework in traditionally graded classes. Quann (1984) insists, "Interest in Pass/Fail and similar grading options appears to be waning, and institutions increasingly place restrictions on use of the non-traditional grading options" (p. 25).

One of the latest tinkering fads was the scheme called "academic forgiveness" or "academic bankruptcy." This scheme was designed to allow students to be considered for readmission by holding in abeyance a portion of the earlier academic record; its main function was to assist students who were immature when they were freshmen (Quann, 1984). Apparently this system has not fared too well, for it is seldom mentioned; one of our respondents in the national survey (Chapters Three, Four, and Five) stated: "Recently I applied for law school. Although I had a LSAT score in the upper 1 percent, admission was denied on the basis of grades earned fifteen to twenty years ago in undergraduate school —even though I have had a successful career in a law-related business."

A recent episode of faculty grade tinkering occurred at the University of Washington (Lunneborg, 1977). The customary symbol system, A through F, was abandoned and each faculty member had three choices: (1) whole numbers instead of letters— 4 = A, 3 = B, and so forth; (2) numbers to one decimal place for the finer delineations of pluses and minuses—3.7 = A−, 2.3 = C+; and (3) the full range of tenths—3.9, 3.8, and so on. A survey of faculty revealed that 70 percent adopted the decimal system (a distinction was not made in the report for number 2 and number 3 separately). The number of faculty hours wasted in discussing and creating these changes is incalculable. Such illusions of precision have nothing to do with student learning and seem best described as exercises in futility designed to distract faculty from their central task—promoting learning.

Grading schemes also vary according to faculty orientation toward grades as well as according to the institutions attended by the student receiving the grade. Geisinger, Wilson, and Naumann (1980), for example, compared faculty orientation toward three grading procedures in three different types of institutions; in addition, faculty members were asked to give an overall evaluation of the usefulness and value of grading. The university faculty was found to favor norm-referenced grading involving the normal distribution, "the curve," more than any of the other groups studied. Community college faculty strongly espoused a self-referenced perspective. While not supporting one particular grading scheme more strongly than another, four-year college faculty were least favorable overall about grading. The evidence that faculty hold widely different views about the basis for assigning grades and that significant inter-institutional differences exist—while not surprising—is important, for it illuminates the impossibility of interpreting the meaning of a given grade across types of institutions.

In one of our early investigations along this line (Milton, 1972), similar findings were obtained. Several experienced faculty were asked: "Imagine that an intelligent well-informed adult (not connected with higher education) asks you: 'Student X received a B in your course. What does that B mean?' " Sixteen of twenty-two respondents gave straightforward replies—each assigned a basic meaning to the grade; none equivocated. Later in the questionnaire the same faculty members were asked: "Imagine that your son or daughter is in college. A final grade of C is received in a very important course. How do you interpret this grade to yourself; that is, what does it tell you about your child?" Only three of the twenty-two respondents said the grade meant "average"; the remaining nineteen were uncertain, equivocated, or wanted to know specific details about the grade. Obviously grades mean different things depending on whether they are given to your child or to someone else's; why do so many people—especially faculty—attribute such definite meanings to a given symbol?

Understanding grades is further confounded by the fact that in the behemoth universities, graduate teaching assistants (GTAs) devise classroom tests and assign grades—in many instances with little or no supervision. In 1967 Koen and Ericksen sent questionnaires to departmental and administrative officers in forty-four universities that collectively supplied approximately 90 percent of the Ph.D. degrees; on-site interviews were conducted at twenty of the schools. Many of the academic departments were among the most highly rated in the nation. Results indicated that GTAs constructed course tests in some one third of the departments and assigned final grades in almost one half. Training or supervision of the GTAs seemed to be perfunctory or nonexistent in most of the schools.

A similar survey of GTAs who had primary responsibility for teaching a section or sections of a course was conducted at the University of Tennessee, Knoxville Campus (Learning Research Center, 1969). Five questions dealt with testing and grading. Ninety-one percent of the respondents reported that they prepared test questions, 99 percent stated that they scored test papers, and 91 percent indicated that they assigned final grades. Eighty-four percent executed all three of those functions. Again, training and guidance were minimal or nonexistent. We have no reason to believe that there have been any appreciable alterations in these GTA activities over the years.

Yet there is only occasional complaining about grades being sacred cows. As one example, Hargadon (1984) lamented, "It never ceases to amaze me that grades and grading systems, characterized as they are by incomparability from school to school, department by department, course to course, and teacher to teacher, generate so little heat and controversy, especially when compared to that which surrounds the use of national standardized examinations" (p. 75). Obviously, Hargadon is interested in tests as well as grades; his query is a good one and is largely unanswered.

Just as grades tend to be determined idiosyncratically by individual faculty members, the GPA is derived idiosyncratically by institutions. In one survey of GPA computation practices from a sample of 448 public and private two- and four-year institutions in the fifty states and the District of Columbia (Collins and Nickel, 1975), great variations were found: For 266 (57 percent) of the schools, when a course is repeated only the last grade is used; in 246 (55 percent) of them, only grades in courses taken in the school doing the computing are used; and in 159 (31 percent), grades from all sources are included. Similar results were found in a more recent survey of grading practices (Quann, 1984)—more about this in Chapter Two.

Most grade interpreters assume the GPA has a definite and clear meaning; these survey results as well as many others indicate this assumption is false. Another interpretative difficulty is the ofttimes complete disregard of grade patterns. The student who receives all C's in many different courses is quite different from the one who makes an equal number of A's and F's; the student who receives A's and B's during the freshman and sophomore years and C's and D's during the junior and senior years is different from the student who receives C's and D's during the first two years and A's and B's during the last two, even though all of our hypothetical students will have the same overall GPA. Finally, the student who takes primarily the traditionally "hard" courses and earns a certain GPA is different from the student who takes essentially "soft" courses and has the same GPA. (We do not have sufficient temerity at this time to identify any of these courses by name. Rest assured, there is more to come about the GPA in Chapter Two and there we do name names.)

College Grades and Future Achievement

Despite all real and potential problems with grades, educational researchers have been obsessed with investigating how well college grades predict future achievement and performance. (There have been even more studies of how well high school grades predict college grades.) These studies have covered two broad areas—those predicting grades in graduate and professional schools and those predicting on-the-job performance.

By far the most common research procedure has been statistical, with the coefficient of correlation being the preferred technique. The coefficient of correlation is simple to calculate but tricky to interpret unequivocally; Kenneth Boulding, the prominent economist, has remarked, "I consider the creation of the coefficient of correlation to be one of the minor intellectual tragedies of our times." Many people who use statistical correlations are unaware of their intricacies; for this reason, the same evidence can be used to support opposite positions as to how well grades predict future performance. One intricacy, often ignored, is the shape of the distributions from which coefficients were derived. As one moves up the educational ladder, grade distributions become more and more truncated and correlation coefficients based on such data are increasingly more difficult to interpret unambiguously. Another intricacy is sample size—the smaller the sample, the less clear the meaning.

A survey of studies (Warren, 1971) using correlational techniques reveals that a correlation of 0.30 is near the median value reported in predicting first-year graduate school and professional school grades from undergraduate GPAs. Warren has provided a clear intuitive analysis of the meaning of a 0.30 correlation; he does this by describing the number of students whose positions will shift from one grade quintile to another. For a correlation of 0.30, one third of the students in the top 20 percent of undergraduate GPAs will remain in the top 20 percent of first-year graduate school grades. Similarly one third of those undergraduates in the bottom fifth will remain there. Ten percent of the top fifth will drop to the bottom fifth and ten percent of the bottom fifth will rise to the top fifth. Still greater numbers will move from the second to the fourth quintile and from the fourth to the second. Even worse, predictions cannot be made for which students will shift from which position to which other position.

Those who have blind faith in the coefficient of correlation are fond of proclaiming something to the effect that "Undergraduate grades are the best single predictors of grades in graduate and professional schools." They do not qualify the statement by noting that the predictions apply only to the first year and are still quite poor. Similar unqualified proclamations are made about high school grades predicting college grades; the limitations appear to be the same.

Donald Hoyt (1965) reviewed forty-six studies, the first of which was conducted in 1917, on the relationship between college grade-point-average and postcollege performance in several fields —business, teaching, engineering, scientific research, medicine, and others. The most recent investigations reviewed by Hoyt used relatively careful and refined methodological procedures. In twenty-four (or about one half) of the forty-six studies, no relationship was found between GPA and adult performance; in nineteen (41 percent), a slight relationship was demonstrated; in the remaining three (6 percent), a high relationship emerged. One study cited by Hoyt is presented to illustrate each category: (1) In 1921 a survey of 392 eminent engineers revealed that 46 percent of them had graduated in the top 20 percent of their class, 28 percent had been in the next quintile, and 4 percent had finished in the bottom fifth. (2) A study of ten thousand employees of the American Telephone and Telegraph Company in the early 1960s is cited frequently in support of the predictive value of the GPA; the criterion measure was salary. It was found that 45 percent of the employees who graduated in the top third of their class earned salaries in the top third; 25 percent of the lowest third academically also earned salaries in the top third. (3) An elaborate series of investigations involving 426 Utah physicians was conducted. Included in this sample were 102 full-time medical faculty members of the University of Utah, 109 board-qualified specialists, 110 urban general practitioners, and 105 rural small town general practitioners. Over 200 measures of on-the-job performance were collected for each physician. It was found that both undergraduate and medical school grades were unrelated to almost all dimensions of physician performance. On the basis of careful evaluation of each of the forty-six studies, Hoyt concluded: "Present evidence strongly suggests that college grades bear little or no relationship to any measure of adult accomplishment" (p. 1).

Ten years later, a more comprehensive literature survey by the United States Civil Service Commission (Nelson, 1975) essentially confirmed these results. Sixty-seven published reports were reviewed and the conclusion was reached that GPA is a poor predictor of vocational achievement. One particularly revealing study is cited that had not been reported elsewhere. Correlations were calculated between final undergraduate GPAs and six measures of occupational proficiency for a group of social insurance claim authorizers who reviewed only complex or unusual cases. All were working at the same salary level and were considered to be fully qualified. Correlations between proficiency and GPA were universally low, ranging between .00 and +.14.

Despite these relatively clear findings, produced over several decades, when 262 well-known companies (almost all of which have recruited college graduates for many years) were asked, "How much importance does your company attach to a high grade-point when evaluating an inexperienced entry-level candidate?" (Lindquist, 1983, p. 17), 68 percent replied "important" or "very important." In a recent study of medical students, Stimmel (1975) reported that the traditional grading system does not ferret out the superior student nor does it predict a student's subsequent performance during hospital duty. Evidence about the instability of the grading system and its inconstancy continues to mount and continues to be ignored "without observation or reasoning."

The recent United States Supreme Court cases involving DeFunis (law) and Bakke (medicine), in which it was argued that other applicants less qualified than DeFunis or Bakke were admitted to professional schools, were based partly on the unvoiced notion that the higher the standardized test score and GPA, the higher the qualification for professional schools and, ultimately, practice of the craft. We do not know of any research evidence to support this position, yet a carefully conducted survey (Oltman and Hartnett, 1985) of graduate program selectivity revealed that graduate departments still assign the greatest importance to undergraduate grades in making admission decisions. This Harvard faculty member must be speaking for many in this declaration that "The grade conveys a relatively unambiguous message about a student's progress, in a universally understood system of academic notations" (Jedrey, 1984, p. 104).

Students and Grades

One explanation for faculty belief in the virtues of grades and the GPA is that most faculty members obtained good grades all along the academic line and, therefore, grades *must* be excellent indicators of future exemplary performance. In our considered judgment, the most significant issues about grades are their influences on students—influences that range from those arousing feelings of success or failure to those inhibiting or enhancing academic achievements. Opinions abound; undoubtedly many stem solely from the experiences of the holders. Note the following generalizations: "Whether a student is trying to maintain a straight A average or simply to keep eligible for the football team, grades are . . . universal incentives" (McKeachie, 1958, p. 580); also: "Many view the competition arising from the grading system as a positive preparation for life" (Miller, 1966, p. 15).

Regrettably, there has been little research about the influence of grades on students. The National Opinion Research Center (Davis, 1964a) surveyed 1,637 students from 135 colleges and universities; all of the students had been National Merit Scholarship holders, finalists, or semifinalists. It was found that 70 percent of that select group had received high grades in lower-quality colleges and universities while only 36 percent had received high grades in higher-quality ones. But many of these intellectually superior young people who had less than a B + average from high-ranking schools chose *not* to pursue graduate study; many underestimated their ability and potential on the basis of feedback provided by GPAs. Thistlethwaite (1965) obtained similar results in a survey of two thousand students attending 140 different institutions, suggesting the damaging personal effects of the GPA on academically talented students.

The fact remains that grades do motivate many students. Therefore, it is important to ask if such motivation produces socially and personally useful effects, and if individual students are motivated differently by grades. As for the first question, detailed and careful observations (Snyder, 1970) in one of our most prestigious institutions of higher learning—the Massachusetts Institute of Technology—revealed marked discrepancies between faculty and student claims about the bases of course grades. For example, Snyder reported, "I observed the professor in one class beginning the term by explaining that the students were expected to be creative and involved.... They would have the opportunity to take intellectual risks, to make mistakes.... Five weeks later the first quiz was given. The students found that they were asked to return a large amount of information that they could only have mastered by memorization" (p. 17). Student reactions varied. Some were cynical; the greatest number approved information-type examinations because memorizing details facilitated their efforts to make good grades. In a somewhat similar vein, an investigation (Davis, 1964b) at eight schools—including Amherst, Cornell, Dartmouth, and Stanford—showed that faculty evaluations of students on a creativity scale correlated very poorly with assigned grades. Cross (1967) reported that among students attending three highly regarded schools, those who tended to approach academic matters in ways characteristic of creative people were less likely to graduate than those who chose a more workmanlike approach to academic matters. Evidently grades stimulate memorization and the mechanical pursuit of information at the expense of creativity and intellectual risk taking.

As for the second question—are individual students motivated differently by grades—287 students were asked to indicate (Zimmerman, 1956) the three factors that motivated them most and those they disliked most. Findings revealed that grades motivated less than 25 percent of the students; an additional 15 percent included grades among those factors most disliked. Despite this dislike by some, grades continue to be important to students. For example, a survey of students at a midwestern state university (Polezynski and Shirland, 1977) asked business administration students to make the following rating: "On a scale of 0 to 10, with 0 being of no importance and 10 being exceptionally important, rate the importance of your attaining your expected GPA for the semester." For one sample of 203 students, the mean rating was 8.60; for a second sample of seventy-seven, the mean rating was 8.62. In a more recent survey (Astin, 1982) of almost two hundred thousand freshmen attending 368 institutions of higher learning, only 15 percent agreed "strongly" or "somewhat" with the statement: "college grades should be abolished."

Experimental studies tend to confirm the view that grades are important but not very significant. An early study by Goldberg (1965) involved five instructors teaching five different sections of an introductory psychology course. For each instructor, five different grading policies—strict, lenient, bimodal, normal, rectangular—were used in reporting results of the midterm examination to students. Results of these procedural variations produced small differential effects on grades on a test administered one month later.

A second empirical study (Cullen and others, 1975), conducted with 233 high school students enrolled in ten different classes, produced different effects. All students were requested to complete a "one-page, written library assignment in two days." In some classes students were offered points (either $+2$, $+3$, $+5$, $+8$, $+10$, or $+12$) toward their final grades; in other classes students were threatened with loss of points (either -1, -2, -3, -4, -5, or -7) for not completing the assignment. The following percentages of students did *not* complete the assignment: (1) approximately 58 percent in the positive-incentive group, (2) approximately 36 percent in the negative-incentive group, and (3) approximately 14 percent in the no-incentive or control group.

The method of participant observation was used in a sociological investigation (Becker and others, 1968) of college life at the University of Kansas. Observations derived from field notes and student interviews revealed that students developed a "grade-point-average perspective" toward academic work; this perspective reflected the institutional emphasis on grades. It was noted that this emphasis on grades did not mean there was a unitary standard for all students—students varied in the extent to which they personally accepted and lived according to the grade perspective —nor that the F students adopting this standard actually made higher grades. The strong and many times unsubstantiated opinions, the sweeping generalizations, and the mixed and sparse research results about the influences of grades on students prompted us to devote careful attention to the issue. Two chapters (Six and Seven) are devoted to what we did and what we found.

Some of the influences of grades are very personal and painful and not easily captured by statistics or experimental work. One of our faculty respondents in the national survey commented: "I have always been an A student—I feel I was more damaged than encouraged by grades. As a child, I was always waiting, in dread, for the course or test I would finally fail. As unrealistic as it may seem, there was no middle ground between A and F; the fear of failure was haunting."

Grades, Tests, and College Learning

Any discussion of grades must include something about the tests from which they are derived. As we have pointed out elsewhere (Milton, 1982a; Milton and Eison, 1983), both anecdotal and research evidence support the proposition that college classroom tests influence to a marked extent how students study and what they learn. Research evidence supporting this view began to appear in the early 1930s and continues to produce consistent findings today. Anecdotal evidence strongly confirms research conclusions; it is familiar to all instructors and is ignored by most. The two most frequently asked questions on all campuses are: "Will that be on the final?" and "Will the test be objective or essay?" If the answer to the first question is "no," studying and learning often cease. If the answer to the second question is "multiple-choice," students will memorize isolated facts; but if the answer is "essay," students will attempt to exercise higher-order mental processes such as critical thinking and evaluating.

Despite these findings, a number of research studies (Milton, 1982a) document the fact that the majority of test questions—especially multiple-choice and true/false—in undergraduate courses seek simple factual information and little else. Publisher-supplied questions that accompany many textbooks are equally limited (Evans, Dodson, and Bailey, 1981; McMillan, 1979; Mentzer, 1982). The highly regarded Educational Testing Service has begun to emphasize the value of tests for the purpose of teaching and learning (Frederiksen, 1984), and has even criticized some of its own standardized tests for containing too many simple memory items and too few questions that require higher-order mental processes. You as an educated person should know the answer to this current question:

> Tradition has it that the Compromise of 1877 was worked out:
>   a. by President Ulysses S. Grant
>   b. between Hayes and Tilden
>   c. at the Wormley Hotel
>   d. both *a* and *c*.

This question is not atypical. (The answer is *c;* you have now attained a new level of erudition by having read this far.)

Consider a different type of trivia item for which the instructor assigned fourteen journal articles in a senior course in psychology. The one and only examination question required students to match authors with titles. Upon challenge by a colleague, this full professor maintained that correct matching indicated a student understood the material.

Essay questions are not without faults. Try answering this one (coherently and using correct grammar) in, say, ten minutes (there were four others on the fifty-minute test): "Discuss the need for governments with respect to the public good." This question demands "shooting the breeze" in order to "psych the prof," in the words of students. Students must guess what points are wanted so as to touch upon as many as possible. The pressures of limited time, coupled with the breadth of the question, promote poor-quality written expression. Furthermore, how can the meaning of a letter grade based on "Wormley Hotel" trivia be compared to the meaning of the same letter grade based on the "government–public good" question? Most important, how can either of those grades be similar in meaning to a grade derived from a carefully constructed test dealing with fundamental concepts in the field or requiring the solution of significant problems?

The most telling study we have seen about college classroom tests was conducted at the University of Kansas (Semb and Spencer, 1976). Seventeen faculty members (teaching courses in anthropology, art, art history, biology, chemistry, economics, English, geology, history, linguistics, math, music, philosophy, physics, political science, psychology, and sociology), reported that 31 percent of their test questions tapped complex cognitive skills (such as problem solving) in their students. Careful categorization by independent judges of test items actually used by these instructors revealed that only 8.5 percent required complex skills; the remainder (91 percent) were of the recall or recognition variety. It was concluded that "many instructors are testing mainly over recall tasks. What is disturbing is that they do not even know it" (p. 121).

Summary

A review of the grading practices of five early schools— Yale, Harvard, Mount Holyoke, William and Mary, and Michigan —revealed that there were frequent alterations in the types and numbers of symbols used. By around 1900 the five-letter system was gaining favor; although it has been changed almost constantly, it remains the predominant grading system. Grading on the curve was introduced shortly after 1900, and Pass/Fail began its brief popularity in the mid-1960s. Seemingly, the tinkering with grading has resulted in little significant benefit to student learning.

Just as grades tend to be determined idiosyncratically by individual faculty members, the GPA is derived idiosyncratically by institutions. Despite these facts, the letter symbols and the metric are interpreted as absolutes—that is, they tend to have the same meanings in both individual and institutional usage.

Educational researchers have been obsessed with investigating how well college grades predict future achievement in graduate and professional schools and in business and industry. The preferred research technique has been the coefficient of correlation, even though it has important limitations. Numerous studies going back at least seventy-five years reveal that there is little or no relationship between grades and any measures of adult accomplishment. Despite these clear and consistent findings, considerable emphasis continues to be placed on grades during selection for postgraduate activities.

There has been a paucity of research about the influences of grades on students—it has been assumed that they provide universal incentives. That assumption is false, and a few studies suggest that grades produce damaging personal effects on talented students. Nonetheless, the majority of students appear to believe that grades are important.

An even more significant reseach omission is the study of the influences of tests and grades on the learning of content. A few studies began to appear as early as the 1930s; the results are consistent—if students know the type of test (objective or essay), their studying is affected. Even more compelling anecdotal evidence supports this finding; students tend to memorize isolated factual information for multiple-choice tests, and they attempt to exercise higher-order mental processes (such as critical thinking) for essay tests. A few studies suggest that most classroom tests (both objective and essay) are seriously flawed, and that instructors are not even aware that most of their tests require simple recall rather than complex cognitive skills.

The most telling study cited was one in which faculty members reported that almost one third of their course test questions tapped complex cognitive skills, for example, problem solving skills. Careful evaluation of the questions from seventeen fields revealed that less than 10 percent of the items required such skills; 90 percent of the items were of the plain recognition or recall variety.

Consider the words of St. Augustine: "For so it is, O Lord my God I measure it! But what it is I measure, I do not know." Or Dressel's (1983) modern description of a grade: "An inadequate report of an inaccurate judgment by a biased and variable judge of the extent to which a student has attained an undefined level of mastery of an unknown proportion of an indefinite material" (p. 12).

TWO

Contexts for Understanding the Meanings of Grades

This chapter is an extension of the first; it presents a continuing analysis of the vagaries of grades. For this reason, there may be some slight repetition across chapters—such repetition is for the sake of emphasis. We have witnessed so frequently individuals attaching incorrect meanings to grades that we are employing several different approaches to convey the extensiveness and fixity of these beliefs. In the National Grade Survey of faculty, students, parents, and business people, we were struck by the extent to which grades and GPAs are believed to reveal significant student characteristics such as achievement, self-discipline, motivation, and so on. Well over half of the respondents in all four groups agreed that these characteristics are indexed by grades, and one third agreed that grades and GPAs serve to indicate intelligence, communication skill, and ability to cope with stress. As one illustration, a parent stated without qualification that "determination, ambition, and so forth, mean a lot in how well you do in life. Grades reflect these traits." We can only marvel at the wonders one letter (A, for example) or one number (3.20, for example) can perform.

Assigning a college student a letter grade for a course appears to be a simple and straightforward act. Behind this appearance of simplicity, numerous factors operate to endow each grade with meaning. Some factors are quite limited, such as the student's field of study; others are extensive and entail nothing less than the attitude a given historical era holds toward the evaluation of people in general and of students in particular. If we examine grades carefully, we must come to the realization that each grade can be understood only within the context of many different frames of reference. These serve to imbue the grade with a unique meaning, both for the student and for the society. A proper appreciation of the true meaning of college grades, therefore, depends on a proper appreciation of the multiple contexts in which the grades are the common element. Although it is difficult to specify all contexts that might be relevant, it seems reasonable to offer the following set of factors as significant for a thorough evaluation of grade meaning: (1) socio-historical era (including grade inflation and deflation), (2) educational institution, (3) academic discipline, (4) instructor policies, and (5) student characteristics.

Socio-Historical Era

The broadest frame of reference for any grade is provided by the socio-historical era in which the grade is assigned. Some of the ways in which this context moderates grade meanings can be presented impressionistically by mentioning certain developments during the last twenty years or so. For example, in the mid-1960s and early 1970s, many colleges went from a grading scale consisting of A+, A, A−, B+ ... F to one consisting of Pass/No Credit (P/NC) or variations thereof. Such a radical shift in the category system used to evaluate students surely had profound effects on grade meanings that accorded with the more lenient attitude toward the evaluation of individuals. The present trend toward more differentiated grading systems (Quann, 1984) accords with changes in societal values toward more stringent accountability in all areas.

Shifting the number of units in a grading system is not unique to the contemporary era. A number of authors (Cureton, 1971; Kirchbaum, Simon, and Napier, 1971; Johnston and Simon, 1976; Geisinger, 1982; Smallwood, 1935; Quann, 1984) have examined various changes in grading systems from as early as 1650 to the present. Considering the specifics at either a single institution or across a collection of institutions, the overall impression is that of cyclic variation. It seems as if faculties are engaged in a continuous search for a golden metric by which to record their impressions and evaluations of students. We have heard that Harvard has gone to a 15-point scale which is oddly tied to only twelve numbers (1, 5, 9, and 13 are omitted) and which, in turn, is related to letters A through F including pluses and minuses.

An examination of the vicissitudes endured by the units comprising grading systems in use at other universities shows similar variations. Prior to 1800, faculties used from 2 to 4 units; from 1800 to 1900, grading systems employed from 2 (P/F) to 100 (percentages) units; and from 1910 to the present, we have varied around a modal value of 5 (A to F), with excursions going as low as two (P/NC) or as high as 13 (A+ to F). While it is possible to see a trend in modal value—from less (2) to more (100) to less (5)—we should not lose sight of the point that grading systems have undergone continual (and continuing) variations in the number of units used. Although 5 units may now seem a "natural" value, we must bear in mind that there is no historically natural unit and that dramatic changes have occurred over the 300-year period of American higher education.

While this exercise in numerology may provide its own satisfactions, we still need to ask what a change from a 2-unit to a 10-, 20-, or 100-unit system suggests about the meaning of grades. At a minimum, a scale having more extensive units implies a willingness to differentiate individuals into relatively precise categories. As such, it suggests the society (or at least the educational establishment) is comfortable with the appearance of evaluating individuals in a highly differentiated way. A well-differentiated system connotes comfort with rigorous evaluation; a less differentiated one connotes relative discomfort with rigorous evaluation.

Accompanying relative comfort/discomfort is the issue of sharp distinctions among individuals. With a less differentiated system, distinctions and rankings are minimal and cross-student equality is emphasized. With a more differentiated system, distinctions and rankings are maximal and individual achievement is emphasized. Within the context of education, less differentiated systems connote a relative sense of cooperation and general worth, whereas more differentiated ones suggest a relative sense of competition and individual excellence. To some degree, the fluctuations of American grading systems may reflect a societal ambivalence about cooperation and the communal good on the one hand, and competition and individual ascendence on the other. Colleges and universities sometimes emphasize strict evaluation, competition, and the individual student; at other times, they emphasize relaxed evaluation, cooperation, and the common good.

What does all of this have to do with grading? One implication certainly entails what any given historical period would view as the standard system. Historical analysis reveals that wide swings in category value occurred in the period from 1800 to 1900, and that much more restricted swings occurred in the period from 1910 on. American grading practices from 1800 thus divide themselves into two major periods: one in which there was no standard number of categories, and a second in which 5 units served as the standard. An examination of early sources (Smallwood, 1935) shows that many faculty attempted to evaluate on the basis of 100 units. One hundred represented expert performance—presumably how a faculty member would perform—and students were marked off as fractions on their way toward expert status (that is, faculty). This notion of 100 units as "perfect" came under experimental attack in the classic studies of Starch and Elliott (1912, 1913a, 1913b), who showed variability among different graders using the 100-point scale—sometimes as much as 40 or more points. These studies indicated that it was no longer possible to maintain the "100 points-equals-perfection" scale, and most universities and colleges went to the 5-unit A to F scale within the next decade. Although we no longer need to consider changes from 2 units to 100, variations from 2 (P/F) to 13 (A+, A, A−, B+ . . . F) can still be discerned and provide a fairly rigorous indication of the attitude a given socio-historical era holds toward the evaluation of students.

One more wrinkle remains in the history of grade units—the summary statistic known as the GPA. Although the contemporary grading systems used for individual classes mostly vary around a modal value of 5 units, the GPA introduces a much more differentiated scale of 400 units. Therefore, it is more precise and extensive than any of its ancestors. The GPA is a completely second order metric—a statistical creature—derived from the properties of the number system (numbers can always be added and divided to yield an average) rather than from the teaching/learning/testing/grading situation known as the college or university classroom.

Thus, there are two separate systems for evaluating and grading students, one containing anywhere from 2 to 13 units and the other containing 400 units. This state of affairs further reinforces the notion that we are ambivalent about the ways in which we evaluate college students: While we know we cannot (should not) make more than a small number of discriminations, nonetheless we feel the need to put each student into a precise rank location for honors, graduate school, jobs, and so on. In addition to our tendency not to trust our classroom judgment beyond 5 or so units but to trust the number system to be accurate to one unit in 400, we use the GPA to make serious decisions about our students' lives and concerns. Clearly, college professors (and teachers generally) allow their judgments to be subordinated to the extra-classroom world that demands supposedly more precise and differentiated metrics, even though such metrics violate the teaching/learning/evaluation context that is the college or university campus. We should not permit our evaluations to be quantified to a level of precision beyond the resolving power of our judgments.

A seldom noted but nonetheless significant socio-historical force—operating on an institution as a whole and on some individual faculty members—is finances. We cannot provide statistics about how the availability or nonavailability of financial support influences grading, but we are inclined to believe this comment made to us by a business recruiter: "My experience in working with college professors has convinced me they felt pressure from the department and the dean to keep many students enrolled for federal funding." In many cases, state funding of its colleges and universities is based upon enrollments. In turn, internal funding of academic departments is based upon number of students in courses; to fail students is thus to lose money.

Grade Inflation and Deflation

Further evidence of fluctuation in our society's concern over student evaluation is grade inflation and deflation. Grade inflation is when a grade is viewed as being less rigorous than it ought to be; grade deflation is when a grade is viewed as being more rigorous than it ought to be. Since the late 1950s there have been public outcries over each of these circumstances, although certainly not at the same time. One early study of grade deflation was reported by Aiken in 1963. Aiken found that although the mean Scholastic Aptitude Test (SAT) verbal score rose from 453 to 485 during the years 1959 to 1961 at the Women's College of the University of North Carolina, the average freshman grade did not, thereby leading to the conclusion that "grading students shifted with the ability level of the class, being more stringent in each successive year" (p. 320). A similar analysis at the University of California, Berkeley—this time covering a thirteen-year period—revealed that the mean SAT verbal score rose from 487 to 550, that the mean SAT quantitative score rose from 459 to 556, and that the average GPA remained constant at 2.34 (Miller, 1966). In both cases, there seems to be clear evidence of grade deflation.

Turning now to concerns about grade inflation, the alarm was first sounded publicly by *Newsweek* in 1974. Conscientious reporters discovered the following facts: The number of A's at the University of North Carolina doubled between 1962 and 1972, and the proportion of seniors graduating from Harvard with honors increased from 50 to 82 percent between 1961 and 1974. Burwen (1971) surveyed grading practices in 435 colleges and universities and, for the seventy-two schools providing pertinent information, found that GPAs rose from 2.40 to 2.56 for undergraduates and from 3.22 to 3.42 for graduate students.

Although this is not the place for an extensive analysis (or defense) of the Scholastic Aptitude Test or the American College Test (ACT), we do feel obliged to note that while we do not consider performance on these tests to provide a perfect measure of "native intellectual ability," we do see such results as providing a reasonable baseline against which to discuss the periodic rise and fall of student GPAs. Scores from both the ACT and the SAT are more reliable and valid than the scores from most classroom tests. Furthermore, when comparing the academic attainments of two or more students, the same measuring instrument should be used. This common measure exists in any comparison involving the SAT or ACT scores of two or more students; it usually does not exist in comparisons involving the GPAs of two or more students.

With this attitude (disclaimer) in mind, what relationships do we find between GPAs and SAT (ACT) scores? Taking all available results into account, it is possible to produce a schematic graph showing the rise and fall of both GPAs and SAT scores over the period 1950 to 1980. Probably the most obvious feature of Figure 1 is that the curves for GPA and SAT are mirror images of one another: When one goes up the other goes down. What this means for flesh-and-blood students is that as students get higher SAT (or ACT) scores the overall GPA goes down, and as students do more poorly on these measures the overall GPA goes up. Although these effects have been labeled as deflation and inflation, respectively, their implications for what grades are worth have not been explored systematically.

If one were to take a dispassionate look at the relationship between SAT scores and GPAs, the situation depicted in Figure 1 represents absolutely the worst case. Consider these two contrasting sets of circumstances:

1. As SATs increase or decrease, GPAs remain stable. This circumstance would reflect a rigid definition of grading despite wide variations in the SAT levels of students then attending college. Such a situation might occur if there was rigid adherence to some external criterion, such as the normal curve. Under these conditions, for example, 10 percent of students would get A's, 15 percent B's, 50 percent C's, 15 percent D's, and 10 percent F's. This distribution of grades would apply regardless of the SAT (ability) levels of the students currently enrolled in college classes. Because this seems too rigid a phenomenon, consider a second possibility in which grades and SATs seem to be related more sensibly.

2. Both SATs and GPAs assume the same curve—when SATs go up so do GPAs, and when SATs go down so do GPAs. The parallel curves of this situation suggest that classroom instruc-

Figure 1. SAT Scores and Average GPAs for the Years 1950–1980

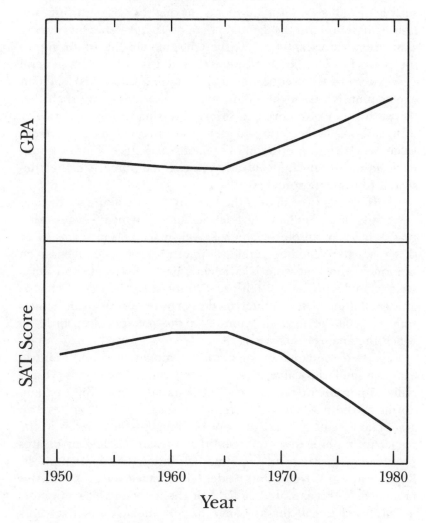

tors are grading in accordance with the presumed quality levels of their students: better students, better grades; poorer students, poorer grades.

The actual case of the GPA in Figure 1 shows neither a straight line nor one parallel to the SAT (ACT) curve. Rather, the relationship is best described as a mirror image. Thus faculty members are responsive to changes in SAT scores alright, but in such a way that "poorer" students get higher GPAs during one historical period (on the average) than do "better" students during a different historical period. Although some may see in this figure the pernicious effects of "lowered standards" (that is, a general decrease in society's educational and grading standards), such an explanation is beside the point: over time, grades vary such that the performance required is different during different eras. For this reason, it is necessary to view grades as not having a fixed value over different eras, and to take the specific era into account in deciding the meaning of any given alpha-numeric cipher designed to evaluate students.

If grades vary all over the lot, why do we still use terms such as "grade inflation" or "grade deflation," which suggest that grades have an absolute value? The primary reason seems to be that grades are equated carelessly to other economic tokens such as money, and that what is at issue is presumed value and not a serious analogy that will tell us anything about either money or grades. Rather, the economic metaphor is used to provide grades with a social value, and "money" is the metaphoric vehicle by which the analogy is carried.

Given the equation of grades to money, it is important to examine similarities and differences between the two. This is especially important in regard to grade inflation, since the ups and downs of the national GPA are often reacted to as if it were an academic variant of the Dow-Jones Averages—fluctuations in the respective index generate a good deal of name-calling by groups presumably in favor of a sound education (economic) policy. Republicans and Democrats aside, GPAs vary over time and this fact needs to be explored in light of the unexamined metaphors usually used to call for a change in educational/evaluative practices.

When faculty and society in general talk about grade inflation, they are describing their own attitudes toward a perceived leniency in evaluation, something that might accurately be rendered as: "Those kids are getting away with murder. The professors are too easy on them—not like when I was a student. How are those kids ever going to grow up and take their place in the real world where everything is not so lenient?" Their talk about grade deflation also involves a social attitude rather than a system gone wrong and might be rendered as: "School is a time for individual growth and discovery, and any attempt to straight-jacket the process by capricious evaluation does a disservice to the student and the society."

Although a number of cogent reasons have been offered to explain why GPAs move around so much (Birnbaum, 1977; Arreola, 1978; Quann, 1984), we should not lose sight of the main point: Grade-flation (either up or down) represents then current American attitudes toward the evaluation of students and education. While there undoubtedly always will be individual professors who feel their colleagues grade too stringently or too leniently, an articulated public concern over either form of grade-flation represents a social attitude, a background important to an understanding of any given grade or GPA.

There is one final implication of systematic increases and decreases in grade valuation. People who use grades for purposes of selection (graduate school admissions officers, government and business personnel specialists, and so on) are likely to be making decisions today about college graduates and other students on the basis of grade values and information formed a decade or more ago. Since there is no guarantee that present values are similar to those prevalent during the user's college career—in fact, there is evidence to indicate they are not—it is clear that decisions are being made on the basis of an outdated understanding of what grades mean.

Think about the following hypothetical cases: A personnel officer who graduated in 1960 is asked to make a job decision about a recent graduate. This official had his or her attitudes toward grades formed during the period of high SATs and low GPAs; hence for this official a grade of B would be an extremely good one. Evaluating the credentials of a student who graduated in 1982, this individual would still be likely to evaluate B as a "good" grade, although the judgment might be affected somewhat by discussions of grade inflation. In contrast, a personnel officer who graduated in 1970 had his or her attitudes about grades formed during the period of lower SATs and higher GPAs; hence this individual would consider a B an "average" grade. Same grade, different personnel officers, different meanings. The point to these examples is not that personnel officers do not keep up with grades, but that grades are always relative to a specific socio-historical era and that various gate-keepers who use grades are likely to be making decisions on the basis of outdated standards. While the problem may be somewhat less serious in academic contexts, business users should realize that "the grade of B" is not always what it used to be or what it will be in the future.

Educational Institution

A second frame of reference serving to inform the meaning of a college grade is provided by the educational institution the student attends. College catalogues provide some clues as to the overall institutional attitude toward grades and grading. Note the following statements from recent undergraduate catalogues offered by the College of William and Mary and by Reed College.

The Reed College statement occurs under the general heading *Teaching Methods and Student Evaluations:* "Students at Reed are not formally divided by academic ability or promise. Although academic work is observed closely and evaluated frequently by instructors, students are encouraged to measure success not by grades or other labels, but by self-assessment of their grasp of course material and intellectual growth." The statement in the William and Mary catalogue is under the general heading *Requirements for Degrees:* "Obligation to its educational mission gives the College the right and responsibility, subject to the employment of fair procedures, to suspend, dismiss, or deny continuance of a student whose academic achievement does not meet established college standards. . . . A student must receive a minimum quality point average of 2.00 for all courses at William and Mary in the field of concentration for which he receives a grade of A, B, C, D or F."

In addition to the attitude expressed in the college catalogue, there is the implicit attitude motivating the grading and grade-reporting practices of the institution. Replies from over one thousand six hundred institutions detailed in the most recent report of the American Association of College Registrars and Admissions Officers (AACRAO) indicated both diversity and similarity across different institutions and institutional types (Quann, 1984). To emphasize similarity, we merely need note that about 92 percent of all institutions surveyed use letter grades and only 1 percent use narrative records, and that the GPA used in about 95 percent of all institutions is a 4.00 scale with A = 4.00 and F = 0.00. Regarding differences, 53 percent of all institutions allow the student to take only one P/F course per term and 31 percent have no limit on the number of P/F courses per quarter. If we examine the number of P/F courses permitted in an undergraduate career, we find that 25 percent of schools now allow only four such courses and 28 percent have no limit. Of the schools using P/F notation, 33 percent require a traditional letter grade of C for a passing grade whereas 42 percent require a grade of D.

Falling somewhere between the similarities and differences is the question of what happens to the grading of courses that are repeated by students. There are two alternatives: (1) averaging, in which the prior grade and the repeated grade are combined in computing the GPA; and (2) replacing, in which only one grade is used—usually, the higher one. Across the great variety of American academic institutions, about 68 percent use the replacement procedure and 24 percent use the averaging method. (Figures add to 92 percent since some institutions use a combination of the two or a completely different method of calculation.) Results by institutional type reveal that fewer two- and four-year colleges average grades (20 percent) than do universities (31 percent). Conversely, universities are less likely to replace grades (60 percent) than are two- and four-year colleges (71 percent). Finally, there is the matter of transferring grades from one institution to another. Here, 28 percent of academic institutions reported that such grades are included in the GPA and 72 percent indicated they were not.

There is much in these bits of information for the numerophile. For the individual who is not so afflicted, there is still something of interest. If there were only similarities, the institution attended would not have to be taken into account in understanding the meaning of a given course grade or GPA. But a B on one's transcript from University X may be the result of having repeated a course three, four, or five times, whereas from University Y it may be the result of a one-to-a-customer policy. Under this condition of cross-institutional difference, it is apparent that the two grades are not equivalent.

What is most remarkable about the patterns of institutional record keeping is that almost all of the schools surveyed use the same alphabetical grading system, which is then converted into the same GPA metric of 4.00. This near identity in the specific symbols and numeration is in marked contrast to the relatively great differences in the procedures used to compute (and recompute) the GPA. No one seems to be bothered that similar GPAs computed from similar A to F systems are the result of widely discrepant record-keeping procedures; somehow or other, it is enough that the letters and numbers are the same.

A less formal aspect of the role played by the educational institution in affecting the meaning of grades is the institutional context created by the contemporary student culture. Some estimate of this factor can be gained by considering the SAT or ACT scores and high school grades (not to mention socioeconomic level or region of the country) of students attending a certain college or university. Generally speaking, the term *prestigious school* is applied to those institutions having a relatively select student population—select, that is, on the basis of academic and, to a lesser extent, social attributes. While it is not completely apparent that being in a college or university composed of students having high GPAs, ACTs, or SATs necessarily results in a more (or less) demanding grading scale, it is apparent that the academic abilities and achievements of students attending a given school influence grading practices by setting higher faculty expectations and by providing greater competition among students. Without taking a stand on whether these conditions are good (or bad) for student learning, we must recognize that they affect the academic ambience not only of individual classrooms but of the institution as a whole.

Although not strictly related to the issue of educational institution, a recent analysis published by the National Center for Education Statistics (1984) revealed that high school grading standards vary in different parts of the country. The most rigorous standards seem to be in New York, New Jersey, and Pennsylvania, whereas the least rigorous seem to be in the states that touch the Pacific Ocean. For the three East Coast states, 20 percent of the grades were A and the percentage of A's was about equal to the percentages of D's and F's. On the West Coast, 30 percent of the grades were A and there were at least twice as many A's as there were D's and F's. Runner-up for "stringent" grading was the South Atlantic region ranging from Delaware to Florida; runner-up for "lazy" grading was the region encompassing Minnesota, Iowa, Mississippi, Nebraska, the Dakotas, and Kansas.

It does not require high-powered statistical analysis to see that state universities in certain parts of the United States will enroll students who experienced tough grading standards in high school, whereas state universities in other parts of the country will enroll students who experienced easier standards. All of these experiences will contribute to the grade ambience at a particular school. For high school students who become college students, West Coast kids may be in for a shock when they come in contact with East Coast kids. How long the shock lasts and whether it is worse at public or private schools are questions left unanswered by this report.

Academic Discipline

The phrase "preventive medicine" usually refers to what the Public Health Service does; within the context of college life it refers to a course in organic chemistry that keeps many students out of medical school. More broadly, this means that certain courses have a reputation of being inordinately difficult or, more important for our purposes, inordinately difficult in which to get a good grade. The student culture is often able to label, with a fair degree of accuracy, those courses that are graded in a relatively "easy" way and those that are likely to wreak havoc on one's GPA. Certain disciplines—usually in the natural sciences—publicly pride themselves on sparingly assigning A's and B's and being much more "liberal" in assigning D's and F's. In addition, certain disciplinary courses (for example, organic chemistry for medicine, statistics for psychology) strongly affect the competitive ambience of the classroom and the degree to which getting a good grade stands out for the student. Thus, both the role of the course in the student's career plan as well as the attitudes characteristic of the discipline toward the class strongly affect the specific meaning for the student of grades received in that disciplinary area.

One of the most complete and rigorous attempts to define precisely the differential effects of academic discipline on grades —both actual and predicted—has been presented by Goldman and his associates in a series of papers dating back to the early 1970s (Goldman, 1973, 1974; Goldman and others, 1974; Goldman and Hewitt, 1975; Goldman and Slaughter, 1976). Starting with the fact that different disciplines in the same school—in this case, the University of California, Riverside (UCR)—differed in their average class grade by as much as a grade unit (the average grade for psychology was 3.20; the average for biology, 2.43), Goldman became interested in transforming grades in one field into those of another.

To accomplish this, Goldman and others (1974) attempted to predict hypothetical GPAs for students in major fields other than their present majors. For example, using predictions based on high school GPA, SATV, and SATM, it was possible to estimate what grades a student now majoring in chemistry would get if he or she were majoring in Spanish. For students whose present GPA at the University of California, Riverside, was in the 3.00 GPA range, the predicted value was 3.28 in Spanish for a student majoring in chemistry and 2.56 in chemistry for one now majoring in Spanish. Comparable cross-field predictions between biochemistry and political science indicated that a biochemistry student would attain a 3.30 GPA in political science whereas a student in political science would attain a 2.60 in biochemistry. Similar analyses conducted on data provided by the California Universities at San Diego (UCSD), Davis (UCD), Irvine (UCI) and Los Angeles (UCLA) all produced comparable cross-field results (Goldman and Hewitt, 1975).

Looking at these grade asymmetries more generally leads us to expect a negative relationship among disciplines. In other words, major fields that have relatively high-ability students (as measured by SAT scores and so forth) will receive low predictions

from other fields whereas disciplines enrolling relatively low-ability students will receive higher predictions. These patterns will occur despite the fact that students are matched on present college GPA. It seems reasonable to conclude, as did Goldman and Slaughter (1976), that the stringency of grading is directly related to the ability of students majoring in the field.

A few points concerning these conclusions deserve comment: Goldman and others (1974) applied cross-disciplinary prediction formulas to three groups of students differing in what they termed "ability level." So, for example, the lowest of their groups had college GPAs less than 2.70 and a composite mean SAT score of 1050; the highest group had college GPAs greater than 3.30 and a mean composite SAT score of 1192. Taking this factor of "ability" into account, results showed that for low- and middle-ability students, those fields with the low-ability students adopted lower grading standards whereas those fields with high-ability students adopted higher grading standards. Results for high-ability students showed this same pattern at some schools (UCSB and UCI) but not at others (UCLA, UCD, and UCR). Although the effect of ability level clouds the picture, the overall conclusion is sustained: Fields with lower-ability students grade more leniently than fields with higher-ability students. That differential grading standards are more prominent for low- than for high-ability students suggests that high-ability students are less affected by differential standards and tend to get good grades regardless of the severity of the criteria used.

While these results indicate differential grading standards, it is important to note that using high school GPAs and SAT scores as predictors only accounts for a relatively small portion of the range of differences in GPAs obtained by students majoring in different fields. One can offer a number of reasons why prediction is not better than it is, with two significant ones being that students only take some of their classes in their own field and that grades are determined by traits other than those assessed by SAT scores. Perhaps the most crucial reason predictions are not better has to do with the fact that GPA is a poor statistic to predict. On the basis of an attempt at predicting overall college GPA through the use of successive predictions made for individual class grades,

Goldman and Slaughter (1976) concluded that the GPA is a composite "made of decidedly *nonequivalent* components" (emphasis in the original) that reflect different standards of grading in different disciplines.

Perhaps the best way to appreciate what this means for student behavior and instructor grading patterns is to retell Goldman and Slaughter's parable concerning the relationship between shoe size and body weight: Shoe size is correlated with body weight. It is not a perfect correlation, but it is positive and even fairly high. Consider an imaginary experiment. We ask 100 college students to weigh themselves on bathroom scales and to report their weights and shoe sizes. Assuming all students carry out these instructions honestly (replies are anonymous), we will have obtained numbers with which to estimate a correlation between weight and shoe size. Two obvious sources of unreliability that can reduce this correlation are the readings of weight and the readings of shoe size. Both are somewhat unreliable, but for the sake of argument consider shoe size perfectly reliable. We all know that bathroom scales are notorious liars. Some are set heavier than others, some do not work well, some are hard to read accurately, and so on. Thus, we would expect to increase the correlation between weight and shoe size if we took as our measure of weight an average of ten weigh-ins on ten randomly chosen scales. This should provide a more reliable estimate of weight thereby rendering it more predictable.

Imagine that twenty scales are accumulated in two rooms— ten in each. In the first room all scales weigh too light, while scales in the second room weigh too heavy. Imagine now that all weigh-ins are public and that subjects want to avoid embarrassment. Therefore, heavy subjects will drift toward the room with the "light" scales and light subjects will go to the room with the "heavy" scales. Now our investigator will find that, even though weight is the average of ten separate weigh-ins, there is a lower correlation between weight and shoe size than was the case with only one weigh-in. This is precisely what seems to be happening in college. The light (low-ability) students gravitate toward the heavy scales (easy grading classes) and the heavy (high-ability) students gravitate toward the light scales (hard grading classes). The resulting difference in grading standards operates to blunt the prediction of GPA by academic predictors.

As this parable suggests, the problem is in the criterion and not in the predictor. The GPA is a composite value that is composed of grades obtained on heavy and light scales. Different studies, done in different classes, lead to the somewhat surprising conclusion that it is easier to predict grades in a single class than it is to predict overall GPA. Although the SAT, ACT, and the like are not infallible, they are better than the GPA, which is about as reliable as a bathroom scale at a dishonest health spa.

All of the issues raised thus far concern statistical facts and relationships; can we supply any psychological meat to cover these numerical bones? First consider the issue from the side of the grade giver: Assigning a grade indisputably represents a judgment by some instructor, and that judgment is rendered on the basis of a personal standard developed over the years. This standard is not independent of the particular sets of students from whom it was derived—an instructor who has had only high-ability students is likely to have a very different standard from that of an instructor who only has had low-ability students. Any grade judgment is therefore always relative to a historical and contemporary student-defined frame of reference, with the present grading scheme representing an attempt to locate Student X's performance in relationship to performance by Students 1 to 100 in years 1 to n.

In psychology, the tendency of a person's unique frame of reference to affect a judgment about events is known as Adaptation Level Theory (Helson, 1948, 1964). This theory, originally developed in the context of perceptual judgments, suggests that each student's performance is judged as relative to the performance of other students in that discipline or in that class. If we consider college grades as an adaptation level phenomenon, then the grader's standard for a given grade category will depend on the ability level of the students he or she teaches and has taught. For this type of analysis, grade inflation can be defined as the use of constant grade distribution in the face of lowered student ability levels and grade deflation can be defined as the use of constant grade distribution in the face of raised student ability levels.

What about the student's side of the grade question? How are we to understand what frame of reference students have for grade values? Perhaps the most direct implication of Goldman's analysis is that students having lower abilities—in whatever it is that is measured by the SAT—are attracted to fields having easier grading standards. This does not necessarily mean that these fields have intrinsically lower standards, but only that at certain universities, certain departments become known—either on the basis of word of mouth or direct experience—as easier to compete in successfully. In the case of direct experience, something very much like an adaptation level explanation seems to apply. That is, the student judges his or her ability relative to the abilities of classmates and decides "this is a class in which I can do well"; the student builds up an expectancy of getting a B or even an A.

Both from the side of the grade giver and from that of the grade receiver, we have conditions appropriate for different standards in different disciplines: Professors make their judgments in the context provided by the ability levels of students in their classes, and students make their judgments in the same frame of reference. Over time, differential cross-field standards will tend to attract students of lower (or higher) ability, which in turn will affect the context in which a given instructor will evaluate new students. This is not to say that easy or hard grading is the major factor determining student majors, but only that in cases where there is no initial (or present) content preference, grading standards may exercise a relatively strong effect. No one is to blame since context effects are inevitable aspects of human judgment and experience. To ignore this fact is to reify the grade and to forget that grades are always relative to contexts, among the most significant of which is provided by the students presently (and previously) studying a specific discipline at a specific school, with some specific professor who has a specific history of experiences with students in this specific category.

Related to the issue of academic discipline is that of the classroom ambience in which learning, teaching, testing, and grading take place. Included here are such factors as course level (freshman versus senior), lecture, discussion, and others. There is a different approach to grading and grade distributions in large lecture classes (for example, the ubiquitous introductory psychology class) than in small senior-level honors discussion classes. Although little research has been conducted evaluating these obvious demographic factors, there is the well-known increase in GPA from the freshman to the senior year.

While such an increase is easy to document, its causes and implications are more subtle. In an incisive discussion of how professors calibrate their grading schemes, Huntley (1976) notes that one approach is to develop a feeling for the mythical "average" student. Unfortunately, colleges and universities regularly demand progressively higher cut-off GPAs at the upper years of school, so that by the senior year the less qualified presumably have dropped from school and the faculty never experiences students whose work embodies the "average" (Huntley, 1976). The progressive rise in GPA, which is intended to promote and indicate higher quality, ends up forcing the faculty to use an absolute standard that has little or no grounding in what a normal student might be like. Institutionally mandated cut-off points leave us little choice but to evaluate students by the somewhat tarnished standard: Who are the people most like me? A faculty member admitted this frailty, according to a student respondent in the national survey: "I received a B with a 96 percent average; I had made straight A's in the program. Some fifteen years later, I get nauseated when I think of the guy. His rationale was that if he gave me an A, I would appear to be as knowledgeable as he."

One respondent recalled this episode from early in his faculty career: "As a student, I had viewed grades as the validation/vindication of the talent and effort (or lack thereof) displayed in each course. Therefore, a departmental policy that failed half of the juniors in a circuit theory course because they only wanted thirty, not sixty, physics majors still rankles me."

Instructor Policies

While all the preceding factors influence how a given grade is to be interpreted, probably the two most significant influences are the frames of reference brought to the learning endeavor by the student and by the instructor.

Although the role played by the instructor as the giver of a grade is obvious, what is not so evident is the network of implicit choices that lie behind the instructor's assignment of a particular class grade. For example, any instructor has at least the following six (usually implicit) choices:

Choice 1: What evaluation procedure should I use? Term papers, classroom discussion, tests, and so on.

Choice 2: If I choose tests, what kind(s)? Essay, true/false, fill-in-the-blanks, matching, multiple-choice, and so on.

Choice 3: If I choose multiple-choice, what grading model should I use? A B C D F, normal curve, percent-correct, and so on.

Choice 4: If I choose percent-correct, how many tests should I give? Final only, two in-class tests and a final, midterm and a final, and so on.

Choice 5: How should I weight each test if I choose the midterm/final pattern? Midterm = final, midterm = 2 × final, final = 2 × midterm, and so on.

Choice 6: What grade report system should I use? P/F, A B C D F, A+ A A− B+ ... F, and so on.

An examination of this sequence of questions and choices indicates that instructors have many different possibilities. If we take the six choices described above and assume a minimal figure of three alternatives for each, a bit of arithmetic (3^6) indicates that any given instructor's specific evaluation procedure is just one of 729 different plans that could have been used. Add in the fact that many instructors use various combinations of alternatives (that is, a given scheme may consist of two multiple-choice tests of equal weight and a term paper equal in value to both tests), and the number of alternatives increases dramatically. Similarly, combinations of many different types of classroom tests may be given and many different grading models used. Although large classes often are graded on the curve (and there are numerous curves), some instructors use absolute percentage correct or a combination of both absolute pecentage and normal distribution grading. Evaluation may take the form of a prearranged contract between amount of work done and grade received, a possibility not even included in the calculation of alternatives. In light of these analyses, 729 alternatives represents a minimal and not a maximal figure.

In one survey of faculty grading practices (Lunneborg, 1977), members at a large state university were asked to select one class as a reference and to indicate how much importance they attached to a dozen sources of information in assigning a course grade. To quantify the degree of relative importance attributed to each source, instructors were asked to distribute a total of 100 points across all twelve items. In decreasing order, the bases for grading were as follows (average number of points are in parentheses):

Objective examination (37)	Laboratory performance (5)
Essay examination (17)	Other (4)
Term papers (11)	Effort (3)
Recitation/problem sets (7)	Attendance (2)
Term projects (6)	Laboratory reports (2)
Class discussion (5)	Ratings by teaching assistants (1)

As can be seen, a single class grade depends upon a relatively large number of different criteria as judged by a relatively large number of different instructors.

The point is not to argue that one evaluation pattern or method of assigning a grade is more desirable than another. Rather, the point is to show how complicated the whole issue is and to suggest that an attempt to equate a B from one instructor given during one academic year with a B from another instructor given during some other (or even the same) year is likely to yield an erroneous impression of equality. The purpose of this discussion is not to suggest a standardized testing and grading procedure but simply to recognize, explicitly, that presently there is no standard procedure (nor do we necessarily believe there should be one).

The problem is further complicated because different instructors differ in the types of grades they assign and these differences are stable over time (Geisinger and Rabinowitz, 1982). Such differences seem to relate to the basis on which the instructor gives grades. Generally speaking, three frames of reference have been defined to describe the explicit standard by which a grade is given: the absolute norm, the relative performance by classmates, and the change in performance during the term. Thorndike and Hagen (1977) have proposed that these three frames of reference respectively be termed *Perfection, Peers,* and *Potential.*

Using these concepts, Geisinger (1980) demonstrated that instructors using the Peers or Perfection models of grading tend to assign relatively lower grades than instructors using a Potential or growth model. The grading model used also has been shown to affect how importantly or positively a student evaluates the grade received. For example, Eizler (1983) asked students to rate the value of the grades A, B, and C depending on whether instructors graded on the basis of peer competition, mastery of course content, or personal improvement. Students rated all grades more valuable and significant if they were assigned on the basis of either a mastery or growth model rather than on a competitive model. Thus, not only do different evaluation procedures turn out to be important for the types of grades instructors assign, they also affect the nature of personal meanings ascribed to them by students.

Finally, faculty rigidities and idiosyncrasies sometimes influence grade meanings, as indicated by a business recruiter replying to the national survey: "Grades have caused me great disillusionment with universities in that on at least five occasions I was denied a higher grade because of just *one* option on an examination. Frequently this figured out to less than one percentage point away from the cut-off point. When I discussed the situations with professors (after realizing that there were abuses), they adamantly refused my additional work offers that might have lifted me into a higher grade. So far in real life I have not experienced anything of similar inflexibility." We know of a situation in which departmental policy dictates grades almost without concern for student performance: "We do not believe in A's for freshmen. No matter how good your papers, the highest final grade you will get is a B." Notes about such limitations do not go on transcripts to aid readers in making interpretations.

Student Characteristics

Although more could be said about the frame of reference associated with the instructor (is he or she a clear and interesting lecturer, available for consultation, sarcastic or understanding in class, and so on), we now move on to the final component of the grade system—the individual student receiving the grade. Prior empirical work on this topic (to be reported in greater detail in Chapter Six) suggests that the student attributes significant to grade meaning can be grouped into two large categories best described as educational and personal. In the former group are such classic educational characteristics as study habits, knowledge, intelligence, as well as some recently evaluated traits such as learning- versus grade-orientation and the personal incentive of grades. In the second group are attributes such as personality structure, personal value areas, family influence, socioeconomic level, need for achievement, and so on.

As an example of the way in which one of these characteristics affects grade meanings, consider how a student values a given grade category. For some students a grade of B is not only good but one that is highly valued as indicating a personally pleasing performance. For other students only an A will provide the feeling that they have succeeded intellectually. If one of these students were to receive a B, he would undoubtedly feel that he had fallen short of the mark. This difference in value of the grade of B implies that for some students this grade will not be viewed as a valued achievement; indeed, it may be viewed as a small failure.

The situation will be different for a student who takes the grading system at face value and considers a C as indicating acceptable work and D as indicating passing work or, at least, not failing work. For these students, the grade of B will be valued as indicating an extremely good job. Notice that no mention has been made of ability—we have been concerned only with student feelings toward the various grade categories. If we throw in the factor of equal ability, the suggestion is that different grades, presumably reflecting different levels of learning, will satisfy students of equal ability.

Although this description may be unidimensional in detail, it is not unreasonable in outline and leads to the question of whether it is possible to determine if students who have different standards of what constitutes a good, bad, or average grade will tend to value the various grade categories differently. Exploring this question experimentally, Pollio, Eison, and Milton (in press) asked about 150 undergraduate students to state what they considered a good and a bad grade for their family, their friends, their discipline, and themselves. On the basis of a formula taking all of these influences into account, a standard value was determined for each student. This value, which determined the student's adaptation level (AL), was used to sort students into six categories.

When students in all groups were asked to rate the grade of C on a scale of 1 to 7 (with 1 meaning a very, very bad grade and 7 a very, very good grade), there was a clear downward trend for the value of the *same* grade of C for each of the six student groups. Students with the lowest standard valued a grade of C as 4.05, whereas students with the highest standard produced a value of 3.19. For students in the latter group, a grade of C is valued almost one unit less than for students with the lowest standard, for whom a grade of C is about an "average" grade—that is, one worth a neutral rating of 4.00.

For all groups except the lowest, a grade of C falls closer to the "bad" than the "good" end of the value scale. For all groups, the average value for a grade of C was about 3.80—or 0.20 less than a rating of neutral.

In another study, Stancato and Eizler (1983) asked students to rate all thirteen grades in the A to F system (including pluses and minuses) on a series of polar-opposite scales such as good/bad, important/unimportant, rewarding/punishing, and so on. When the rated distance of the A to F grades was computed and compared with their usual numerical values on the 0.00 to 4.00 GPA scale, dissimilar continua resulted. Specifically, B − was rated considerably above its location on the GPA scale and C+ was rated considerably below. In general, these results suggest that A's and B's are overvalued and that C's and D's are undervalued.

For student groups studied in both experiments the definition of a C as a neutral grade is incorrect; students at widely differing universities assessed by differing procedures nearly all perceive the grade of C as more punitive than its location in the quantitative GPA system would suggest. Whether we should term this *student grade deflation* is not clear; what is clear is that the meaning of every grade depends upon the evaluation of a specific student from a specific family, learning a specific discipline at a specific educational institution at a specific historical time in a specific society. In short, grades are always relative to contexts, never independent of them. To reify grades and assume a cross-situational stability is to abuse both the student and the evaluative meaning of the procedure.

On a more theoretical level, the problem comes down to one of grade validity. Educators, no less than psychologists and parents, often forget that grades are the outcome of judgments made both by a rater and a student being rated. As is true of all behavior, these judgments are subject to an enormous variety of personal, situational, and historical factors. Just as any given action is never context-independent, so too grade meanings are never free of their context. Theoretically, the real meaning of any particular grade is never given by the metric or statistical sophistication used to produce it but only from a series of constantly shifting frames of reference. For this reason the only justifiable approach to the meaning of college grades is to recognize them as context-dependent phenomena and to accept all of the social, theoretical, and educational implications such recognition entails.

Summary

We often forget that assigning a student a grade is a human act and, like all such acts, is dependent for its meaning on the context. Such a contextual approach suggests that the meaning of a grade is moderated by a number of different frames of reference, of which the most important are (1) the socio-historical era in which it is given, (2) the educational institution at which it is given, (3) the academic discipline in which it is given, (4) the instructor giving it, and (5) the student receiving it.

Among the more important socio-historical contexts are society's attitudes toward evaluation and accountability. We discussed evaluation in terms of cyclic variations in the number of units comprising the grading system and we discussed accountability in terms of articulate public concern over grade inflation and deflation.

Differences in educational institutions and their attitudes toward grades can be detected relatively directly in the statements made in the institution's catalogues as well as by the personal and intellectual attributes characterizing its students. More subtle influences are the record-keeping practices of various institutions. While there are many cross-institutional similarities, differences are also numerous and make comparisons difficult if not meaningless—a B recorded by one institution is not often arrived at in the same way as one recorded by another institution.

Academic disciplines, both within and across institutions, also vary in their understanding and use of the major grade categories. Certain disciplines pride themselves on being tough; others do less talking. Attempts to equate grade values across disciplines indicate differences as large as half a GPA unit (that is, a 2.50 in one field is equal to a 3.20 in another). On the basis of these (and other) considerations, it is apparent that a student's overall GPA is composed of decidedly unequal components and that a student may get a high or low GPA simply by being good or poor at playing the course selection game.

Instructor policies significantly affect grade meanings in a number of ways. Different instructors use different evaluation schemes. In addition, the quality of students seen over the years influences the standard set by the instructor. Finally, instructors attempt to implement different values by their grading models— some use an absolute norm (Perfection), some use relative student performance (Peers), while still others use personal student change over the term (Potential).

Student attributes also provide a significant context for moderating the meaning of a grade. For some students a grade of

C indicates a personally successful academic performance; for other students, only an A is valued. Grade valuation is always relative to the student's frame of reference and to the labels (or numbers) attached by the educational institution. In fact, recent evidence suggests that the "average" grade C is experienced by most students as below average.

The proper meaning of any grade (whether for the society, the professor, the student, the parent, or whomever) is not given by its metric properties but by a consideration of the various frames of reference within which it was produced. Grades are context-dependent phenomena, and any use or understanding of grades that does not take this fact into account will reify the grade and misinterpret its meaning. To fall victim to the illusion of precision is potentially harmful to both the student and the society within which he or she learns and will later work.

THREE

Current Attitudes
About Grades:
The National Survey

What are the attitudes toward and beliefs about college grades and grading practices today? We were interested in this question because we had observed that grades were central to so many of our students. Consequently, there was continuing conflict between our desire to help students learn and their desire to make good grades. Have you ever heard a student say, "I made an A" and another one say, "He gave me an F?" We do not believe that a good grade in a course necessarily means that learning has occurred. Unfortunately, most people equate good grades and learning; we do not! The educational, psychological, and sociological literature reveals limited and piecemeal information on opinions about the pervasive grading enterprise. We knew that more complete information from those directly affected by grades—givers, receivers, and users—would be interesting and we hoped that such information would assist in making appropriate recommendations for alterations in the grading game. Not to be overlooked in our motivations was the fact that two of us had twice been college grade receivers—once as students and three times each as parents; the latter experiences were the ones that hurt.

Millions of people are involved presently with grades in some way and over the years countless millions have heard about or experienced grades. Generally speaking, the resultant beliefs and attitudes seem to vary from strong to indifferent, and thinking about grades seems to range from rational to irrational. Given this state of affairs, how are researchers to obtain a reasonably comprehensive and representative sample of people who would share their specific attitudes and beliefs? This issue preoccupied us for quite some time, as did the issue of phrasing questions to minimize the influences of our own opinions (sometimes villainously labeled "prejudices"). Undergraduate and graduate students aided in our struggles during lengthy discussions over many months by keeping the research team focused on the complexities of its concerns and advancing many good ideas.

To produce a good machine-serviceable questionnaire (our primary device), we needed to learn some of the questions to ask and, especially, the choices to provide for each one. We began by conducting semi-structured interviews with small numbers of faculty, students, parents, and business recruiters. These interviews helped broaden our views, add flavor to the results, and capture some of the spirit of people's feelings.

We interviewed twenty-two faculty, twenty-four students, and eighteen parents of college students in nearby colleges and universities. We also interviewed eight business recruiters who visited our campus. All those interviewed were pleasant and answered questions readily and thoughtfully. Some were garrulous, some were opinionated, some were uninformed. Each interview lasted approximately one and one half hours and was tape recorded. All tapes were transcribed and studied diligently. The following schools assisted us in this early phase of the research: the University of Tennessee, Knoxville; Maryville College; Roane State Community College; University of the South, Sewanee; Vanderbilt University. These institutions were chosen for our initial reconnaissance because they are very different in outlook and philosophy, and each serves a different constituency.

The following quotations from these initial interviews give some of the flavor of how people feel about grades. We often were surprised by what we heard.

Faculty Comments

- Grade inflation gives the student a false concept of his performance.
- Predetermined levels assume an instructor can write a test with precision that doesn't exist.

- We failed a student on a comprehensive exam and the student's mother, wife, and wife's mother—all three came screaming to the president.
- The whole system is too much a life-or-death thing. Students feel bound to memorize and are not free to learn.
- Multiple-choice tests discriminate against the better student, who recognizes nuances where the lesser student cannot.
- There is a lack of a sense of what we are all about—our own goals, standards, and structures—and so we don't know good work, poor work, so forth.

Student Comments

- The big push for grades is by the parents. Parents are dishing out big bucks and they want some reinforcement.
- Grades are what everything is done for. That's exactly what students are going to class for every day. That's what I go to class for.
- In some ways students become so obsessed with grading that they don't take the courses they should be taking or they don't learn from the courses they are taking.
- I've said more today about grades than I've ever thought about them.

Parent Comments

- When I brought a report card home that had three A+'s and an A, my father would say, "Where's the other plus?"
- I'd never have gotten through freshman English if Joe hadn't been sitting next to me.
- We gave her a dollar for each A she made.
- Sometimes A students are strange, rather weird.
- I didn't know I knew so much about grades.

Business Recruiter Comments

- When I first look at the data sheet, I look at the overall grade-point.

- I'd go with the A+, A, A-, B+, so forth; it is a system of communication everyone understands.
- Using percentages tells me right on the line what they think of the student.
- I don't know how you assign a plus or minus; this applies only if you're working on a car battery.
- I think most recruiters assume grades are the same everywhere.
- Working with manager trainees, we've had straight A students who bombed out and we've had C students who reached high levels of responsibility.

Extensive qualitative analysis of the transcripts led to the development of a questionnaire for each of the four groups. Approximately three fourths of the questions in each were identical; so far as we can tell from extensive reading, some of our questions have never formally been asked before. The common questions across the groups and the new questions are exceptionally notable features of this survey.

Schools were selected to participate in the National Grade Survey on the basis of two factors: type and location. We divided some three thousand institutions of higher learning in the United States into five major types: community colleges, comprehensive universities, four-year colleges, highly selective four-year colleges, and highly selective universities. Our original plan was to choose one representative of each type from each of five geographical regions: Northeast, Southeast, Central, Southwest, and West Coast/Northwest for a total of twenty-five schools. We found later that some regions did not have a sufficient number of each type of school.

We contacted a total of sixty colleges and universities; twenty-three of them (38 percent) agreed to ask samples of faculty and students to complete the questionnaire. For each school we asked a staff member to assist us; that person was given a general description of the contents of the sample and the number of respondents required (desired numbers varied with the size of the institution). We sought experienced and inexperienced faculty from four broad academic divisions: humanities, social sciences, natural sciences, and professional (engineering, education, nursing, and so on). We also sought students from each of those divisions and from each level, freshman through senior.

Some schools seemed extremely sensitive about participating, while others apparently felt they knew all there was to know about grades. In one school, heavy black marks were inked through identifying information—the ink bled through and ruined the questionnaires. A high-level official in one of the most highly regarded universities in the United States informed us, "We cannot bother the faculty with this." These actions, of course, reflect important attitudes; we are afraid they are widespread.

Most students provided the names and addresses of their parents. We then sent questionnaires along with an explanatory letter to 1,463 of them. We did not contact the parents of older students—only those of students younger than twenty-six. The College Placement Council provided an alphabetized list of 3,600 names of companies (and names of individuals in each) that recruited regularly on campuses around the nation. Questionnaires were sent to an official (by name) in every fourth company; they went to officials with such titles as vice-president of personnel, personnel director, director of human resources, and corporate recruiting supervisor.

Demographics of the Sample

The distribution of completed questionnaries, broken down by school type and geographic region, indicated that each of the twenty-three participating institutions provided more than the minimum number needed for useful statistical analysis. The relative proportion of questionnaires received from individual institutions was also well balanced. For example, each school contributed between 3 percent and 12 percent of the total student sample, between 2 percent and 10 percent of the total faculty sample, and between 1 percent and 15 percent of the total parent sample. Because institutional sizes are so different, ranging from the large state universitites to small liberal arts colleges, the actual number of participants from each school varied and results are reported in percentages throughout. Faculty respondents were drawn from a broad spectrum of disciplines and from across the ranks; the collective data well represent faculty on both variables. Approximately 25 percent of faculty respondents were in each of the following disciplinary areas: natural sciences, social sciences, humanities, and undergraduate professional fields. Although a slightly higher percentage were associate professors (39 percent), the remaining professorial ranks were represented in approximately equal proportions.

Student respondents similarly show that our procedures provided a balanced sample of the currently enrolled student population. Of the total student sample, 51 percent were women and 49 percent men. Thirty-four percent were under age twenty, 58 percent were between twenty and twenty-nine, 6 percent were between thirty and thirty-nine, 2 percent were between forty and forty-nine, and 0.4 percent (seventeen students) were age fifty or over. Twenty-nine percent were freshmen, 25 percent sophomores, 21 percent juniors, 20 percent seniors, and 6 percent were in other categories. There was a diversity of majors for students who participated in this multi-institutional investigation.

Colleges and universities were identified as having competitive admission standards on the basis of either self-reported institutional mean SAT scores of 1050 or higher or mean ACT scores of 21 or above in their 1983 listings in Lovejoy's *College Guide*. An analysis of these scores—actually, of the values reported by respondents—indicated that a large number of students (72 percent of the total sample) did not take either examination or did not report their scores. The students providing SAT and ACT data reported scores well above published institutional averages. The significance of this finding is difficult to interpret since nearly three fourths of the sample failed to provide information, but what is important to the discussion of demographics is that the competitive colleges and universities reported higher average SAT and ACT scores than did the open admission institutions.

There are potentially troubling issues regarding the representativeness of our samples and the extent to which generalizations can be made. Since this was the first comprehensive study of its kind, knowing what variables to consider was difficult. Furthermore, when one samples people there are usually unknown factors. Some of the results are consistent with what prior literature and academic practice suggest. We believe that generalizations are warranted even though we could not designate institutions or individuals randomly or on any stratified basis—our colleges and universities and the people in them were all volunteers. We believe the findings are interesting and significant in their own right and would be confirmed by more extensive sampling. We offer the results with considerable commonsense confidence that they will generalize to large populations. Overall, we analyzed questionnaires from 854 faculty, 4,365 students, 584 parents, and 362 business recruiters. This is a grand total of 6,165 questionnaires in the national survey.

We have tried to present the following results accurately, but without inundating the reader with numbers and statistical niceties. Too many numbers can be dull reading, and some of us tend to be numbed and misled by the numbers to the detriment of the broader picture being developed. For this reason, simple declarative sentences will be used rather than sentences with such qualifying phrases as "on the average," "generally speaking," and so on.

Results from Questions Asked of All Respondents

It should be noted that the wording of some of the questions has been changed for ease of presentation (see Appendixes A and B).

1. When a college faculty member assigns a final course grade, to whom do you think it is addressed primarily—the student, the official record, employers, parents, other faculty?

Well over 90 percent in each group believed that grades are intended primarily for students. There was almost equally strong agreement across groups that grades were aimed least at other faculty. A few surprises were noted. Faculty members ranked the audiences in the order: student, *employers*, official record, parents, faculty. Business respondents ordered the items: student, official record, parents, *employers*, faculty. Thus, business recruiters see grades as not heavily directed toward their world at the same time faculty members see business as a significant audience—significant enough, in fact, to be in second place behind students.

2. Please rank order each of the following six grade-reporting systems: A+, A, A-, B+, so forth; Percentages (0–100); A, B, C, D, F; Honors/Satisfactory/Unsatisfactory; Pass/Fail; Written Narrative; Pass/No Credit.

Around three fourths of all groups preferred one of the first three systems—these are historically most familiar and ostensibly differentiate most strongly among students. Our guess is that most of the faculty, parents, and recruiters were graded almost entirely on one of these systems when they were students.

Each of the remaining four systems was preferred by between 5 percent and 20 percent of respondents in each group. All participants preferred quantitative, not qualitative, grading systems. This conclusion is inevitable since written narratives, which potentially provide the most differentiating evaluation for student performance, were preferred by less than 10 percent of respondents in any of the four groups. It is not differentiation per se that is preferred—it is *numerically quantifiable* differentiation!

3. Please indicate how strong a relationship you feel there is between the grades a student receives and success in life: very high, high, moderate, slight, very slight, none.

Approximately one half the participants in each group believed there is a moderate relationship between grades and later success. At the same time, one fourth (students) to one third or slightly more (each of the remaining groups) believed there is a high relationship. About 15 percent of respondents felt there is little or no relation between grades and future success, with the highest percentage—21 percent—produced by students. The next item was designed to clarify question 3.

4. Two students in the same class got different grades from their instructors—one received an A while the other received a C. How long do you think the difference in knowledge (achievement, learning, performance, and so on) represented by the grades A and C will last? (0 to 3 months, 3 to 12 months, 1 to 2 years, 2 to 5 years, greater than 5 years, no real initial difference)

We had more difficulty writing this item than any other, and we have had more criticism of it (from faculty) than any other. It was accused of being ambiguous and unclear (some of the critical remarks have been decidedly nonscholarly). At any rate, one fourth of the students and parents believed there are "no real initial differences"; almost none of the faculty and recruiters believed this statement. The striking finding is that almost half the faculty thought differences would last from two to five years and one third thought five years or more. The student group definitely did not see the difference between an A and a C as very meaningful or long lasting—only 14 percent saw real differences lasting longer than two years. Business people viewed an A and a C as representing a real difference between students that lasts about a year. Parents showed the greatest variability and seemed to hold three quite distinct opinions: For 26 percent there is no real difference; for 22 percent a real difference exists and it lasts for five years or more; for some 40 percent the difference is real but lasts between three months and two years.

What these responses to this question show most clearly is that grades, when considered as an evaluation of performance, have decidedly different meanings for different groups of people and thereby provide strong support for the view that socio-personal factors influence what a grade means even when the grade presumably represents a rigorous evaluation of student performance, knowledge, or achievement.

5. Discussions of grades and grading practices suggest that grades serve several purposes. Indicate the relative importance you believe each purpose currently has; then indicate the degree of importance you would like each to have. (5 = major, 4 = moderate, 3 = some, 2 = slight, 1 = none)

> *Communicates to the student how much learning was achieved.*
>
> *Provides reward (or warning) for outstanding (or unsatisfactory) performance.*
>
> *Provides the student with information for making educational or vocational decisions.*
>
> *Provides other educational institutions, such as graduate or professional schools, with information for making decisions about the student.*
>
> *Provides potential employers with information for making decisions about the student.*

Provides the instructor with information about teaching effectiveness.

Reflects academic standards of a department, college, or university.

Helps maintain academic standards.

Provides a historical record of the student's educational experiences and achievement.

Helps prepare the student for the competitive nature of adult life.

Helps the students learn discipline for later work or job requirements.

Helps remind the student that school is really work, not fun.

Provides a way of pleasing parents and meeting their demands.

Affords an accounting to society of how well the university or college is educating its students.

This is one of the most important items in the national survey because replies can be used to provide direction for future grading practices. For that reason, we have analyzed the results more fully than for any other item.

By combining rating categories 4 and 5 ("moderate" and "major importance"), the most important *current* purpose according to each of the groups is that of providing other educational institutions with information for making decisions about a student. Between 78 and 85 percent endorsed this purpose as being of primary importance—verfication of the fact that colleges and universities serve as personnel selection agencies for society. Three of the groups also agreed that the second most important *current* purpose is to provide rewards or warnings to students for performance; between 76 and 80 percent evaluated this purpose as number 2. (Sixty-seven percent of students rank this as number 3.)

There was much less agreement across groups about ten of the remaining eleven current purposes, but it is interesting that even the lowest percentages supporting a purpose as being of moderate or major importance range between 23 and 30 percent.

It is certainly puzzling to us how a set of letter symbols can serve all these functions. The purpose "providing the instructor with information about teaching effectiveness" was ranked either thirteenth or fourteenth in importance by all groups. Almost half the students ranked "provides the student with information for making educational or vocational decisions" as thirteenth. Almost one fourth of the faculty ranked "affords an accounting to society" as fourteenth. Thirty-nine percent of parents placed "provides a way of pleasing parents" fourteenth, and almost one third (30 percent) of the recruiters ranked "helps remind students that school is work" thirteenth.

Remarkable (and educationally encouraging) shifts occur for the second ranking of these statements; these rankings indicate the degree of importance respondents would *like* each purpose to have. Again by combining ratings 4 and 5, all four groups would *like* the most important purpose of grades to be that of communicating to students about learning—between 76 and 82 percent endorsed it as the most desirable purpose. The only other purpose for which there was agreement across groups was "grades provide a way of pleasing parents and meeting their demands"; all groups placed this one last, and the endorsement percentages are appreciably lower than for any of the other purposes: faculty, 9 percent; students, 17 percent; parents, 20 percent; recruiters, 11 percent. Perhaps this bottom ranking is a reflection of the changed age of majority and the fact that college is no longer reserved for those eighteen to twenty-one years old; many of today's students already are emancipated from the parental family.

High on the list of *preferred* purposes, and ones endorsed almost as extensively as that of communicating to students about learning, were "helps students learn to discipline themselves" and "provides rewards or warnings" to them. Both of these purposes, of course, are central to formal learning. Last on the list were "accounting to society" and "reminding students" that school is work. Faculty were out of step with the other three groups in continuing to place high on the list "providing information to other educational institutions for making decisions about the student."

The results for this item point to significant (for the cause of learning) disparities between the *present* and *preferred* purposes of grades. For a slightly different view of the disparities, we calculated "difference scores" between the preferred and current purposes. Positive values (+) in Table 1 indicate that the specific purpose should be more important; conversely, negative values (−) mean it should be less important. The size of the number is also significant—the larger the positive number the more that purpose should be stressed, and the larger the negative number the less it should be emphasized. The purposes listed in Table 1 have been selected from the total list of fourteen because they best meet the criteria just elaborated.

Table 1. Difference Scores Between Current and Preferred Grade Purposes

Positive	
Communicate to students how much was achieved	+0.49
Provide students information for making decisions	+0.48
Provide instructor information about teaching	+0.79
Help students learn discipline	+0.60
Negative	
Provide information to other educational institutions	−0.49
Provide potential employers with information	−0.25
Please parents	−0.85

The first finding of note by this method of analysis is that "communicating to students how much was achieved" as a desired purpose also was specified as needing greater emphasis. Second, observe that all four major positive purposes refer to students, instructors, or teaching and learning, that is, to actions relating to the academic mission of colleges and universities. In contrast, the major negative purposes (those to be deemphasized) do not concern aspects of teaching and learning. The clear majority of participants in this survey forcefully suggest that *grades ought to refer more to the educational process and less to their evaluative use by society.* We detail ways of improving communication about learning to students in Chapter Nine.

6. *Please indicate your preference for each of the following grading procedures: fixed levels (100 to 90 = A); inspection of scores; normal*

curve; personal change; student self-grading; amount of work completed; students grade other students.

Probably all participants were graded on the basis of one or all of the first three procedures during their student careers; they might not have known which procedure at which time. The "fixed levels" procedure was definitely the preference—slightly over half the faculty and students preferred it, as did two thirds of the parents and recruiters. All seem to feel that quantification of the unknown produces a precise and usable value. Approximately one third of each group desired grading based on the amount of work completed—the faculty were the least enthusiastic about this alternative. The two arrangements of students doing the grading were chosen by almost no one in any of the groups. "Personal change" was preferred by one third of the students and by approximately one fourth of the others.

For some of the procedures, striking differences appear among groups. Less than one fifth of the faculty preferred grading on the normal curve; almost half the students preferred it, as did well over one third of each of the other two groups. Almost half the faculty and students desired faculty inspection of scores, while only a third of parents and recruiters did. On the basis of these results, it seems reasonable to suggest that faculty members prefer more discretionary procedures, such as the inspection of scores, and that business people prefer more "objective" procedures, such as grading on a curve or on fixed levels. While students preferred normal curve grading to grading on the basis of the amount of work, they did not seem to want to deny completely the faculty discretionary power. This may be inferred from their strong preference for the inspection of test scores and by their preference (relative to the remaining groups) for grades given on the basis of personal change decided upon by each instructor.

Results on this question generally indicate that all respondents liked the "fixed levels" procedure and no one liked students controlling grades. Faculty liked more discretionary power for themselves, and parents and business people both preferred "objective" procedures. This was particularly true for the business group, whose top three preferences all have something of an "objective," contractual nature to them.

7. Using a seven-point scale (1 equals a very, very good grade and 7 equals a very, very bad grade) please describe your personal feelings about each of the grades A to F.

Table 2. Values of Grades for Each Group

Grade	Respondent Group			
	Students	Faculty	Parents	Business
A	1.48	1.59	1.42	1.51
B	2.61	2.73	2.48	2.65
C	4.67	3.94	3.58	3.86
D	5.41	5.21	5.07	5.21
F	6.52	6.41	6.33	6.42
Average Value	4.14	3.98	3.78	3.93

The results for this question produce a very clear pattern (Table 2). For the so-called "good" grades of A and B, the order of value—where the lower number means better—is parents, students, business people, and faculty. For the nominally neutral grade of C the order changes slightly; parents still valued this grade higher than did business people, but faculty valued it more than students (who, as noted in Chapter Two, put it below the 4.00 neutral point). Results for the nominally poorer grades of D and F indicate that parents continued to value these grades more highly than did respondents in any of the other groups. Results for faculty and business people indicate a tie-in valuation—both groups rated poorer grades less severely than did students.

The average value produced by all five grades suggests that, relative to other groups, parents overvalue all grades, students undervalue all grades (particularly the lower ones), faculty undervalue higher grades and find lower grades "not so bad," and business people tend to have the most consistent valuation of grade worth across the complete range of values. The same grade has a quite different meaning for each of the four groups. (See Chapter Eight.)

8. Indicate the degree to which you feel each of the following groups should consider changing its emphasis on grades: faculty, students, parents, business. Should they emphasize grades more, no change needed, or emphasize them less?

Essentially half the students, faculty, and parents believed the professoriate should continue its emphasis "as is." Only one third of the recruiters wanted the status quo maintained—almost one half wanted the faculty to emphasize grades more, the highest value for any group.

Well over half the students, parents, and recruiters thought students should emphasize grades more; only one third of the faculty thought this. Almost half the faculty wanted students to emphasize grades less. But remember, the number one present purpose of grades is to inform other educational institutions about students; if students emphasize grades less they will be in trouble with graduate and professional schools. Faculty members know this—in their response to item 5, they ranked that purpose high on both the "current" and "preferred" lists. But they still felt students should emphasize grades less. Is this the indifference of the Ivory Tower showing itself?

Almost half of the participants in each group thought parents should emphasize grades less, and all but the faculty thought the same true for business. Slightly more than one third of faculty wanted business to maintain its present emphasis.

9. A. *Did you ever cheat because you wanted a better grade? (yes, no)*

B. *If Yes, how frequently? (once only, 2 to 5 times, 6 to 10 times, 11 times or more)*

Over one third of all groups acknowledged having cheated to get a better grade and slightly over half of the current students acknowledged doing it. Of those who replied "yes," the majority indicated two to five times. The alternative, eleven or greater, was chosen by between 3 and 11 percent in each group. In a survey conducted twenty years ago (Bowers, 1964), half the students reported they had engaged in some form of academic dishonesty; most were those having grades of C or below, although over a third of those with A's and B+'s also admitted to cheating. (Some of the participants in the present survey were in college twenty years ago.)

10. A. *Did you ever drop (or audit) a course because you were afraid of a poor grade? (yes, no)*

B. *If Yes, how frequently? (once only, 2 to 5 times, 6 to 10 times, 11 times or more)*

Striking differences in frequency emerge across the groups: parents, 18 percent; faculty, 30 percent; recruiters, 40 percent; current students, 47 percent. Across all four groups, 90 percent mentioned equally "once" or "two to five" times.

In our opinion, dropping courses to avoid bad grades is a problem that needs further study. Why there are differences among these groups is not clear and might not be important; the important problem is that half of today's students drop courses to avoid receiving a mysterious and powerful symbol. We do not believe "lowered standards" or "raised standards" are useful explanations, although we do know that contemporary college students are more comfortable dropping courses than were students a generation or more ago. Perhaps the stigma of "drop equals fail" no longer applies with as much force as it did.

On the basis of our personal experiences with students, it seems likely that many of those dropping courses to avoid bad grades are destined for graduate and professional schools or for leadership positions in business, industry, or government. It is our guess, too, that the courses dropped are those designed to broaden and enlighten beyond narrow technical interests. A fairly common complaint nationwide concerns the narrow-mindedness of some professional and business people. Furthermore, one is likely to hear an established physician, or lawyer, or professor, or executive say in effect, "If I had only taken something in philosophy or literature or the like when I was a student." Thus, we hope the reasons for dropping courses will be studied exhaustively.

11. To what extent have you read about . . . or discussed grade inflation? (not at all; a little; a great deal)

Less than one in five of the parents and students selected the alternative "a great deal," and only one in four of the recruiters selected it. One of every two faculty members chose "a great deal." This faculty interest strikes us as odd because essentially the same number indicated that "the difference in learning reflected by grades A and C" will last from two years to more than five. As is to be expected, faculty were more concerned about the value of their symbols than were any of the remaining groups.

12. How strongly on a scale from 1 (not at all) to 5 (very strongly) does grade inflation concern you?

Again, it was the faculty who expressed by far the strongest concern. While there was some general concern across all four groups, the overall average was 2.77, indicating that the majority of respondents were only moderately concerned. While it may be going too far to say that the issue of grade inflation is simply a tempest in an academic teapot, it seems safe to say that academics are much more concerned about it than are most others.

13. Using this five-point scale (1 = excellent, 2 = good, 3 = fair, 4 = poor, 5 = not at all) please indicate the usefulness of student grades or GPA as an indicator of: [the thirteen properties listed to the left in Table 3 were in a different order and not grouped in the questionnaire].

This item was designed to determine the extensiveness and depth of belief about the presumed virtues of grades and that haloed statistic, the college GPA. Because of the abiding faith in grades as assessing the various characteristics mentioned in this item, results for question 13 are presented in detail. Percentages in Table 3 are combinations of the "excellent" and "good" rating.

The first aspect of note in these results is the relative ordering of each of the thirteen characteristics. These range from high rankings for achievement, ability to get grades, self-discipline, and motivation, to low rankings for psychological adjustment, interpersonal skill, and creativity. One is struck by the contrast between achievement-oriented motivation and discipline, characteristics thought to be well captured by the GPA, and more personal characteristics such as adjustment and creativity, thought not to be well captured by this statistic. Surprisingly, two of the characteristics often presumed to be indexed by GPA—intelligence and communication skill—occupy only the seventh and eighth positions, respectively.

A different but related way of looking at these rankings is in terms of the size of the average percentage separating each of the characteristics. An examination of the values associated with each characteristic indicates that the list may be divided into three groups: one ranging from rank 1 through rank 6 (50 percent or greater), a second from rank 7 through 10 (32 to 44 percent), and a third from rank 11 through 13 (9 to 27 percent). The first set of characteristics, almost without exception, deals with motivational

Table 3. Student Characteristics Indicated by Grades

Characteristics	Faculty (1 + 2)		Students (1 + 2)		Parents (1 + 2)		Business (1 + 2)	
First								
Academic achievement	(1)	83%	(1)	74%	(1)	84%	(1)	84%
Ability to get grades	(2)	76	(2)	66	(3)	72	(2)	80
Motivation	(3)	71	(4)	60	(4)	70	(4)	60
Self-discipline	(4)	69	(3)	65	(2)	73	(3)	66
Ability to work within a system	(5)	64	(5)	55	(5)	64	(5)	54
Ability to compete	(6)	59	(6)	52	(6)	62	(6)	52
Average		70%		62%		71%		66%
Second								
General intelligence	(7.5)	46%	(8)	34%	(7)	53%	(7)	45%
Communication skill	(7.5)	46	(10)	31	(8)	46	(9)	27
Conformity	(9)	38	(9)	34	(9)	44	(8)	37
Ability to cope with stress	(10)	35	(7)	35	(10)	35	(10)	18
Average		41%		33%		44%		32%
Third								
Psychological adjustment	(11)	19%	(12)	20%	(12.5)	23%	(11)	14%
Interpersonal skill	(12)	15	(11)	21	(11)	29	(13)	9
Creativity	(13)	14	(13)	17	(12.5)	23	(12)	10
Average		16%		19%		24%		11%

Note: Value in parentheses indicates rank order of characteristic.

factors, the second (in three of four cases) with academic characteristics, while the third reflects personal virtues not restricted to the academic environment and—according to our respondents—related only slightly to grades and GPAs.

A second conclusion to be drawn from the table is provided by the average percentages of 1 (excellent) plus 2 (good) ratings for each group of characteristics. Parents and faculty view grades and GPAs as better indicators of the first and second set of characteristics than do students and recruiters. Put in a somewhat oversimplified way, parents and faculty overvalue the significance of grades and the GPA compared with students and business people.

In addition to overall differences, individual characteristics have different average values in each of the four groups. For example, students produced somewhat different (and less optimistic) values for "academic achievement" than any of the remaining three groups. A similar result describes the pattern of responses for "intelligence," where students produced a value of 34 percent and the remaining groups varied between 45 percent and 53 percent. Results for "ability to cope with stress" showed a clear division between business (18 percent) and all other groups (35 percent), with business finding grades and GPAs less useful metrics for this characteristic than any of the other groups.

Finally, the pattern produced by business deserves some comment, particularly since business is viewed by many people as one of the major users of grades and GPAs. For the two items at the top of the list, business valued GPA as much or more than any other group; for items at the bottom of the list (ranks 9 to 13) they valued GPA less than any other group. This suggests that business people value grades as indicators of little other than an ability to get grades and tend to undervalue them as indicators of more broad-ranging personal abilities and skills. This should serve to make all the more surprising the finding, to be discussed later, that in over 80 percent of initial decisions to hire a college graduate, recruiters reported that GPA is at least of moderate importance to their decision, and in almost half of the cases GPA is of either great or crucial importance.

To emphasize further the idiosyncratic nature of beliefs about grades and GPAs, it is well to recall both Dressel's definition of a grade ("an inadequate report of an inaccurate judgment . . .") and the conglomerate structure of GPAs as reported by Goldman and his associates (see Chapter Two). If one adds to these metric difficulties the fact that the qualities of tests from which the grade has been derived vary from unbelievably poor to extremely good, who can know the meaning of a grade or GPA? In the light of these difficulties, it is tragic that three fourths or more of our respondents believe that grades indicate academic achievement. Ask an expert in any field (including faculty experts in different disciplines) about the meaning or significance of any given "fact" and invariably the answer will be prefaced by "Well, it depends." Not so for the meaning of a B or a GPA of 2.99.

The next five items, numbers 14 to 18, examine certain developmental aspects of attitudes toward and beliefs about grades. We were curious and hope others will be, too.

14. In general, what type of grades did you receive in elementary school, junior high school, high school, and college?

The total group is remarkably homogeneous on the basis of self-reporting, having made mostly A's and B's up to and through high school. At the college level, the percentage of faculty receiving top grades increases, the percentage of students decreases, and the percentages for the other two groups remain constant.

The students continue to be embroiled in the grading game and for that reason may be reporting more accurately than those in the other groups; memories often soften with the passage of time.

15. Using the following five-point scale, please indicate how important grades were to you at the following levels: grades 1 to 6; grades 7 to 9; grades 10 to 12; college.

This is one of the few items for which there are no essential differences among groups. Grades increase in importance as one goes up the educational ladder—starting with a moderate degree of importance in elementary school and increasing to a much more important level during college. Replies to the next item should help to clarify the dynamics of this increasing importance.

16. Students report they work for grades to satisfy or please different groups of people. Rate on scale of 1 to 5 the relative importance each of the following had (has) for you for grades 1 to 6, 7 to 9, 10 to 12, and college: self, parents, teachers, friends, future educational institution, future employers.

For grades 1 to 6 there are remarkable similarities; almost two thirds in each group tried to please parents, one half wanted to please teachers, and one third or more worked to please themselves. For grades 7 to 9 the pattern is similar to that of the first six grades, although shifts begin to appear: Pleasing oneself increased from one third to almost one half for all groups. For grades 10 to 12, pleasing parents continued unabated; pleasing oneself increased to two thirds, and slightly over one half were concerned about satisfying educational institutions.

At the college level, real shifts occur but certain similarities and differences continue to exist across groups. Around three fourths worked to please themselves and from one third to one half to satisfy parents. Some three fourths of the faculty and students were concerned about other educational institutions, and about three fourths of the students were concerned about employers. As for relative importance (average value 3.00 or more out of 5.00), the significant groups are ordered: self, future educational institutions, future employers, and parents.

The pattern presented by these results seems to describe the developmental cycle of human growth in contemporary American society. At the elementary school level, the first four places are occupied by significant people in the student's immediate environment. At this level some students may be working for themselves but most are working primarily for parents and parent-surrogates—teachers. Not surprisingly, no real importance is attached to future educational or employment issues. At the junior high school level, a significant reordering occurs: Parents are still most important, but students now find self-evaluation more important than that of their teachers. Friends begin to be less significant—a trend that will continue over all subsequent levels—and the future is still far away. By high school, the future has moved closer (presumably in regard to the role grades will play in the selection of a college), and the person's own evaluation of grade significance has become of primary importance. Parents and teachers are still significant; future employers are not yet a main focus.

At the college level a noteworthy reordering occurs. Although grades are still most important for satisfying the student, future education or employment is now more imminent. Parents still fall in the group of people of moderate importance to satisfy; teachers and friends are no longer in that group. The relatively low position afforded teachers with respect to grades provides a sad commentary on the fact that students and teachers are no longer in a meaningful social-interpersonal relationship; that is, teachers are no longer part of the primary group a student feels satisfied by pleasing. Teachers do receive an average score of 3.13 at the postgraduate level, although two of the four groups (parents and business) produced average values of less than 3.00 (more important). As at all levels beyond elementary school, friends are not important influences on grade-pursuit.

Given these general trends, did any of the various respondent groups produce different results? There were only two significant exceptions: (1) Business respondents reported that at the high school level parental sources of satisfaction were of primary importance and self-satisfaction was in third rank; and (2) faculty respondents continued to rate teachers as sources of significant satisfaction at the college level, even more significant than parents. The latter exception is readily interpretable: Students who later became faculty seem to have experienced a mentor-like relationship during the college years. The first exception, that parental values were of primary importance during the high school years to individuals who became business people, does not have an easy or ready interpretation. Perhaps an examination of how parents dealt with such individuals during the high school years (the next two questions) may provide some insight into this finding.

Results for the overall question reveal a pattern that accords with broader issues concerning the progressive significance of self-evaluation and an orientation toward the future at the expense of an evaluation by powerful others. Such changes seem quite reasonable as the person progresses from elementary school through the college years.

17. For grades 1 to 6, 7 to 9, 10 to 12, and college, please indicate which of the following actions describes your parents' typical response to any good grades or report cards you received. [The actions were in a different order and not grouped in the questionnaire.]

Category 1 Made no mention of it

Category 2 Joked and/or made other appreciative comments

Remarked that good grades were expected

Praised and encouraged

Gave monetary (or other tangible) rewards

Were supportive, proud

Said "grades are not worth killing oneself over"

Discussed the general importance of grades

Said "you're doing better than I did"

Said "what is important is that you do your best"

Category 3 Asked if I were "turning into a bookworm"

Reminded that "there is more to life than just good grades"

Cautioned against getting a "swelled head"

This item is one of the more unique in the questionnaire and one in which we were most interested. For purposes of analysis, parental actions are divided into the three categories indicated above—the first being "made no mention of it." The second and largest category contains two kinds of appreciative remarks—those that praise, reward, or indicate personal support, and those that suggest a relatively intellectual reaffirmation of the importance of grades. The third category is best defined as a somewhat negative reaction or as a teasing warning.

The consistent finding for all educational levels and across all four groups is that good grades produce parental actions of some sort. The category "made no mention" was marked by very few participants; the percentage ranges from 4 to 16 percent, the 16 percent being for faculty at the college level.

Between one fourth to two thirds of all groups reported positive parental reactions (the second category) to good grades through high school. These percentages continue for both the business and student groups in college (the parent group was not analyzed beyond the high school level because 26 percent did not attend college). Positive parental reactions dropped rather markedly for the faculty group during the college years—this finding is consistent with the increase for that group of the parental reaction "made no mention." By far the most common positive actions were "praised and encouraged" and "were supportive, proud." The positive actions of "tangible rewards" were more common for present students during grades 1 to 9 than for any other groups.

A careful evaluation of changes across the various school levels reveals changes in "good" responses and some reasonably strong differences for each of the four groups. The most striking trend is that positive reactions to good grades reached a peak for all groups during the high-school years and, in agreement with results involving the no-mention category, dropped off sharply during the college years. For business and faculty groups, the pattern seems to be that parents of respondents who became business people were more active in responding to good grades than was true for respondents who became college professors. Although the student group provided the greatest overall proportion of responses, differences between business and faculty can be considered meaningful since members of both groups were describing events retrospectively. In contrast, students were describing contemporary actions and the higher level of response reported by them does not necessarily represent a difference in "amount" of parental activity in the same way as it does for the other two groups.

The category of somewhat negative warnings was used infrequently. What is interesting about this category is that at the college level its use increased rather strongly for students and less so for faculty and business. One suggestion from these results is that while parents actively reward good grades in high school, thereafter their reactions are more oriented to the world beyond the classroom. As said in one of the alternatives, "there is more to life than good grades," and some 16 percent of parents of current students begin to push such an evaluation during the college years.

18. For grades 1 to 6, 7 to 9, 10 to 12, and college, please indicate which of the following actions describes your parents' typical response to any bad grades or report cards you received. [These actions were not grouped in the questionnaire.]

Category 1 Made no mention of it

Category 2 Asked for an explanation

Made demeaning jokes

Gave me "the cold shoulder"

Expected even less from me in the future

Were sarcastic

Accused me of laziness

Nagged

Showed anger

Withdrew privileges

Lectured or verbally scolded me

Administered physical punishment

Category 3   Said "what is important is that you do your best"

Helped me study afterwards

Told me not to worry

This, too, is one of our unique items. Again for purposes of analysis, the parental actions are grouped into three categories. The first of these is "made no mention." The second category is a punishment or unpleasant-consequences category, whereas the third consists of supportive or positive actions.

Overall, bad grades were ignored more often than were good ones—the percentages for the "made no mention" category are slightly higher here than for good grades. Such reactions ranged from 4 to 14 percent with one exception—the faculty group reported 23 percent "made no mention" at the college level. This category was slightly higher for the faculty group throughout all educational levels.

Although bad grades tended to be ignored slightly more than good ones, all groups reported a greater frequency of negative actions for bad grades than positive actions for good grades. At least one third of all groups reported unpleasant consequences of one sort or another. At all levels, grade 1 through college, the most common was "asked for an explanation," with current students and recruiters being the most pressured. The second most common unpleasantness was "lectured or verbally scolded"; this one tended to cease during college. As was true for the rewarding of good grades, there was an increase in negative reactions from elementary school through high school, with peaks tending to occur during junior and senior high school.

Approximately one third of all groups indicated support in the form of parents saying, "what is important is that you do your best." For grades 1 to 6, for approximately one fourth in all groups, support included being helped to study; such offers were less frequent as the students got older. One encouraging aspect of the results is that the students reported an increase in supportive remarks—"what is important is that you do your best"—from high school to college. About 40 percent of the student sample reported such actions by their parents during this period.

Grades 7 to 12 was the period for "accused me of laziness," "nagged," or "showed anger." Current students report more of this behavior than do members of the other groups. Memories of those in the other groups may be fading.

Parental reactions to both good and bad grades provide a picture of differential reponse for respondents in each of the four groups as well as at each of the various grade levels. Peak parental activity for both good and bad grades occurs in high school and drops off dramatically in college. Although negative parental reactions begin in junior high school, they continue at a relatively high rate through the high school years and decline sharply at the college level. For the various populations studied, the general order of groups (from most to least parental reactions) was students more than business or parents, and business and parents more than faculty. Looking only at the two professional groups—faculty and business—it seems clear that parents of those students who grew up to work in the business community were more responsive both to good and bad grades than was true for students who grew up to be faculty members. Faculty generally reported earning better grades than business people, but this does not seem to account for the relatively marked differences since such differences applied to good as well as to bad grades. It appears, rather, that parents of future faculty members just left their children alone more throughout the educational process and that parents of future business people monitored their children's activities—good and bad—more carefully and more continuously. Perhaps the choice of business rather than teaching as a career represents a continuing interest in public evaluative reactions that let the person know how well he or she is doing. Also, life in a university is much less structured than in business.

A final item in this section requested respondents to state in their own words the manner in which they felt grades had had the greatest impact on their lives. Approximately 50 percent of the total number of people sampled chose to write something. As a whole, the comments were on what one would expect: (1) the competive pressures caused by grades, (2) the positive motivating effects of them, and (3) the assertion that good grades led to needed financial aid. Some of the noteworthy negative remarks are scattered throughout the book.

Summary

A total of 6,165 people—4,365 students, 854 faculty, 584 parents of college students, and 362 business recruiters—completed a machine-scoreable questionnaire about their attitudes toward and beliefs surrounding grades and grading practices. Certain common questions were asked across the four groups and several questions were asked that have not been asked previously. Samples of faculty and students were drawn from twenty-three colleges and universities representing five institutional types throughout five regions of the United States. The business recruiters were sampled from companies that recruit regularly on college campuses. We believe our results would be confirmed by more extensive sampling.

The salient findings include the commonly held belief that the current major purpose of grades is that of communicating about students to graduate and professional schools; encouragingly, though, all four groups expressed a desire that the primary purpose of grades be that of communicating about learning to students. At the same time, and contradictorily as we see it, grading practices that reflect numerically quantifiable differences among students were preferred by all groups. Such reporting systems as A+, A, A−, and so on, represent the overwhelming choices. Faculty believe that the learning or achievement indicated by course grades lasts for much longer periods of time than do those in the other three groups. All groups believe grades predict future achievement to some degree, although faculty believe this most strongly and students least strongly. In general, parents value all five grades more than does any other group; students value them least. All groups report having worked to satisfy their parents at the lower educational levels and to satisfy themselves at the upper levels. Not surprisingly, faculty reported getting higher grades in college than did those in the remaining groups.

Good course grades receive favorable parental reactions, especially at the elementary and secondary levels, while bad course grades arouse fewer parental reactions. Recruiters reported more parental reactions to grades, especially to bad ones, than did faculty. Currently, some one half of college students drop courses for fear of receiving bad grades; between 30 and 40 percent acknowledge having cheated in order to get a better grade. Such cheating was reported to occur relatively infrequently over the course of a college career.

Grade inflation was found to be of little interest to any group other than faculty. When all groups were asked to describe the student characteristics they thought were represented by grades and GPAs, all four groups thought grades have most to do with student motivation and drive, less to do with intelligence and communication skills, and least to do with interpersonal skills or psychological adjustment. At the same time, most of the qualitative comments point to the significant roles grades have played in the lives of our respondents, whether these individuals are now students, parents, college professors, or business recruiters.

FOUR

What Employers
and Faculty Members
Think About Grades

There are certain common interests about grades among faculty members and business people—perhaps the major one is their use in the selection of college and university graduates for either graduate or professional school or for positions in business or industry. For this reason, in the National Grade Survey members of the two groups were asked several of the same questions as well as distinctly different ones. Before turning to these results, we will extract and review sources of agreement and disagreement for common questions between the two groups described in the last chapter. This review is offered as a summary of the major attitudes held by faculty and business. It is intended to highlight, in as clear a way as possible, their unique perceptions of grades independent of those perceptions held by students and parents.

1. Both faculty and business people thought the major audience for grades should be students; faculty were much more likely to see business as a target group than were business respondents themselves.
2. Both faculty and business people agreed there is a real difference in knowledge reflected by a grade of A and one of C; almost one half of faculty believed it would last two to five years, whereas only one third of business respondents held the same view.
3. When proposed changes between present and preferred purposes for grades were evaluated, both groups agreed quite

closely on those needed in eight of the fourteen purposes. There were two rather striking disagreements: (1) Faculty ranked "grades provide other educational institutions with information" third and business people ranked it seventh, and (2) faculty ranked "grades provide information to instructors about teaching effectiveness" tenth and business ranked it as 5.5. Faculty believed to a slightly greater extent than business that "grades should reflect and maintain academic standards." At the same time, business people believed to a slightly greater extent than faculty that grades should "prepare students for the competitive nature of adult life" and "help students learn to discipline themselves."

4. While both business people and faculty wanted grades to be based on fixed levels of performance, business people preferred grading on the normal curve more than did faculty. Faculty rated second their personal discretion in looking at test scores, and business people rated it fourth. Thus, faculty like some discretion whereas business people prefer presumably more rigorous and fixed procedures.

5. Both business people and faculty felt that parents and business should reduce the emphasis on the importance of grades; business people also felt that faculty and students should emphasize grades more.

6. There were clear differences in quantity (although not in kind) of reactions made by parents to the grades of students who later became business or faculty people. Reactions to both good and bad grades were more numerous by parents of students who later went into business; parents of future academics tended to leave their children alone during the school years.

7. Faculty members were much more concerned about grade inflation than were business recruiters; both groups were more interested in this issue than parents or students.

8. There was considerable agreement between business people and faculty in the rank order of importance of the characteristics presumably measured by grades. For example, both placed academic achievement first and interpersonal skill last. Faculty felt much more strongly than did business people

that grades reflect communication skill, ability to cope with stress, motivation, and ability to work within a system.

Items Common Only to Business People and Faculty

In addition to items that were similar across all four groups, there were pairs of parallel items specific to business and faculty participants. These items are discussed next.

1. When you are reviewing materials of recent college graduates for employment in your firm (admission to graduate or professional school), how strongly would you value each of the following pieces of information? Assign a number from 1 (minimum) to 7 (maximum) indicating the degree of importance.

This is a very significant item because personnel selection for postcollege activities continues to be a primary function of institutions of higher learning. We present the results in some detail because we believe there is considerable misunderstanding about these matters. Average ranks of importance were calculated for each set of materials. The materials are listed from highest to lowest for each group (see Table 4) and placed in three categories—those with ranks of 5.0 or greater, those with ranks between 4.0 and 4.9, and those with ranks of 3.9 or less. These three categories represent three levels of importance and for convenience sake are labeled Most Important, Moderately Important, and Slightly Important.

Note first the top category—Most Important. It is apparent immediately that there is little overlap in the kinds of information used for selecting young graduates for the marketplace or for further schooling. Faculty emphasis is on academic matters entirely, while only one of three sorts of information for business concerns academic matters. Now note the bottom category—Slightly Important. Here there is no overlap between the interests of the two groups. It is noteworthy that one of the features of most importance to business—"nature of noncollege jobs"—is of minimal importance to faculty and that one of the features of maximum importance to faculty—"samples of student writing"—has little significance for business. Yet *business is among the major complainers about young graduates being unable to use our language properly.* We

Table 4. Importance of Personnel Selection Materials for Postcollege

Business	*Faculty*
Most Important (5.0 or higher)	
Personality of student	Grades in major courses
Grades in major courses	Number difficult courses completed
Nature of noncollege jobs	Breadth of courses taken
	Samples of student writing
Moderately Important (4.0 to 4.9)	
Overall GPA	Overall GPA
Publications, awards, honors	Publications, awards, honors
Reputation of school attended or of recommenders	Reputation of school attended or of recommenders
Breadth of courses taken	Standard test scores
Breadth of personal life experiences	Letters of recommendation
Participation in extracurricular activities	Personality of student
Number of difficult courses completed	Breadth of personal life experiences
Contributions to the school	
Affirmative action needs	
Slightly Important (3.9 or less)	
Samples of student writing	Contributions to the school
Letters of recommendation	Participation in extracurricular activities
Standard test scores	Affirmative action needs
	Nature of noncollege jobs

were surprised that standardized test scores, graduate record examination (GRE) and others, are of such little interest to business.

In the Moderately Important category four of nine sets of material preferred by business are identical to those preferred by faculty. These similarities suggest some slight agreement between groups on what constitutes good credentials. The overall differences between the two should not be surprising since the postcollege worlds of business and industry on the one hand, and undergraduate and professional schools on the other, require different interests, qualities, and abilities. Business, in the main, is selecting young people in hopes of immediately using their skills. Faculty are selecting young people for further development of their talents and skills; use of these skills and talents will be delayed for several years.

Within the context of selection it is important to recall that faculty believed that the second most important audience for grades is employers (Chapter Three). Business respondents saw employers as a much less important audience for grades than did faculty. It is also useful to recall that faculty continued to rank "providing information to graduate and professional schools" high on their list of preferred purposes for grades and GPAs— third among fourteen to be exact. One conclusion to draw is that college professors cannot simultaneously provide the kinds of information desired by business for selection purposes and those desired by graduate and professional schools. In our view, serving as personnel selection agents for society is a distortion of the faculty role in the first place; the job should require them to focus on promoting learning in the classrooms and not on classifying students for industry.

For those who might maintain that we have magnified the significance of small differences between numbers (for example, the difference of one tenth of a point between 4.9 and 5.0), we remind you that our interpretations are consistent with those made from student GPAs. Much smaller differences between GPA numbers result in profound differences in the lives of students. For example, a student with a GPA of 3.50 receives consideration for admission to a professional school, while one with a GPA of 3.49 may be rejected summarily. One hundredth of a GPA point is very small, although it often seems much larger and significant in regard to student careers.

2. A. Do you think it necessary to control grade inflation? (yes, no) Three fourths of the participants in each group responded "yes".

2. B. If Yes, for which of the following reasons?

Dilutes the value of the only reward feedback system we have for students

Gives students a false concept of their ability and performance

Is just another example of lowered standards

Lessens the ability of graduate schools and businesses to make knowledgeable decisions

Reduces the value of a college degree

There are two interesting differences between the two groups: (1) More recruiters (two thirds) than faculty (one half) endorsed the statement "gives students a false concept of their ability and/or performance"; and (2) fewer recruiters (one third) than faculty (one half) endorsed the statement "lessens the ability of graduate schools and businesses to make knowledgeable decisions." Aside from these differences, the percentage of endorsements by each group is approximately one half.

2. C. If No, for which of the following reasons?

Nothing can be done

Grades are detrimental to students anyway

There is no real standard against which alleged inflation can be compared

Grades do not necessarily reflect student ability and performance

The system will ultimately correct itself

Fewer than 10 percent in either group endorsed any item except "grades do not necessarily reflect student ability and performance." Sixteen percent of the recruiters agreed with this reason but only 8 percent of the faculty did. (The faculty is consistent over several items in manifesting its reverence for grades.)

3. In the following list, please mark the three most important factors that you believe have led to grade inflation.

Faculty wanting to maintain high student enrollment

Faculty showing less concern for maintaining standards

Students being more competitive for grades

Use of Pass/Fail grading systems

Liberalization in course withdrawal policies

Students repeating courses more often to raise grades

Faculty expecting less of students

Students on the whole not being as bright as they used to be

Declining quality of education in elementary and secondary schools

Overcrowded classes forcing a change in grading standards

Product of the student movement of the 1960s

Close to one half in each group chose the alternatives "declining quality of education in the lower grades" and "faculty expecting less of students." The third most important factor for business was "faculty showing less concern for maintaining standards"; for faculty the third factor was "faculty wanting to maintain high student enrollments." There were similarities, too, about factors of least importance—"students repeating courses more often to raise their grades," "overcrowded classes forcing a change in grading standards," and "students on the whole not being as bright as they used to be."

Business Recruiters

Several items were unique to recruiters.

1. Please indicate the extent (little, slight, moderate, great, crucial) to which college grades and grade-point-averages influence the following decisions made by your company:

Initial hiring

Initial salary

Selection for special training programs

Subsequent promotions

In well over one third of the cases, grades are of great or crucial importance for initial hiring; in another one half, grades are of moderate importance. Thus, in 84 percent of the companies, grades are of moderate to crucial importance for obtaining that first job. (In the Lindquist study mentioned in Chapter One, the GPA was considered by 68 percent of 262 well-known companies as Important or Very Important for initial hiring.) Recall from an earlier item in this survey that the second most important feature to business was "grades in major courses." After the applicant's foot is in the door, according to replies to this item, college grades have little to do with future decisions about the applicant. This fact is consistent with the repeated research findings (Chapter One) that grades do not predict future performance in industry or, for that matter, anywhere else.

It is interesting, though, that the group that prides itself on being "hard-nosed about the bottom line" responded as it did to the question, *Has your company conducted any studies relating college grades to on-the-job performance?* Eighty-nine percent said "no." Of the few reporting (11 percent) that studies had been conducted, companies reported that in one fourth of them grades were excellent predictors of job performance. At the other end of the spectrum, 34 percent said that college grades turned out to be fair or poor predictors of success. The results only confirm those of numerous studies over the years, which have shown that grades do very little in the way of predicting postcollege job success. Perhaps we should have asked, "Have you read the research literature about grades and occupational success?"

In the thirty-ninth annual survey of employment practices for college graduates conducted by Northwestern University (Lindquist, 1984; this is a separate study from the Lindquist study mentioned above), 250 companies were asked, "Do you feel that grades are a predictor of future success in your company?" Forty-eight percent replied "yes." Yet almost all "yes" respondents qualified their opinions; for example: "Too many other factors affect grades. . . . The ability to take exams doesn't equate with leadership, integrity, motivation, and the interpersonal skill it takes to succeed," and "While grades are important, many other factors may be important to a higher degree, such as productivity, energy, communication skills, honesty, tact, and other such personal characteristics" (p. 17).

Here we must ask, "Do the different findings from different surveys of business people mean that their beliefs about the sanctity of grades are diminishing, or are the differences merely reflections of differently worded questions?" In any case, it is clear that contradictions and inconsistencies occur frequently in the attitudes business holds toward grades.

2. *When comparing the GPAs of interviewees from different schools, how much importance do you place on the reputation of each educational institution? (little, slight, moderate, great, crucial)*

Forty-eight percent rated the reputation of the college or university as being of great or crucial importance; only 15 percent indicated this factor was of little or slight importance.

3. *When conducting initial employment interviews, do you ever ask interviewees to explain their grades to you?*

Thirty-seven percent indicated "always" or "often," 41 percent stated "sometimes," 22 percent marked "rarely" or "never."

4. *How would you react to an interviewee who said that his or her grades did not give a good indication of ability?*

Slightly over half the recruiters maintained they would accept the explanation with reservations; only 17 percent would react with strong reservations or dismiss the explanation totally. Surely there are instances in which grades' meanings must be clarified. One student responding to the national survey explained: "Grades that have determined my GPA as a C average have indicated to prospective employers that my intelligence and ability are only average. What they do not tell is that I also worked forty hours per week and paid my way through school."

Business recruiters were also asked, "In general is there a minimum GPA or cut-off score used by your company for initial hiring of recent college graduates? (Assume A = 4.00, B = 3.00, and so on)." Forty-five percent indicated that their company did not have an established minimum GPA cut-off. Of the 55 percent that did, the following minimums were reported: 2.00, 19 percent; 2.25, 6 percent; 2.50, 28 percent; 2.75, 19 percent; 3.00, 25 percent; 3.25, 3 percent. In light of the number of companies that consider grades of great importance when making decisions about initial hiring, it is somewhat surprising to find that nearly half do not have established minimum grade cut-offs, and of those that do, only 28 percent require a GPA of 3.00 or better as their minimum. Given the ambiguities of grading perhaps this is not such a bad idea—after all, business would seem more interested in doing and not in thinking about doing.

Faculty

The number of students a faculty member grades each term varies greatly from institution to institution, from department to department, and from individual to individual; so, too, do individual grading practices. Since few would argue with the educational truism that "no two students are alike," we wanted to learn if, and how, faculty in the privacy of their classes individualize grading practices. During our initial interviews, we had asked faculty if they had ever given a student a final course grade on the basis of some information or criterion not used for the remainder of the class. The diversity of their answers can be seen in these replies:

No. I wish I could have at times. Some poor souls had troubles that were no fault of their own.

Two or three times in sixteen years.

I had a student recently who had leukemia and was having to undergo special radiation therapy (half way across the country). The student had to take two weeks out in the middle of the semester. I knew that student rather well because she had taken a course with me two years earlier when a freshman. I knew perfectly well she was an A student; she got an A in that freshman seminar. She could have gotten an A in this course. I ended up giving her a B on less than the full quota of work.

Once in a while, I will know a student, and know that she had real tough luck. I remember a case two years ago where a student missed the final because her mother died. She took a make-up three weeks later and on the basis of numbers would have merited a D, but she had been doing C work all semester—I gave her a C. In a very rare instance, an older student who had just been widowed—her work

and her papers were C level. . . . We gave her an A
for the course because she had vastly improved from
the beginning to end . . . because of effort.

We then formally asked the following question of over 800
faculty members: *Have you ever given a student a final course grade on
the basis of some information or criterion not used for the remainder of the
class? If Yes, approximately how often?* The picture that emerged is
striking—nearly half of all faculty reported they never made exceptions to the "rule," and of those who did, 66 percent did so
only once or twice in several years. Of the total number surveyed,
a minuscule 10 percent did so once or more per term. Greater
frequencies rarely occurred. *If Yes, for which of the following reasons?*
(Eight reasons were listed.)

The two most frequent occasions prompting faculty to alter
their grading schemes were progressive improvement from an exceptionally poor start (28 percent) and personal crisis (27 percent).
It is not surprising that personal crisis ranks high on the list—after
all, most faculty have experienced one or more such events in
their own lives. Progressive improvement from an exceptionally
poor start is a testament shared by both the student and the hard-
working faculty member, and accomplishments of this type merit
special consideration. It is interesting that physical illness (19 percent), language disabilities (13 percent), and certain personal responsibilities such as the student being sole provider for the family
(4 percent), received little consideration when course grades were
assigned. It is also significant that even when a faculty member
had other knowledge of a student suggesting the grade did not
reflect the student's ability, only 15 percent reported a willingness
to use this information to alter a grade. Somewhat facetiously, we
might advise students to get a note from a psychiatrist rather than
from a physician if they want to get an instructor to change a
grade.

Though it is impossible to know from an examination of
student transcripts the grading policies and practices used by individual faculty members, it seems reasonable to anticipate that in
the vast majority of cases these unspecified standards were applied
consistently to all students. A second set of considerations must be

noted. Few scholarly thinkers in any disciplinary area would disagree with these three observations: (1) Measurement of any kind cannot be made without error (often the magnitude of error is considerable); (2) exceptions to every rule exist; and (3) judgments, however carefully derived, can produce errors. In this light it is paradoxical that college and university faculty are bound so inflexibly to idiosyncratic grading systems that they refuse to acknowledge unique circumstances that might justify altering the system. In the end, for the majority of faculty members, it is the grading system and not the student that prevails.

Faculty and Students

The academy has two major constituencies—faculty and students—and it seemed important to find out how well these groups feel about grading practices. The following summarizes and highlights the sources of agreement and disagreement between students and faculty:

1. Both students and faculty viewed the student as the primary audience for a grade and other faculty members as the least important audience.
2. Students tended to view the relationship of grades to success in life as less significant than faculty; 21 percent of students felt there was only a slight relationship, whereas only 10 percent of faculty felt this to be the case.
3. Perhaps the major difference between students and faculty was regarding how long the difference in knowledge reflected by a grade of A and a grade of C would last. Some 53 percent of the faculty felt it would last two to five years or more; only 14 percent of students felt this way. Forty-five percent of students felt such differences were nonexistent or would last only zero to three months; the comparable value for faculty was 14 percent.
4. Faculty and students agreed fairly well on changes needed to make grades merit their preferred purposes. The major exception was that of "preparing students for the competitive

nature of the postcollege world"—students wanted this purpose emphasized more; faculty wanted it emphasized less. All other disagreements were those of degree; students wanted grades to provide more intense feedback to them about learning and to faculty about their teaching.

5. Faculty and students agreed that fixed levels were a good way to go about assigning grades and that having students grade other students was not a good idea.

6. As for changing the emphasis students place on grades, faculty felt students should emphasize them less and students felt they should emphasize them more. They both agreed that parents and business should emphasize them less and that professorial emphasis should remain as is. Yet we find one student commenting: "Grades seem to have warped the concept of learning. A student will ask a question about the material being studied. The professor will respond 'You don't have to worry about that; it's not on the test.' One professor said, 'We're not learning today, we're preparing for the test.' "

7. The tendency to cheat on an exam or to drop a course was acknowledged more frequently by current students than by faculty.

8. Students were much less concerned about grade inflation than any other group and especially less concerned than faculty.

9. Faculty and students generally agreed on the rank order of personal characteristics presumably indicated by grades and GPAs. Faculty members considered grades to reflect academic achievement, motivation, intelligence, and communication skill to a far greater degree than did students. Regarding communication skill, students agreed with business and parental respondents much more closely than with faculty, who felt that grades strongly reflect this characteristic. Dare we hope the faculty are telling the nation something about what they look for in giving good grades? Recall that the faculty placed top emphasis on samples of student writing for postcollege selection purposes.

Common Items on Student and Faculty Questionnaires

The unique item sections of the student and faculty questionnaires had two common questions. The first of these asked faculty, *How strongly does the fact that you assign grades influence your relationship with students?* Students replied to a companion question, *How strongly does the fact that faculty members are required to grade students influence your relationship with them?*

Almost one third in each group felt that grades had a moderate influence on student/faculty relationships. Twenty-five percent of the students and 14 percent of the faculty reported that grades have little or no influence, but one fifth of the students and one fourth of the faculty felt that grades exert strong or very strong influences. With these results, it is certainly not surprising that in-class, postexamination discussions so often produce ill will, chaos, and confusion.

As an elaboration of the previous item, each group was asked to identify all of the consequences that follow from the fact that faculty grade students—that is, to detail the influences grades have. The first part of Table 5 shows professorial consequences; the second part shows those for students.

Students and faculty hold significantly different views

Table 5. Influences of Grades on Student/Faculty Relationships

	As Viewed by	
Professorial Consequences	*Faculty*	*Students*
Puts instructor in a position of power over students	43%	64%
Helps create a reputation for fairness	45	23
Helps create a reputation for having high standards	50	24
Helps create a reputation for unfairness	4	20
Prevents me from viewing them as friends	8	25
Helps our roles—mine as instructor and theirs as students	43	48
Prevents them from viewing me as a friend	16	19
Student Consequences		
Causes students to put pressure on instructor to give higher grades	33%	17%
Causes students to take classes more seriously	55	59
Makes students try to meet requirements of instructor	68	73
Reminds students that instructor must judge (assess) them	52	50

about six of these consequences. Approximately half the faculty members thought grades help create a reputation for fairness and for having high standards; only one fourth of the students thought this. More students than faculty felt that grades helped to create a reputation for unfairness and prevented them from viewing faculty as friends. One third of the faculty, in contrast to less than one fifth of the students, believed that grades cause students to put pressure on faculty to give higher grades.

Both groups believed that grading puts an instructor in a position of power over students, but many more students (almost two thirds) felt this than did faculty (less than one half). One faculty member stated forthrightly, "Grades are means of control and regulation rather than means of facilitating learning." All of these strikingly different views of grades indicate that the educational ideal—in which students and faculty recognize that they are partners in the learning endeavor—is far from being realized. The results for this item reveal some of the influences of grades on students that we alluded to earlier and which need considerable exploration. Despite these differences, there are some consequences that are viewed in a similar way; two of the most important of these agreements are that grades cause students to take class more seriously and that they make them try to meet the requirements of the instructor.

An interesting observation about the influence of grades on learning came from a parent: "An incident in college left an indelible mark on my life. A respected professor graded a question as incorrect when it was quoted as given in the text. When challenged, and *the only reason I challenged was for the A,* he replied, 'Gracious, Pat, a young lady of your intelligence should know more than a statement from a book.' He taught me more by that statement than anything taught in the regular course, but the situation would not have arisen had a grade not been in question."

Summary

When faculty and business groups were asked to respond to some of the same items, certain striking differences appeared. There is little overlap in the kinds of information business recruiters and faculty members view as most important in selecting college graduates. As for the least important information the two groups consider, there is no overlap. A surprising finding was that samples of student writing fell in the latter category for the business group. Both groups agree that grade inflation should be controlled, and both agree on the chief causative factors: the declining quality of precollege education, and the point that college and university faculty expect less of students.

There were several items responded to solely by the business recruiters. In well over three fourths of the companies, grades are reported to be of moderate to great importance for initial hiring. The vast majority of companies have not conducted any studies about the predictive validity of grades. Almost half of the companies surveyed consider the reputation of different schools when comparing GPAs of interviewees. Over one third of recruiters ask candidates to explain their grades, and around one half accept the explanations with some reservations. Forty-five percent of companies do not have a minimum GPA cutoff; of those that do, the majority fall in the B− to C+ range.

As for replies to items unique to the faculty, approximately one half reported having given a student a grade on the basis of information not used for grading the class as a whole. The two primary reasons were personal crisis for the student and progressive academic improvement over a term. In general, faculty make exceptions infrequently, with the modal value being only once or twice every several years.

Student and faculty agreements (and disagreements) about grades and grading practices reported in Chapter Three were reviewed, and we reported two additional questions asked of both groups. For the first question, almost one third in each group felt that grades have a moderate influence on student/faculty relationships; an additional one fifth of the students and one fourth of the faculty believe that grades exert strong to very strong influences on such relationships. For the second item, there were marked differences in opinions about the specific influences of grades on student/faculty relationships—students were especially sensitive to issues of power and control, and faculty were uniquely sensitive to issues of being perceived as having high (and fair) standards.

FIVE

Students' and Parents' Attitudes Toward Grades

There ought to be a strong relationship between the attitudes and values one holds and those held by one's parents. Folk wisdom, no less than social science and genetics, attests to this relationship via maxims such as "As the twig is bent so it will grow" and "The apple doesn't fall far from the tree," as well as plenty of others that do not invoke an arbor as their metaphoric locale. In fact, one of the major purposes of the National Grade Survey was to determine the degree of correspondence between student and parent replies because we have been intrigued by the continuing tradition of inconstant grade standards and hoped to understand some of the ways in which parents communicate the value (or nonvalue) of grades to their children. Recall that 584 parents of our college student sample returned completed questionnaires; this group comprised about one third of the total parent sample contacted. Though this return rate is well within acceptable limits for unsolicited mail surveys (with no follow-up contacts to encourage cooperation), recognize that these respondents are parents with a strong interest in their children's college grades.

Before going into details, we will review similarities and differences between parental and student attitudes compared to each other and to faculty. In this review, no attempt is made to summarize differences for parent/student interaction questions; these are dealt with as the major focus of this chapter.

1. Parents felt grades are addressed more to them than to future employers; students reversed the order and see future employers as a more significant audience.

96

2. Parents saw grades as more predictive of future success than did college students.
3. Students saw the difference in achievement reflected by a grade of A and one of C as much less long lasting than did their parents.
4. Parents and students agreed on fixed levels as their first choice for a grading system.
5. Across all five grades, A through F, parents gave a higher rating for each grade than did students—this suggests they value each grade more highly than do college students.
6. More students (56 percent) than parents (34 percent) indicated they had cheated because they wanted a better grade.
7. Far more students (47 percent) than parents (18 percent) reported having dropped a course for fear of getting a poor grade; 53 percent of students reported once only, another 45 percent reported two to five times.
8. Parents were slightly more concerned about grade inflation than students, although not nearly as concerned as faculty.
9. Parents valued the following characteristics presumably indexed by grades and GPAs more strongly than did their college-age children: intelligence, communication skill, conformity, motivation, and interpersonal skill. Students saw grades and GPAs as indicating only a greater ability to withstand stress.

How can we summarize these points of difference between students and parents? Perhaps the most obvious difference is that parents think grades are more significant, "objective," long lasting, and so on, than do college students. Despite the fact that parents seem to want, ideally, to reduce the competitive and worklike nature of the college environment, they tend to see grades as far more important than do students.

Students, Parents, and College Professors

In addition to results for students and parents, we must describe briefly the ways in which both of these grade-receiving groups differed from the grade-awarding group—college and university faculty. Starting from those closest together in this pairing, what differences can be noted between students and faculty? As before, only points of difference between common items are described.

1. Compared to professors, college students did not view business as a prime audience for grades.
2. College students did not think that the difference between a grade of A and C represents a very strong difference in achievement; 53 percent of faculty believed that the difference is not only real but that it will last from two to five years or more.
3. Students preferred being graded on a curve; their professors preferred more discretionary procedures.
4. Student and faculty groups differed in the degree to which students were seen as needing to change their emphasis on grades: students—like parents and business respondents—felt students should increase their emphasis; faculty felt students should decrease their emphasis. Both groups felt faculty emphasis should remain as it is.
5. When students and faculty rated the usefulness of a student's GPA to assess various educational and personal characteristics, the following characteristics were considered more useful by faculty than by students: academic achievement, motivation, ability to compete, intelligence, and communication skill. These differences suggest that faculty members think student GPA provides a relatively good picture of some of the major personal attributes thought to be important in the university context.
6. When students and faculty were asked to indicate how strongly they felt student/faculty relationships were influenced by the fact that faculty assign grades, over 50 percent in both groups agreed that it had a moderate or stronger effect. Students emphasized that grades put faculty in a position of power and this thereby made it more difficult for students to view faculty as friends; faculty emphasized that this position enabled students to exert pressure for higher

grades. Faculty also noted that they could use grading to show they were fair and had high academic standards.

The most significant difference appears to be that faculty members—like parents—value grades far more highly than do students. That is, faculty view grades as indicating significant and enduring personal and intellectual characteristics. From the student's point of view, grades interfere with the public affirmation of the instructor's fairness and high standards. Faculty members, paradoxically, would like students to emphasize grades less than they now do.

Faculty and Parent Perceptions

As a final piece to the puzzle it is worthwhile to summarize differences between faculty and parent perceptions of grade meanings and influences.

1. Parents, more so than faculty, tended to view college grades as addressed to them.
2. Unlike faculty, who believed differences between a grade of A and one of C would last for two years or more, parents fell into three distinct groups. For 26 percent there was no real difference, for 22 percent the difference was thought to last more than five years, whereas for 33 percent the difference was thought to last between three months and two years.
3. Parents did not want colleges and universities to use grades to "help students prepare for the competitive nature of adult life" nor to remind them that school "is really work and not fun"; college professors would like to emphasize these purposes more strongly.
4. Parents believed college students should emphasize grades more; college faculty believed students should emphasize them less.

In general, there is fairly strong agreement between faculty and parents; both groups tend to see grades and the resulting GPA as significant indications of student performance and potential. These two groups differ primarily about the parent's own degree of involvement in the grading game. Thus, parents see grades as addressed to them and, while they would like their children to emphasize grades somewhat more, they also would like to see the role of grades deemphasized as harbingers of the more competitive and work-oriented adult world.

Cross-Generational Patterns for 584 Families

One of the original features of the national survey is that it attempted to assess parental reactions to student grades across three generations. Within the context of our analysis it is possible to examine (1) what present students say their own parents did in reaction to good and poor grades, (2) what the students' parents say they did in response to good and bad grades received by their own children, and (3) what the students' parents say *their* parents (that is, the students' grandparents) did in response to good and bad grades received by parents of students now in college. Each of these three sources of information was collected in a different section of the questionnaire, and each of three possible cross comparisons—parent-student, grandparent-student, and grandparent-parent—offers a unique look at cross-generational patterns of reactions to student grades.

Consider the first of these pairs—students and their parents. A comparison of parental actions as reported by the doer (parent) and by the receiver (student) offers two perspectives on reactions to good and poor grades received by the current student. It also offers what in the psychological literature is called a reliability check—that is, do students and parents agree in their reporting of past parental actions? When they do agree that the parent did or did not do a particular something (for example, offer praise for good grades), we can be reasonably sure of the accuracy of the reports. When they disagree, things are not so clear: Does a disagreement mean that the action was/was not remembered or reported correctly by either party, or does it mean that the student did not know a certain action was taken, or does it mean that both the student and the parent perceived the action differently?

These are difficult questions to resolve. What is clear is that our best results are those where both students and their parents agree that the same action was or was not taken. The other two situations—in which the parent reported taking the action and the student did not so report, and vice versa—present unique possibilities for assessing differences in perspectives; for this reason, such disagreements will be presented as appropriate.

There are four possibilities for parent-student reports:

1. Parent reported a parental action; student reported the same action (Yes/Yes).
2. Parent reported a parental action; student did not (Yes/No).
3. Parent did not report a parental action; student did (No/Yes).
4. Parent did not report a parental action; student did not (No/No).

Both 1 and 4 indicate agreement between parent and student; thus the sum of the frequencies for these two divided by the total number of child-parent pairs gives the proportion of agreement between parents and students about a given parental action.

For example examining the parental reaction of praising the student for a good grade, we found reasonably strong agreement. Sixty-seven percent of the paired respondents agreed—61 percent agreed there was parental praise and 6 percent agreed there was none. For 22 percent of the pairs, parents reported they praised for a good grade when the student did not so report. In 11 percent of the pairs, students reported that their parents praised for a good grade and their parents did not so report.

These latter two values, 22 percent and 11 percent, indicate that parents more often reported having praised than their children reported. Although the meaning of this asymmetry is not clear, two possibilities are suggested: Parents think praise for a good grade is a socially desirable action and thus over-report it, or some students did not experience praise in response to a good grade as an especially noteworthy action and therefore did not recall its occurrence. A pattern of student/parent asymmetries occurs across the various alternatives, making it somewhat easier to interpret the meaning of the disagreements.

Patterns of Agreement and Disagreement

With all this computational machinery and its underlying logic now in place, we can turn to an analysis of the patterns of agreement and disagreement across the three comparison groups —parent-student, grandparent-student, and grandparent-parent. As a historical place-marker, bear in mind that the two college generations span the period from around 1950 to around 1980— certainly a lively and crucial period in the history of American higher education.

Table 6 presents average values for each of the four possibilities—Yes/Yes, Yes/No, No/Yes, and No/No—for the three cross-generation groups. For group PS, which includes responses by parents and their college-age children, results indicate that for parental responses to good grades there is 77 percent agreement between reports by parents and children about the actions parents took (Yes/Yes = 15 percent) or did not take (No/No = 62 percent). There is even a slightly higher degree of agreement, 84 percent, about bad grades because the much higher value for the No/No entry (79 percent) more than offsets the lower value for the Yes/Yes entry (5 percent).

Table 6. Patterns of Agreement for the Three Pairs of Subject Groups

a/b	PS Good	PS Bad	GS Good	GS Bad	GP Good	GP Bad	Average Good	Average Bad
Yes/Yes	15%	5%	10%	3%	13%	5%	13%	4%
Yes/No	11	8	9	5	6	4	9	6
No/Yes	13	8	18	10	12	8	14	9
No/No	62	79	64	82	70	84	65	82
Y/Y + N/N	77	84	74	85	83	89	—	—

Note: For group PS, the *a* term is parents and the *b* term is students; for group GS, the *a* term is grandparents and the *b* term is students; for group GP, the *a* term is grandparents and the *b* term is parents.

Comparisons of groups GS (grandparents and students) and GP (grandparents and parents) indicate similar high degrees of agreement in reporting actions for good grades (74 percent and 83 percent, respectively) as well as for reporting bad grades (85 percent and 89 percent, respectively). In all cases, the highest values are for the No/No category, indicating agreement on the nonoccurrence of certain parental or grandparental responses. If we look once again at values contained in Table 6, we see that Yes/Yes values are higher for reactions to good grades than to bad grades for all comparisons; the same pattern is true for Yes/No and No/Yes entries. Finally, for all three groups—PS, GS, and GP —No/Yes values for good grades are higher than Yes/No ones; for reactions to bad grades, No/Yes values are higher than Yes/No values in two of the three groups.

What do all these Yes's and No's mean? For group PS, the Yes/No pattern means that parents said they did a certain action and their college-age children said they did not; for group GS it means that grandparents were reported as having done a certain action and their grandchildren said their parents did not; for group GP it means that grandparents were reported as doing an action and the students' parents said they did not. For all three groups, the No/Yes pattern indicates that parents did not report having done an action but the student reported that the parent did. This is true whether the recipient was a contemporary student or a parent, and whether the parent was the student's parent or grandparent. Some things just do not seem to change across the span of thirty-five to forty years of academic history.

Inspection of Table 6 also reveals that while the No/No category accounts for between 62 percent and 82 percent of the entries, between 18 and 38 percent of the actions fall into one of the other three categories—Yes/Yes, Yes/No, or No/Yes. These three categories, in combination, represent the total value for each of the various actions taken by parents. As such, each of these sums tells us which of the various categories represents the major actions taken by parents in response to good and bad grades brought home by their children.

Parental Reactions to Good Grades

Table 7 presents total values for actions by parents and grandparents to good grades for each of the major comparison groups. The first feature to note is the degree of agreement across groups; with few exceptions, the rank order for each of thirteen categories is identical. Also note that the reactions seem to organize themselves into about five groups. For example, each of the first three parental reactions was reported in an average of two thirds or more of the cases. In the second most frequent category of reactions, each was reported to have occurred in around 40 percent of instances; those in the remaining three categories occurred in around 20, 10, and 5 percent of the cases.

Table 7. Reactions to Good Grades: Total Percent Reporting

Reaction	PS	GS	GP	Average
Praised	94%	85%	88%	89%
Proud	91	87	82	87
Do best	74	66	60	67
Discussed importance	47	38	38	41
Joked	47	42	29	39
Expected	46	51	36	44
Rewarded	28	25	10	21
Better than me	21	19	14	18
Don't kill self	15	15	4	11
More to life	13	12	7	10
Swelled head	7	6	4	6
Bookworm	3	4	2	3
No mention	8	15	10	11

The top eight reactions to good grades seem to fall roughly into three groups. One of these (involving "praising," "being proud and supportive," and "rewarding") seems to represent a direct positive reaction to the student having received a good grade. A second cluster (involving "what is important is that you do your best," "discussed the general importance of grades," and "remarking that good grades were expected") seems to represent more sober, almost intellectualized, reactions in which the meaning of a good grade is affirmed and discussed in a less emotionally rewarding way than is true for the first cluster. The next two reactions ("joked" and said "you're doing better than I did") represent lighthearted reactions that nonetheless provide emotional support for the student. Almost all the remaining reactions, which are of very low frequency, caution the student against overinvesting or trying too hard to get good grades. As for cross-generational patterns, there is some suggestion that group GP (grand-parents responding to parents) has lower reactivity to grades in general. Despite this difference, the order of reactions is essential-ly the same for all three groups.

Parental Reactions to Bad Grades

Into every life a little rain must fall, and the same appears to be true of grades. Very few of us have gone through a student career without receiving a bad grade. Table 8 presents what parents and students report parental reactions were to periods of in-clement weather. Each entry represents the total degree of re-sponse checked for each alternative and includes the categories of Yes/Yes, Yes/No, and No/Yes.

As is the case for good grades, the alternatives fall into a number of clusters. The first one, which was endorsed by over half the respondents in all three groups, involves both a request for an explanation and an encouragement to "do your best." The second cluster continues this potentially helpful tack by offering to "help the student study" and by telling the student "not to worry." The last item in the 20 to 30 percent range concerns the negative reaction of scolding. This type of reaction is picked up in the next two clusters, which include (at about a 10 to 15 percent level) call-ing the student lazy, withdrawing privileges, nagging, and becom-ing angry. Actions in the final cluster, which were reported by between 1 and 5 percent of the respondents, include sarcasm, de-meaning jokes, and punishment. The reaction of "no mention" was reported by an average of 14 percent, which is slightly more than the comparable reaction to good grades, where the value averaged 11 percent.

The major impression conveyed by these results is that a direct expression of anger or punishment is not the most frequent reaction to bad grades. Instead, parents try to be supportive by telling their children "not to worry" and "to do their best"; some-times they ask for an explanation. In 14 percent of the cases when a bad grade is received there is no parental reaction. Although there are somewhat larger degrees of difference among the three groups concerning parental reactions to bad grades, the order of

Table 8. Reactions to Bad Grades: Total Percent Reporting

Reaction	PS	GS	GP	Average
Explanation	73%	62%	61%	65%
Do best	66	57	53	59
Help study	37	13	35	28
Don't worry	24	21	16	20
Scolded	24	24	10	19
Lazy	18	19	10	16
No privileges	17	14	12	14
Nagged	14	13	6	11
Angry	12	13	8	11
Sarcastic	5	5	2	4
Cold shoulder	2	3	1	2
Demeaning jokes	3	3	1	2
Punished	2	3	3	3
Expect less in future	1	2	0	1
No mention	10	18	13	14

reactions across groups is roughly the same, suggesting that emotional support and intellectual questioning have been the primary reactions to poor grades over at least two generations of parents and students.

Parent/Child Disagreements over Reactions to Good and Bad Grades

The picture of parental reactions to good and bad grades has been painted on the basis of patterns endorsed by both students and parents. Present procedures permit an evaluation of parent/child disagreements by a comparison of the two categories Parents Yes/Students No and Parents No/Students Yes. Pertinent results for parental reactions to good grades are presented in Table 9 and those for bad grades in Table 10. Only results dealing with contemporary students and their parents are presented.

Table 9 shows differences in the frequencies students and parents reported that certain actions were taken. A plus value indicates what students said their parents did that was not so reported by parents; a minus value indicates what parents said they did that was not so reported by their children. Thus, +14 percent

Table 9. Differences in Reactions to Good Grades Reported by Students and Their Parents

Reaction	Total Percent Reporting, Students and Parents		Students: Yes No Parents: No Yes		Difference
Expected	46%	(5)	26%	12%	+14%
Don't kill self	15	(9)	13	2	+11
Appreciative jokes	47	(4.5)	24	16	+ 8
No mention	8	(11)	7	1	+ 6
Better than me	21	(8)	11	7	+ 4
More to life	13	(10)	8	4	+ 4
Rewarded	28	(7)	12	9	+ 3
Swelled head	7	(12)	5	2	+ 3
Bookworm	3	(13)	2	1	+ 1
Do your best	74	(3)	22	22	0
Discussed importance	47	(4.5)	16	19	− 3
Proud	91	(2)	16	21	− 5
Praised	94	(1)	10	22	− 12

Note: Value in parentheses indicates rank order of reaction.

for the reaction "parents remarked that good grades were expected" was endorsed by 14 percent more students than parents. The value of − 12 percent for the reaction "praised" indicates that 12 percent more parents than students reported that reaction to good grades. Only the reaction of "do your best" showed no difference in the percentage of times students and parents reported that parents reacted in this way to a good grade.

The first noteworthy aspect of the table is that among the most frequent reactions reported by both groups, "discuss importance," "proud," and "praised," are the ones parents reported doing more frequently than did their children. Only for the reaction "discuss importance" do the two nonagree values (of 16 percent and 19 percent) exceed the percentage (12 percent) of students and parents who agreed in reporting this reaction (47 − 16 − 19 = 12). While there is some disagreement (parents reported these actions more frequently than students), there is fairly strong agreement and we can be reasonably confident that such reactions represent the major ways in which parents do respond to good grades.

When we turn to the other end of the scale and consider

those reactions students uniquely say their parents exhibited, we notice that the top three ("expected," "don't kill self," and "appreciative joking") are not nearly so frequent overall. In fact, for none of the first nine items is the number of Yes/Yes items equal to the combined Yes/No + No/Yes total. This finding suggests fairly strong disagreements between students and their parents on these items. From the student's point of view, we can see that, contrary to results presented earlier, parents seem a little less rewarding, a little less intellectual, and a little more emotional. That is, two of the top three parental reactions to good grades that students reported involve more joking than discussion. Whether parents highlighted a more formal type of reaction because they wanted to answer the questionnaire in a more "parent-like" way cannot be decided; what can be decided is that students reported that parents react to good grades in somewhat more relaxed and low-key ways than parents reported.

What sorts of differences do we see in reactions to bad grades? Results are presented in Table 10, which is organized the same as Table 9—plus values indicate greater student endorsement and negative values indicate greater parental endorsement. Even a cursory examination reveals that the four minus values all reflect reasonable, supportive actions and that the majority of plus values represent direct, negative emotional reactions. For bad grades, the difference in perspective produces a clear difference in the major reactions described: Students more frequently reported that their parents behaved in an emotionally negative way, and parents tended to report either that they offered support or that they asked for a more intellectual "explanation."

It is difficult to know how to interpret these results; did parents try to present a more socially acceptable evaluation, or did both sets of respondents report what was meaningful or impressive to them? Without attempting to decide the issue, it appears that parents emphasized the supportive, intellectual reactions and their children emphasized more directly punishing or emotional reactions.

If we apply this difference in emphasis to parental reactions to good grades, we see a similar pattern: Students selectively high-

Table 10. Differences in Reactions to Bad Grades Reported by Students and
Their Parents

Reaction	Total Percent Reporting, Students and Parents		Students: Yes No Parents: No Yes		Difference
Lazy	18%	(6)	13%	4%	+ 9%
Nagged	14	(8)	10	3	+ 7
No mention	10	(10)	8	2	+ 6
Angry	12	(9)	8	4	+ 4
Sarcastic	5	(14)	4	1	+ 3
Cold shoulder	3	(12)	3	0	+ 3
Demeaning jokes	3	(13)	2.5	0.5	+ 2
Scolded	24	(5)	11	9	+ 2
Punished	2	(14)	1	0	+ 1
Expected less in future	1	(15)	1	0	+ 1
No privileges	17	(7)	7	7	0
Do your best	66	(2)	20	24	− 4
Explanation	73	(1)	19	25	− 6
Don't worry	24	(4)	13	5	− 8
Helped study	37	(3)	4	29	−25

Note: Value in parentheses indicates rank order of reaction.

lighted emotional reactions (pleasant joking and lighthearted ban-
tering—don't kill yourself), whereas their parents emphasized
more formal, intellectual, and relatively lighter emotional reactions. Their children were more impressed by the emotional reactions, either positive or negative. Both agreed that some reaction
was usually forthcoming by parents to a grade report. These results only further confirm that grades are significant events not
only for colleges and universities but for the students (and their
families) who receive them. Grades evoke a wide variety of reactions in the families of student receiving them, and of this there
can be no doubt.

Changes in Parental Reactions from Elementary School to College

The national survey asked parents to describe not only how
they reacted to good and bad grades received by their college-age
children, but also how they reacted at earlier educational levels:

elementary school, junior high school, and high school. This part of the survey was designed to determine what changes, if any, occurred over the sixteen or more years of formal schooling.

Table 11. Reactions to Good Grades at Various Grade Levels

	Grade Level			
Reaction	1 to 6	7 to 9	10 to 12	College
Proud	53%	54%	58%	54%
Discussed importance	7	12	18	12
Expected	8	10	12	8
Appreciative jokes	7	8	9	7
Better than me	1	2	5	4
Swelled head	0	1	1	0
Praised	66	62	61	56
Rewarded	11	8	6	1
Do your best	25	25	32	39
More to life	0	0	2	3
Don't kill self	0	1	1	2
Bookworm	0	0	0	0
No mention	0	0	0	0

Table 11 gives results for parental reactions to good grades; these values are the total Yes/Yes entry for each reaction. This value was used since it offers a single value agreed on by both parents and students. Although these values tend to be small in absolute percentages, they do have the advantage of being endorsed by two independent groups of people who sometimes have different perspectives on the matter. Although conservative, the numerical values are ones in which we can put a good deal of faith.

What patterns stand out? Perhaps the most obvious is that different reactions—more precisely, different sets of reactions—have different patterns over the various grade levels. The largest set, encompassing the first six of the thirteen reactions, shows a pattern in which parental reaction is lowest during the elementary grades, increases during the junior and senior high school years, and decreases during the college years. No one type of reaction seems to predominate; some are emotional reactions such as pride, some are more intellectual reactions, such as discussing grades or telling the student good grades are expected; and some reactions are more gentle, such as appreciative joking—in short, there exists the full complement of possible reactions.

A second pattern, shared by the next two entries, shows a decrease in parental reaction over the years, with the peak occurring in elementary school and the low point during college. These reactions involve direct rewards—either emotional or monetary—for good grades. The third major pattern shows a regular increase in parental reaction over the years. Although three different reactions follow this trajectory, the major one is the intellectual type of support, "what is important is that you do your best." Together, the second and third patterns in response to good grades indicate that direct rewards decrease and more philosophical/intellectual types of parental support increase as students progress from elementary school to college. However, these two patterns involve only five different reactions; the more usual pattern seems to be one of maximal parental reactivity to good grades during the high school years.

Table 12. Reactions to Bad Grades at Various Grade Levels

| | Grade Level | | | |
Reaction	1 to 6	7 to 9	10 to 12	College
Explanation	24%	33%	38%	22%
Scolded	3	5	6	3
No privileges	2	4	4	1
Lazy	1	3	3	1
Nagged	0	2	2	1
Angry	0	1	3	1
Helped study	14	1	1	0
Do your best	18	20	24	26
Don't worry	2	2	3	4
Sarcastic	0	0	0	1
No mention	1	1	1	1
Demeaning jokes	0	0	0	0
Cold shoulder	0	0	0	0
Expected less in future	0	0	0	0
Punished	0	0	0	0

An examination of parental reaction patterns to bad grades also shows three patterns (see Table 12); as in the case of reactions to good grades, values contained were computed only from responses falling in the Yes/Yes category, where both students and parents independently endorsed the item. The first major pattern (the first six reactions) is a progressive increase from elementary school to high school and a decrease for the college years similar to the pattern reported for good grades. The second pattern, involving only the reaction "helping the child study," shows a precipitous decline from elementary school to junior and senior high school. Beyond elementary school, parents may not be comfortable helping their child with school work and therefore do not offer except when they are relatively sure of the material. The third and final pattern shows an increase in the percentage of parents who react by telling their child "do your best" or "don't worry," or, for one percent, "by being sarcastic." Both major reactions in this pattern represent a reflective type of support for the student-learner, and parents seem to feel more comfortable giving this support to older than to younger children. This pattern is in contrast to five of the first six reactions, which peak during the high school years and are best described as direct negative reactions to bad grades. Even the reaction of "asking for an explanation" has something of a negative quality to it, although it is more "under control" than any of the other five.

The best summary of reaction patterns suggests that parents are primarily reactive to grades—both good and bad—during the high school years. In general, good grades generate at the high school level a wider range of reactions—including both intellectual and emotional reactions—than do poor grades, where direct negative reactions dominate. Supportive reactions of a reflective nature show a continuous increase in response to both kinds of grades. Included in this set of reactions are such remarks as "try to do your best," "there is more to life than grades," "don't worry," and so on. Finally, direct reward (either in the form of praise or more tangible goods) for good grades and more direct help in response to bad grades decrease over the four periods. Parents are reactive to good and bad grades in a wide variety of ways throughout the student's academic career; a lot of somebodies out there really do care about grades, and this concern, in both its benign and more negative forms, reaches its peak during the high school years.

Parental Reactions and Student GPA

Now that we know about parental reactions to good and bad grades and how these reactions do or do not change with the student's educational level, it is reasonable to ask if any of these reactions make a difference to performance. If a parent responds by praising his or her child for good grades or by getting angry about bad ones, does it affect what kinds of grades the student will receive in college? We are not interested in advising parents how to rear children to get high grades in college, but we are interested in using our results to document relationships between parental actions and the academic metrics of the GPA and the ACT (or SAT) score. We do not believe that SAT or ACT scores index "native intellectual ability," and a college GPA is not one of our favorite statistics. But it is necessary to examine the effects of parental reactions to grades using college GPAs and SAT scores because these two values are the most frequently employed metrics of student potential and student achievement. In this chapter, the GPA is used in its most neutral sense (as an average of all grades received by a student during his or her college career); no further implication is intended. We hope that our efforts will prompt further studies dealing with the effects of parental behavior on student learning rather than focusing on the more narrow subject of GPAs, SATs, and ACTs.

The student GPA was asked for on the national survey and, given this manner of determining GPA, the suspicious among us will want to know if this procedure can be trusted. Fortunately for the grade researcher, a study by Maxey and Ormsby (1971) indicated that student self-reports of GPA correlate in the 0.80 to 0.90 range when compared to official school records. On the basis of these unambiguous findings, self-report provides a reliable source of information.

To relate student GPA to parental behavior, we next examined whether or not a given reaction—for example, praising a student for a good grade—was done by a particular parent. Here again, whether or not the parent took the action in question could be defined in one of four ways: (1) Yes/Yes responses by both parents and students, (2) Yes/Yes + Yes/No responses (a parents-only definition), (3) Yes/Yes + No/Yes responses (a students-only definition), and (4) all possible Yes categories (Yes/Yes + Yes/No + No/Yes). Because the use of the Yes/Yes value provides only a relatively small number of cases for many of the reactions and because the patterns it produces are similar to those reached on the basis of each of the other definitions, we chose to use definition (4), which gives the greatest number of total cases. This definition seemed more advisable than either the parents-only (2) or students-only (3) definitions since it does not favor either perspective.

One final decision still remained: Which of the four educational levels—elementary school, junior high, senior high, or college—should we investigate to see if a given reaction did or did not occur? To produce the greatest number of possible differences, the sum of reactions at all four levels was used. This decision meant that any given action could receive a value of 0, 1, 2, 3, or 4 and thereby provide a measure of both the relative frequency and persistence with which a given parental action occurred. A value of 4 means that the parent did that action at all four educational levels; a value of 0 means the parent never did so. With this method of bookkeeping, all parents who yielded a value of 4 were considered to have produced a particular reaction very consistently and those yielding a value of 0 were considered never to have responded to any good (or bad) grade with that reaction.

As an example of results produced by this type of accounting, consider what the reaction of "took away privileges" (for bad grades) looks like in Figure 2. The solid line indicates that parents who did this frequently tended to rear children whose college GPAs are *lower* than children whose parents took away privileges less frequently. For this class of parental reaction, there seems to be a negative relationship between college GPA and privileges having been taken away as a reaction to poor grades all along the educational way.

The right hand axis of Figure 2 presents the average ACT score for these same students; as before, a higher number on the bottom axis indicates more sustained parental reaction. Results for ACT (the dotted line) show little systematic relationship between the number of times a parent took away privileges for poor grades and the ACT scores achieved by their children. In conjunction

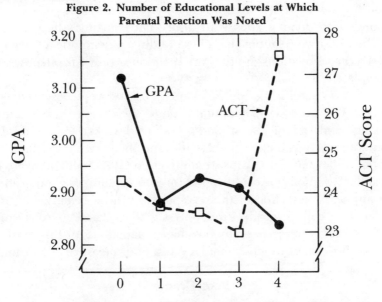

Figure 2. Number of Educational Levels at Which Parental Reaction Was Noted

Number of Educational Levels

with other results involving student GPA, such findings suggest that the differences in GPA presented in Figure 2 are not related to differences in ACT scores. A similar analysis employing SAT scores produced similar results.

Good Grades

Using this type of analysis for all thirteen reactions to good grades revealed that there was only one significant effect relating GPA to any of the reactions; the parental reaction "discussed the general importance of grades" had a slightly negative effect on GPA. That is, the greater the number of times a parent reacted to good grades by discussing the general importance of grades, the *lower* the student's college GPA. All other reactions to good grades produced essentially no effect on student GPA.

An examination of results involving SAT, likewise, produced only two significant relationships between specific parental reactions to good grades and SAT score. When parents responded to good grades with a monetary reward there was a *negative* rela-

tionship (more frequent reward, lower SAT). When parents responded to good grades with appreciative joking, there was a
slightly positive relationship. These findings are not meant to suggest a causal relationship; they are mentioned only for purposes of
completeness.

Two significant (positive) relationships were observed between ACT scores and parental actions; these were "appreciative
joking" and "telling the student good grades were expected." In
general, it is possible to conclude that specific parental reactions to
good grades have little consistent effect on GPA, SAT, or ACT. It
is almost as if parents can respond (or not respond) to good grades
in any way they choose; their responses will be remarkably unrelated to college grades and only slightly related to ACT and
SAT scores. There are many possible explanations for this finding
—not the least of which is that GPA is a poor measure of learning.

Poor Grades

The picture for responses to poor grades is different, as
may be expected on the basis of results shown in Figure 2. As a
matter of fact, the negative relationship between GPA and frequency of parental reactions to poor grades was significant for
eight of the fifteen reactions, and marginally significant for one
additional reaction. For ACT no significant relationships were
found. For SAT there were two significant relationships, one positive and one negative. The positive relationship indicated that the
more frequently the child was told "not to worry about poor
grades" the higher the SAT score; the negative relationship revealed that lower SAT scores were associated, to a slight degree,
with the parental reaction of telling the student "just do your
best." The absolute size of both effects was quite small. In general,
there seems to be little relationship between the frequency of parental reactions to poor grades and the ACT or SAT levels
achieved by their children.

As suggested, the picture is quite different for GPA. Here a
number of significant effects were found, and all were negative:
that is, the more frequent the parental reaction, the lower the

college GPA. The set of reactions showing such a relationship to poor college GPA include:

1. Asked for an explanation
2. Made demeaning jokes
3. Was sarcastic
4. Accused me of being lazy
5. Nagged
6. Was angry
7. Withdrew privileges
8. Scolded or lectured me

Actions 2 through 8 are best described as negative responses to poor grades, and it is reasonable to wonder how the more benign reactions, such as "don't worry" or "what is important is that you do your best" or "helped me study," affected college GPAs. A careful examination of the relationship between GPA and the frequency of these presumably more benign reactions indicated no systematic effect—either positive or negative. All that can be said with certainty is that they did not adversely affect GPA; we cannot say they led to higher GPAs. Finally, it seems clear that the reaction "asked for an explanation" is best construed as somewhat negative from the perspective of the student. Originally, we viewed this reaction as relatively intellectual and unemotional, but results suggest that when parents ask for an explanation for a poor grade, such an action is seen by the student as emotional in nature and negative in tone.

Suppose someone were to ask what advice we would like to pass on to parents who want their small children to get high college GPAs. Somewhat irreverently, we offer the following two suggestions: If your child gets a good grade, do whatever you feel comfortable doing—such action apparently has little or no effect on a GPA. If your child gets a bad grade, do not react negatively; if you feel you must do something, a bit of support will not hurt— then again, it will not help either. (Neither suggestion has anything to do with learning.)

Perhaps the major conclusion suggested by these results is that, contrary to parent perceptions and folk wisdom, grades should be thought of as a communication between teachers and students, not teachers and parents. Few types of active intervention by parents during the school years seem to yield higher college GPAs (if we assume this is a major purpose of the intervention) and some types of intervention may actually yield lower GPAs.

Parental Reactions to Unfair Grades

One area that emerged during open-ended interviews with parents was the diversity of parental reactions to claims made by their son or daughter that they were graded unfairly. Unfair grades were examined in the questionnaire by asking, *Before your child was in college was he/she graded unfairly? If Yes, which of the following actions did you take?* Eighty percent of the parents reported that their child had indeed voiced a complaint to them about being graded unfairly; 64 percent of the students remember reporting one or more complaints about grades to their parents.

When asked a parallel set of questions regarding their child's college experience, 51 percent of the parents and 45 percent of the students again indicated they had discussed unfair grades. Advising a son or daughter to discuss grade problems with their teacher or college professor was the single most frequent response to reports of unfair grading. At the precollege level, parents also frequently contacted the teacher, other school personnel, and other parents. Not surprisingly, these responses were seldom made to complaints about college-level grading injustices. It is interesting to note how few parents told their child that the grade did not matter all that much (9 percent with precollege-level students and 4 percent with college-age students); most behaved as if it really did.

Parental Concern over Grades

Indication of a high level of parental concern over grades becomes even more apparent in the next set of questions. Parents were asked, *How closely did (do) you pay attention to your child's grades for each of the following grade levels?* Students were asked, *How closely did (do) your parents pay attention to your grades for each of the following grade levels?* Scores were rated on a 1 to 5 scale with 5 defined as "very closely" and 1 defined as "not at all."

Figure 3. Parent and Student Concern About Grades

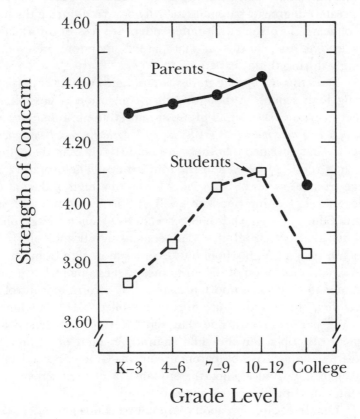

Figure 3 shows that students reported less parental concern over their grades than did parents. Of even greater importance is that on a scale of 1 to 5 the average values given by both students and their parents were considerably larger than the neutral value of 3.00. For our group of parents, paying close attention to grades made by their children at all ages seemed to be the norm. On the average, over 65 percent of students rated parental concern in the 4 or 5 category suggesting that grades were monitored closely.

One other aspect of Figure 3 deserving comment is that parental monitoring reaches its peak during the high school years. As such, these results corroborate those derived from our earlier examination of specific parental reactions to grades. As may be recalled, the major pattern for both good and bad grades was that the greatest degree of parental reactivity occurred during the high school years. Two somewhat independent sources of information thus lead to the conclusion that parents monitor grades most strongly during these years.

Does this mean that grades attain their greatest importance during high school? Although such a conclusion is possible, an earlier question asked of all groups required them to *Indicate on a scale of 1 to 5 how important grades were to you at [various] educational levels.* Results revealed that there are no differences in the pattern of values reported by each of the four groups. The overall values range from a low of 2.87 in grades 1 to 6 to a high of 3.92 at the college level. The intermediate levels of 7 to 9 and 10 to 12 produced values of 3.21 and 3.58 respectively. Unlike the graph of parental reactivity to grades, the personal significance of grades does not peak in high school but becomes most significant in college. The combination of these findings suggests that while grades continue to grow in importance, parental efforts to control or shape their children diminish during the college years. It is almost as if the parent gives it one "last shot" during high school and begins to let up when the child figuratively (and often literally) leaves the home base of parental control. Grades do not grow weaker in importance when the student leaves high school, only parental attempts to control them.

One final question about parental reactions to grades asked of both student and parent groups was, *How often did (do) you (your parent) ask about grades earned by his or her (your) friends?* At no grade level, according to both students and their parents, did the combined category of "often" and "always" exceed 15 percent, suggesting that while parents are interested in grades made by their own children, only a small proportion pay attention to grades made by their children's friends. Not surprising even in this regard both students and parents showed a peak of concern during the high school years. By now we should not be surprised to find that this peak value was preceded by lower values for elementary and junior high school and followed by a small drop at the college level.

A final important point is that parents were asked to indicate whether or not they knew their child's college GPA. A scant 3 percent indicated they did not know this vital statistic. Twenty-six percent reported their child's college GPA was between 3.50 and 4.00 and an additional 35 percent reported it to be between 3.00 and 3.49. In light of these high values, one can only wonder why so large a proportion of these parents felt the need to watch their child's grades so closely—they surely were not doing it to monitor borderline or marginal academic performance. Something more must be at issue, and we can only speculate that in one way or another grades matter very much to parents and their college-age children. And this is no less true for the student who is doing well than for the student who is not. One of our faculty respondents commented, "I was always expected by my parents to do well. A report card with all A's and one A− would be met with 'Why the A−?'"

Grades assume a personal significance far in excess of simply letting a student (or parent) know how well the student is performing academically. It is almost as if grades let both the student and parent know how the student is doing in a personal and important sense. While grades may provide an academic measure, they also provide, appropriately or inappropriately, a more significant personal measure. It is our impression from working with students that grades become equated with the self for far too many. It is as though an A means "I am a good or a smart person" and an F means "I am a failure as a person." For some students, of course, the symbols are a bit different—substitute B for A and D for F. A student captured this meaning of grades in these few words: "To my parents, my worth in their eyes is largely dependent upon my current grade-point-average." We are clearly conjecturing, but perhaps the significance of a student's grades to his or her parents has to do with the parent's self: "When my child makes A's, I am a good parent; when my child makes lower grades, I am a failure as a parent." If these conjectures are correct, they provide some substantiation for one of the opening lines in this book: "And so it is with the auras attached to those ubiquitous educational symbols A, B, C, D, and F."

Does the following story about parents who have students in college illustrate the auras surrounding grades?

The mother of a recently married daughter met a friend, who asked about the newlyweds.

"Oh, they're so happy!" exclaimed the mother. "Just got back from a month in Bermuda, and they're moving into a new apartment. She's getting all new furniture for it, and as soon as they're settled they're buying a car."

"My," said the friend, "your son-in-law certainly must be doing well."

"Indeed he is," said the mother. "He's getting straight A's."

Summary

Two groups most vitally concerned with college grades are college students and their parents. To determine how these two groups look at, value, and react to college grades, questionnaires were sent to about one third of the original sample; completed questionnaires were returned by about one third of this group, yielding 584 usable parent forms. When forms from the two groups were coordinated, one of the first results of importance was that parents view grades as more "objective," long-lasting, and significant than do their college-age children. These attitudes more closely approximate those of college professors and, to a lesser extent, business recruiters.

When cross-generational patterns for 584 families were examined over three generations, results showed a good deal of agreement in how parents of each generation responded to grades received by their children. In general, reactions to good grades involved direct positive rewards and, to a lesser degree, intellectual discussion of the importance of good grades. Reactions to poorer grades are roughly the same and include rewards and intellectual questioning. When differences between parental and student reports of parental reactions to good grades are examined, students selectively highlighted emotional reactions for both good and bad grades; their parents emphasized more intellectual and unemotional ones. For both parents and students, grades are significant events.

Parents were most reactive to grades during their children's high school years. Only tendencies to help students (in response to bad grades) and to provide tangible rewards for good grades decreased from elementary to high school to college. Examination of how the several parental reactions to grades related to college GPA and SAT (ACT) scores revealed little or no consistent effects for reactions to good grades and some negative effects for reactions to poor ones.

Parents generally referred the student to the teacher in a question of unfair grading, and, at the elementary or secondary school level, the parent also contacted the teacher. The level of concern, as reported both by parents and students, reached its peak during the high school years. Concern over grades is significant because grades not only reflect academic achievement but may reflect a sense of self: for students, "I am (am not) a success as a person," and for parents, "I am (am not) a good parent."

SIX

Learning for Grades Versus Learning for Its Own Sake

There is a peculiar omission in the educational research literature on grades: Little is said about how they can motivate students to learn. This oversight creates the impression that grades are of equal importance to all students. Those who have spent time in the college classroom as either a student or a faculty member will know this is erroneous. Some students work very hard for good grades; others do not care about them. This chapter describes a few of the efforts that we, and others, have made to address this omission.

One student in the national survey explained how grades affected his motivation for learning in this fashion: "I tried to get good grades to keep my parents off my back." The parental effect on a second student is not clear: "My father told me to make straight A's or else I'd sleep in the garage. That's what I did." According to a third student there were other motivating forces: "After being thrown out of high school indefinitely, I went to work washing pots and pans. A few thousand pots and pans later, I decided an education was my only alternative. I'm presently in aerospace engineering."

One attempt to describe different student orientations toward grades and grading practices was offered by John Hobbs (1974).

1. The Grubber is willing to sacrifice social life, mental balance, and even education to win the solemn game of grades—

this student's self-image is built on the A's and B's received.

2. The Idealist pretends to self and to others that grades are irrelevant to deeper educational goals but still worries and gets anxious over low grades.
3. The Pragmatist, having a clear vocational goal, such as law or medicine, knows it takes a certain GPA for a chance to attain that goal and works at it.
4. The Loser has been on the lower end of the grade spectrum so long that feelings of intellectual inferiority have overcome judgment and eaten away at self-esteem.
5. The Conscientious Objector has won professorial respect by conventional achievement yet has the intellectual and emotional resources to play at the game without becoming addicted.

A somewhat less anecdotal approach was employed in a sociological investigation of college life at the University of Kansas during the late 1950s; Becker, Geer, and Hughes (1968) collected field notes and conducted interviews while participating in student life. From a large body of annotated observations, these investigators inferred that many students develop a certain perspective toward academic work; they labeled this way of looking at things as the "grade-point-average perspective." This perspective reflects the environmental emphasis on grades and describes " . . . the situation in which students see themselves working, the rewards they should expect from their academic work, the appropriate actions to take in various circumstances, the criteria by which people should be judged" (p. 33). The authors emphasize that this perspective does not mean there is a unitary standard among students; there are variations in the extent to which students live according to the perspective.

Support for their claim that the GPA perspective is used ordinarily by students in meeting academic problems comes from items that appeared in their field notes. They report a total of 1,041 items indicating positive student use of the GPA perspective and only 76 negative ones (or 7 percent of the total number of items). Negative items generally concerned incidents in which students indicated they did not accept or act on premises of the GPA perspective. For eleven of those observations, students said they were not especially interested in grades and would not go out of their way to get good ones.

Mindful of the fact that within any large college class there will be some students who are preoccupied with the pursuit of grades while others are genuinely committed to the process of learning, our research efforts to explore differing student orientations toward grades and learning began in 1976. We attempted to develop a psychometrically rigorous questionnaire to assess student attitudes and beliefs about grades. Our early work was based on the following two impressionistic descriptions.

Learning-oriented (LO) students view the college classroom as a context in which they expect to encounter new information and ideas that will be both personally and professionally significant. Grade-oriented (GO) students view the college experience as a crucible in which they are tested and graded and which is endured as a necessary evil on the way to getting a degree or becoming certified in a profession.

Our brainstorming sessions with undergraduate students, graduate teaching assistants, and senior faculty members produced a collection of statements thought to identify students as either learning-oriented or grade-oriented. Further discussion resulted in a twenty-item bipolar scale that included ten items with which learning-oriented students might agree and ten with which they might disagree. Conversely, grade-oriented students would find ten of these same items with which they might agree and ten with which they might disagree. In addition, there were three nonscoreable items that measured factors other than LO or GO. We called our test LOGO.

Though a detailed description of LOGO's psychometric properties (reliability estimates, validity data, and so on) is presented elsewhere (Eison, 1979, 1981), findings from two subsequent studies are pertinent. In the first of these (Eison, 1982), 239 university students enrolled in two introductory psychology classes completed the LOGO Scale as well as a battery of tests assessing personality traits and measuring educational skills. An a priori decision was made to divide the total LOGO score range into thirds, with students scoring 7 or less identified as learning-oriented and those scoring 13 or more identified as grade-oriented.

Compared to grade-oriented students, learning-oriented students were found to be more emotionally stable, trusting, imaginative, forthright, placid, self-sufficient, and relaxed as revealed by the Sixteen Personality Factor Questionnaire, Form C (Cattell, Eber, and Tatsuoka, 1974). These students also were found to have significantly higher scores for delay avoidance, study methods, educational acceptance, and teacher approval as measured by the Survey of Study Habits and Attitudes (Brown and Holtzman, 1967). On the Achievement Anxiety Test (Alpert and Haber, 1960), learning-oriented students reported greater levels of facilitating test anxiety and lower levels of debilitating test anxiety than did grade-oriented students.

At the end of the quarter, teacher-evaluation forms were distributed to all students in the two classes of this first study. Our aim was to challenge the widely held assumption that all students judge faculty performance on the basis of similar criteria. The form for one class contained such statements as:

- The textbook was _____ ("I never read it" to "very helpful").
- The amount of work required outside of the classroom was _____ ("much too much" to "much too little").
- The material covered in this course was _____ ("very interesting" to "very boring").
- I would _____ this course as an elective ("highly recommend" to "actively try to persuade others not to take").
- The instructor summarized material in a manner which aided retention ("always" to "never").

Learning-oriented students rated each of these five statements in a significantly more favorable fashion than did their grade-oriented peers. Moreover, LO students responded in a significantly more favorable fashion on twenty-three of fifty items; GO students did not rate even a single item significantly more favorably than did LO students.

In the second class (taught by a different instructor) a different, less extensive form was used. Learning-oriented students rated the course in a significantly more favorable fashion on four of twelve major subscales (for example, reaction to the textbook, reaction to out-of-class activities such as movies and study sessions, interest in the course, and overall impression of both the course and the instructor). As before, GO students did not rate any of the items more favorably than did LO students.

These findings have several educational implications. Perhaps the most important one suggests that undergraduates who enter a class with differing orientations toward learning and grades will judge, at the end of the term, both the course and the instructor differently and (seemingly) independently of instructor behavior. One cautionary note about this finding—the fact that this class was better liked and more favorably evaluated by LO students does not mean that such would be the case in other classes. It is easy to imagine that on a college or university campus there are teachers who are better liked by grade-oriented students than by learning-oriented ones—the obvious case would be the faculty member known for being an "easy A." In this case, we might expect GO students to evaluate such instructors more favorably.

In a second study (Eison, 1982) evaluating the original LOGO Scale, 272 community college students participated. They completed the LOGO Scale, the Achievement Anxiety Test (Alpert and Haber, 1960), the Survey of Study Habits and Attitudes (Brown and Holtzman, 1967), and the Riechmann-Grasha Student Learning Style Scale (Riechmann and Grasha, 1974). The results were remarkably similar to those produced by university students: Learning-oriented students scored significantly higher on all seven scales of the Survey of Study Habits and Attitudes and showed significantly higher levels of facilitating test anxiety. Grade-oriented students again were plagued with significantly more debilitating test anxiety. Learning-oriented students' scores from the Learning Styles Scale indicated significantly higher levels of participation and collaboration; grade-oriented students' scores indicated their likelihood of being avoidant and competitive.

The contrasting orientations displayed by students who feel it both legitimate and important to ask "Will this be on the final?" and those who remain after class to talk with instructors about exciting implications of the lecture or who ask for additional information, and so on, provided us with the impressionistic bases for developing the initial LOGO Scale. Similarly, the rationale for choosing the tests for investigating differences between LO and GO students was simple and straightforward: Each test measured personality traits or educational skills previously found by other researchers to influence learning in the college classroom (see reviews by Cattell, Barton, and Dielman, 1972; Eison, 1979; Entwistle, 1972; Lavin, 1965). Each test was mentioned frequently in published educational research. The pattern of group differences that emerged in these two independent investigations was consistent with our intuitions, and on the basis of these results, a foundation for further study of the motivational impact of grades on students was established.

LOGO II

Despite these promising early results, additional analyses of the original LOGO Scale suggested a number of minor procedural problems and one potentially more serious conceptual problem. For example, use of a simple Agree/Disagree response format prevented respondents from indicating the relative strength of their agreement or disagreement with each item. A second problem involved item format; each item was essentially of the form: "I like (dislike) . . . ," or "I feel (think) that. . . ." Thus, items identified student attitudes without necessarily attempting to identify personal actions that might serve to differentiate the LO from the GO student.

A critical conceptual problem was whether LO and GO should be considered as opposite ends of the same continuum (as originally implied by the LOGO Scale) or whether these attitudes should be conceptualized as representing two different, and potentially independent, orientations of students toward the college experience. For real, flesh-and-blood students it is possible to be high (or low) on both learning- and grade-orientation. For example, many premed students hold competitive attitudes toward grades and are also interested in learning. Thus, we were led to the idea that LO and GO items ought to be presented in separate questions and not as Agree/Disagree choices to the same question. With this approach it was possible to describe four different categories of students resulting from the crossover of high and low endorsements of both LO and GO statements. This procedure allowed a more precise description of students who had a mixed orientation.

With these considerations in mind, a new list of sixty items was developed. Thirty of these items were attitudinal, such as "I dislike extra assignments that are not graded," and thirty reflected overt actions, such as "I browse in the library even when not working on a specific assignment." Thirty of the items (fifteen attitude and fifteen action) were phrased to elicit attitudes and actions potentially descriptive of LO students; the remaining thirty were phrased to elicit attitudes and actions potentially characteristic of GO students. All statements were accompanied by a 1 to 5 rating scale with endpoints defined as "strongly disagree" and "strongly agree" for attitude items and "never" and "always" for action items.

A statistical analysis of data provided by several hundred university and community college students was used to select the final set of the thirty-two items that comprise the LOGO II Scale (see Table 13). Part I of LOGO II contains the attitude items and Part II contains the action ones; within each part, LO and GO items have been arranged randomly. Testing of LOGO II's psychometric properties—including reliability estimates, interitem correlations, and a second factor analysis—has been described elsewhere (Eison, Pollio, and Milton, 1982). Results indicated that LOGO II was an even more useful research instrument (and potentially applicable one) than the original LOGO Scale.

Considering learning-orientation and grade-orientation to be essentially independent categories, and recognizing that each orientation can be subdivided into high and low levels (using a simple middle split of the distribution of scores), allowed us to develop a four-fold typology of student orientations:

1. High Learning-Orientation/High Grade-Orientation (High LO/HIGH GO)

2. High Learning-Orientation/Low Grade-Orientation (High LO/Low GO)
3. Low Learning-Orientation/High Grade-Orientation (Low LO/High GO)
4. Low Learning-Orientation/Low Grade-Orientation (Low LO/Low GO)

Our original notions about the types of students represented by each of these groups were straightforward. For example, the first of these groups—High LO/High GO—represents a recognizable type on most college campuses and, as a first approximation, seems best characterized as preprofessional students (premed or prelaw). Presumably these students are motivated both to learn and to achieve high grades, the former perhaps out of personal interest and avocation, the latter out of necessity.

The second of our major groupings—High LO/Low GO—reflects the original LOGO intuitions about LO students. The central focus of classroom attitudes and actions for these students is the pursuit of educational enrichment and personal growth. Although grades are viewed as an unavoidable part of the classroom experience, they are incidental to understanding the student's reason for being and doing in college. Grades serve neither as a uniquely relevant goal nor as a means to achieving some goal.

The third type—Low LO/High GO—likewise reflects our initial intuition about the GO student. These individuals view all aspects of the classroom in terms of their effects on a course grade. Instructional procedures and policies that make getting good grades easier are valued highly; activities not related to course grades are viewed as inconvenient wastes of time and may be ignored.

Finally, the fourth major type—Low LO/Low GO—represents something of an enigma, although such students are often those who go to college to have a good time or avoid having to get a job. In this situation, neither LO nor GO describe this student, and the student's motivation must be sought outside the context of learning or grades.

Having devised this typology, our next step was to explore the ways these four student groups differ on the educationally

Table 13. LOGO II
Student Survey of Attitudes

Part I

Directions: Below is a series of statements taken from interviews with a large number of college students concerning their reactions to various courses, instructors, and classroom policies. Please read each statement carefully, and indicate how strongly you agree or disagree with each item using the following rating scale:

1. Strongly disagree
2. Disagree
3. Neither disagree nor agree
4. Agree
5. Strongly agree

___[a]___ 1. I enjoy classes in which the instructor attempts to relate material to concerns beyond the classroom.

___[b]___ 2. I think it is unfair to test students on material not covered in class lectures and discussions, even if it is in reading assignments.

___[b]___ 3. I dislike courses which require ungraded out-of-class activities.

___[a]___ 4. I prefer to write a term paper on interesting material rather than take a test on the same general topic.

___[a]___ 5. I get annoyed when lectures or class presentations are only rehashes of easy reading assignments.

___[b]___ 6. Written assignments (such as homework, projects, and so on) that are not graded are a waste of a student's time.

___[a]___ 7. I appreciate the instructor who provides honest and detailed evaluation of my work, although such evaluation is sometimes unpleasant.

___[b]___ 8. I think that without regularly scheduled exams I would not learn and remember very much.

___[b]___ 9. Instructors expect too much out-of-class reading and study by students.

___[a]___ 10. I find the process of learning new material fun.

___[b]___ 11. I dislike courses in which a lot of material is presented in class, or in readings, that does not appear on exams.

___[a]___ 12. Easy classes that are not pertinent to my educational goals generally bore me.

___[a]___ 13. A teacher's comments on an essay test mean more to me than my actual test score.

___[b]___ 14. I do not find studying at home to be interesting or pleasant.

___[a]___ 15. I am more concerned about seeing which questions I missed than I am with finding out my test grade.

___[b]___ 16. I think grades provide me a good goal to work toward.

Table 13. LOGO II—*(continued)*

Part II

Directions: Please read each of the following statements. Indicate how frequently your behavior coincides with the action described using the following rating scale:

1. Never
2. Seldom
3. Sometimes

4. Often
5. Always

_____ [a] 17. I do optional reading that my instructors suggest even though I know it won't affect my grade.

_____ [a] 18. I try to make time for outside reading despite the demands of my coursework.

_____ [b] 19. I try to get old tests when I think the instructor will use the same questions again.

_____ [b] 20. I will withdraw from an interesting class rather than risk getting a poor grade.

_____ [b] 21. I get irritated by students who ask questions that go beyond what we need to know for exams.

_____ [a] 22. I stay after interesting classes to discuss material with the instructors.

_____ [a] 23. I discuss interesting material that I've learned in class with my friends or family.

_____ [b] 24. When looking at a syllabus on the first day of class, I turn to the section on tests and grades first.

_____ [a] 25. I participate in out-of-class activities even when extra credit is not given.

_____ [a] 26. I buy books for courses other than those I am actually taking.

_____ [b] 27. I borrow old term papers or speeches from my friends to meet class requirements.

_____ [b] 28. I cut classes when confident that lecture material will not be on an exam.

_____ [a] 29. I try to keep all my old textbooks because I like going back through them after the class is over.

_____ [b] 30. I try to find out how easy or hard an instructor grades before signing up for a course.

_____ [b] 31. I'm tempted to cheat on exams when I'm confident I won't get caught.

_____ [a] 32. I browse in the library even when not working on a specific assignment.

[a]Indicates a LO item.
[b]Indicates a GO item.

---

[a]Indicates a LO item.
[b]Indicates a GO item.

relevant dimensions identified with the LOGO I Scale. For this reason, an examination of personality traits, study habits, and test anxiety levels of each of these student types was undertaken.

Educational and Personal Characteristics
of Four Student Types

Two hundred fourteen students in eight freshman/sopho-more-level psychology classes at a state community college participated in the study; these participants constituted approximately 93 percent of the enrolled students. Because the classes were required, these students were probably quite representative of the general student population. Nearly total cooperation was obtained —most who chose not to participate also withdrew from the classes.

Each of the participants completed LOGO II and the three instruments used in earlier research with LOGO I: the personality questionnaire of Cattell, Eber, and Tatsuoka (1974), the study habits inventory by Brown and Holtzman (1967), and the anxiety test of Alpert and Haber (1960). In addition, the Levenson IPC Scales (Levenson, 1981) and the Myers-Briggs Type Indicator (Myers, 1962) were used to show locus of control and personal type, respectively. A median split of the distribution of total LO and total GO scores was used to define the four student groups: High LO/High GO, High LO/Low GO, Low LO/High GO, and Low LO/Low GO. A detailed description and interpretation of the statistical procedures used to compare these four groups appear elsewhere (Eison, Pollio, and Milton, in press).

When considering students in the High LO/Low GO group, one finds the following distinguishing personality traits: greater abstract reasoning ability; higher levels of sensitivity, self-motivation, and inner directedness; and a greater interest in new ideas and intellectual matters. These students also report lower tension and frustration levels. They are more inclined to trust personal hunches, preferring to look for possibilities and relationships rather than to work only with known facts. These students acknowledge the highest level of responsibility for personal actions (that is, high internal locus of control) and pay least attention to the importance of luck or fate (low chance locus of control scores) in determining their successes or failures. Academically, they employ the most effective study methods, hold the most positive educational attitudes, and report both the highest levels of facilitating anxiety and the lowest levels of debilitating test anxiety. In short, they can be expected to impress instructors as intellectually and emotionally able, willing, and interested—and they are.

Students in the Low LO/High GO group, on the other hand, are distinguishable by personality traits that include a strong desire to do the right things and to act in conventional ways; they tend to take a tough-minded and realistic approach to personal and social issues and to show the greatest respect for established ideas. As with students in the Low LO/Low GO, they also report the highest levels of tension or anxiety. The Low LO/High GO students approach the world in a nonintuitive and relatively concrete way. They report the lowest degree of internal locus of control. These students reported the lowest levels of facilitating test anxiety and a consistent pattern of low scores on the study habits and academic attitude dimensions. Although these learners are anxious to do well in established and traditional sorts of ways—for example, they have a high level of concern for the grades they receive—they have poor study skills, high levels of debilitating anxiety, and a generally concrete manner of approaching tasks.

Students producing the Low LO/Low GO pattern on LOGO II appear to be the most difficult group to identify in a college classroom. Personality measures reveal only that these students reported high levels of tension and frustration. Such students reported the lowest level of extroversion and the highest of introversion. Along with those in the Low LO/High GO group, these students have the lowest levels of internal control but do not place much importance either on chance or on powerful others as determining their fate. Students in this group reported midrange levels of both types of test anxiety and only average study skills.

Turning now to students with high levels of both learning- and grade-orientation (High LO/High GO), we find a composite personality profile containing the lowest scores on abstract reasoning combined with a tough-minded realistic approach to situations and ideas—quite the opposite from our original expectations. Students in this group show a relaxed disposition and, in this regard, are similar to students in the High LO/Low GO group. High LO/

High GO students approach the world in an extroverted manner. Of the four groups, they attribute the greatest importance to luck and fate as powerful influences in their lives, and they report the highest level of debilitating test anxiety. On the remaining educational dimensions, students in this group did not differ markedly from other student groups. The overall picture is one of an extroverted yet relaxed person who takes a realistic and tough-minded view of the world while still placing great importance on fate and being quite tense when taking tests.

Although these results conform to prior expectations of students in three of the four LOGO groups, they do not agree with our original conceptualization of the High LO/High GO student. As may be remembered, these students were assumed to be following preprofessional curricula and primarily learning oriented, but also strongly concerned about grades (for admission to a professional or graduate school). The portrait that emerges is not one of a learning-oriented student burdened with excessive concern over grades but one of an extroverted, but relatively less able student seeking concrete information (grades) concerning how well he or she is doing. Although students in this group appear to have relatively low levels of general anxiety, they are quite anxious about course tests. The college context is a stressful one for these students; they are less able intellectually and view college as a somewhat chancy environment. While these characteristics may also occur in other situations, they are especially evident in the college context. Although such students score high on both learning- and grade-orientation, they do not, as originally predicted, appear to have the personal and educational skills that many faculty believe are characteristic of preprofessional students. They are interested in learning but seem to need the reassuring anchor provided by grades to let them know that they are doing alright as college students.

Responses to Selected Items of the National Grade Survey by LO and GO Students

To help us learn more about the personal worlds of LO and GO students, 196 community college students completed both the

LOGO II Scale and the National Grade Survey. We will focus attention selectively on survey items involving both classroom and instructional matters, and in addition, we will look at items involving parental and student reactions to grades at precollege educational levels.

Using our standard research procedure (a median split of the distribution of LO and GO total scores), four groups were formed. The number of students in each group is indicated in parentheses:

High LO/High GO (N = 35)   Low LO/High GO (N = 52)
High LO/Low GO (N = 52)   Low LO/Low GO (N = 57)

Readers are cautioned that this sample is much smaller than the national student sample. Statistically-minded readers will know that considerably larger between-group differences are needed to reach usual levels of statistical significance. Obtaining educationally meaningful group differences necessitates even greater differences among LO and GO groups.

Most striking were the similarities observed among students in all four LO/GO groups. Although LO/GO student responses to almost all survey items showed considerable variability—as was true for general student responses to the national survey—the relative number of items clearly distinguishing LO and GO students was quite small. Students with strong grade orientations had no more confidence in the relationship between grades and success in life than did their learning-oriented compatriots. There also were no significant differences among the four groups in their beliefs about knowledge represented by the grades of A and C; all believed that the presumed differences would not last long. Thus, GO students appear to value grades despite the fact that, like LO students, they do not view grades as predictive of future success or as indicating long-lasting differences in knowledge.

Another instance in which LO/GO standing was unrelated to student responses is seen in the item requiring the student to rank order preferences for various grade-reporting systems. These were ranked from high to low: letters with pluses and minuses; letters only; percentages; Honors, Satisfactory, Unsatisfactory; Pass/Fail; Pass/No Credit; written narrative. Aside from a slight tendency for Low LO/High GO students to like percentages less than students in the three other groups, no significant group differences were obtained.

Learning- and grade-oriented students did not differ greatly in their perceptions of the many purposes grades presently have in higher education. There were noticeable differences only for two of them: "Grades currently help prepare students for the competitive nature of adult life," and "Grades currently help students learn to discipline themselves for later work or job requirements." Students with high grade-orientation scores endorsed these statements more strongly than did students with low grade-orientation scores. When students described the relative degree of importance they would *like* each grade purpose to have, high grade-oriented ones endorsed the following two purposes more favorably than did learning-oriented ones: "Grades should provide a way of pleasing parents and meeting their demands," and "Grades should afford an accounting to society of how well the university or college is educating its students."

The open-ended interviews conducted prior to the development of the National Grade Survey indicated that some students work for grades to satisfy or please different groups of people. When the present 196 students were asked to rate the relative importance the following six groups (self, parents, teachers, friends, future educational institution, future employers) had on them during each of four school periods (grades 1 to 6, grades 7 to 9, grades 10 to 12, and college), only one consistent LO/GO difference emerged: High grade-orientation students rated working for grades to please oneself as significantly less important than did low grade-oriented students; this was true at each grade level. Though high grade-oriented students attached less importance to "self," they did not indicate a greater interest in working for grades to satisfy members of the other groups in a fashion different from other less grade-oriented students. Comparisons among the four LO/GO student groups failed to identify any pattern of parental reactions to either good or bad grades that might have influenced the differing orientations.

Two areas in which learning- and grade-oriented students

did clearly differ involve cheating and the dropping of courses. Sixty-nine percent of the Low LO/High GO students reported having cheated, whereas only 50 to 55 percent of the students in the other three groups reported having done so. Twenty-two percent of these Low LO/High GO students reported cheating eleven times or more in contrast to the 6 to 13 percent of the students in the remaining LO/GO groups. Since cheating is a purely grade-oriented action (one does not cheat on exams to learn), such a result is not surprising. Low LO/High GO students are also more likely to drop or audit classes because they fear getting a poor grade. Both groups with low grade orientation (the High LO/Low GO and the Low LO/Low GO) were least likely to drop courses because of anticipated poor grades. Here again, grades, not learning, are the issue.

Students were asked to describe their personal feelings about each of the grades A through F. A comparison among the four LO/GO groups revealed significant differences between high grade-oriented students and low grade-oriented ones for the letter grades of A, B, and D. In each instance, High GO students rated these letter grades more positively than did their peers with lower grade-orientation. Although they did not reach statistically significant levels, similar trends were observed for the grades of C and F. High GO students simply value all grades more positively than do their LO counterparts.

On first glance, the nonsignificant differences between LO and GO students observed on many of the items appear puzzling —after all, we anticipated a clear and consistent pattern of differences to emerge from the four LO/GO groups. Another equally plausible hypothesis is that an individual student's total collection of attitudes toward grades is filled with confusion and contradiction. That is to say, the reliably different patterns of attitude and action measured by LOGO II represent varying approaches students adopt to help them function in classroom settings The development of these approaches appears unrelated to the particular way the individual's parents responded to good and bad grades received in elementary and secondary school. The student's approaches seem unrelated to his or her current views of the overall relationship between grades and later success in life. Though a

large number of students (38 percent of the present sample) believed that no real difference exists between those students who
receive an A and those who receive a C, this too appears unrelated
to the degree to which students are learning- or grade-oriented.

One finding does stand out in helping us understand the
pattern of differences and similarities between LO and GO students: Students in both the High LO/High GO and the Low LO/
High GO groups did not report experiencing an internal locus of
control. They saw either luck or powerful others as determining
what happened to them in general and, more parochially, in the
college or university environment. The differences between the
GO and the LO student—seeing the purposes of grades as to
please parents and employers, to discipline oneself for adult life,
and to provide an accounting to society, as well as viewing the
importance of grades as not terribly significant—indicate that the
GO student experiences the forces beyond the self as determining
what the self will do, who the self will please, and how well the self
will succeed in life. High GO students find themselves in an uncertain world—the world of higher education—and look to external
supports to evaluate how well or poorly they are doing. They are
uncertain young people, and powerful others, such as parents,
teachers, and future employers, as well as powerful public symbols, such as grades, all provide a structure within which these
students can at least find some comfort and possibly some satisfaction.

This lengthy analysis of the GO student is necessary to
counteract an initial prejudice on our part (and we believe on the
part of other faculty members) against the GO student. Maybe
Hobbs's (1974) concept of the Grubber comes closest to expressing
the usual faculty attitude toward the GO student. While we do
think that an orientation toward learning is the proper one for an
"ideal" university or college, we have come progressively to be
more sympathetic toward the lot of the GO student in a society
that demands at least a modicum of success in higher education as
a prerequisite for any sort of reasonable occupation.

Once we turn from derision to concern or even sympathy
for GO students—from seeing them as Grubbers to seeing them as
people trying to come to terms with a complex and personally

disorienting situation—we must then ask if there is anything faculty members can do to help alter their single-minded attitude toward grades that almost excludes learning. In framing an answer to this question, it is important to remember the national survey revealed that faculty members value the grades they dispense more than does any other group. Faculty may emphasize grades in their classrooms more than they need to or should. Faculty members have it within their power to reduce this pernicious and distorting aspect of educational practice that often seems to work against learning. If faculty would relax their emphasis on grades, this might serve not to lower standards but to encourage an orientation toward learning. A strong emphasis (either implicit or explicit) on grades as indicative of standards does not necessarily raise standards; it may, however, reduce the value of learning unencumbered by external rewards. To be sympathetic to the varying needs and personal values of all students is not a call to reduce standards but a call to increase the intrinsic value of learning. In the final analysis we are interested in learning, not grades.

At the moment, most students, parents, and even grade researchers view grades as an inescapable fact of life, an inherent part of a compulsory educational system that makes its presence felt from the very first day the child enters the classroom. It is easy to understand how individuals adopt inflexible attitudes and strong and contradictory personal convictions about grades and their meanings. Inconsistencies in beliefs and understandings exist and endure in large part because they are not subjected to thoughtful scrutiny and discussion. Faculty—viewed by students as the purveyors of truth and enlightenment and the dispensors of grades—seldom encourage critical thinking about the meaning of the grades. Parents respond in various ways to both the good and bad grades their child receives at each grade level, but few tell their children grades are not to be taken all that seriously. Representatives of the business community have all but ignored empirical investigations of their own hiring practices and grade orientation; once again the utility of grades remains unchallenged. Thus the orientation toward grades and learning that students develop —and the actions that these orientations engender—endure side by side with other beliefs that challenge the notion that grades have a clear meaning, purpose, validity, or value. But then, no one ever said that students—no more than other mere mortals—had to be consistent in their beliefs and actions.

Implications

American college students differ from one another in a number of relatively obvious ways. This chapter has attempted to develop a typology of students based on what they consider to be of importance in directing their actions during the college years: grades or learning. There is no alternative but to recognize that the four categories of LO and GO students defined by LOGO II are distinctly different types of folk, not only in their attitudes, beliefs, and personality patterns, but also in what they value and do during their college years. These differences have significant and clear implications not only for colleges and universities but for the business community as well. In fact, the purpose of this section is to suggest at least some of the implications of LO and GO differences for each of these audiences: students, faculty, and business people.

Students. As noted, faculty members tend to view the learning-oriented individual as the most desirable type of student and to blame students for being "so grade-oriented." We feel that a student may be grade-oriented not because he or she necessarily wants to be, but because such an orientation is a plausible and situationally effective way of dealing with the traditional classroom environment as well as with early postcollege endeavors. In many instances, an instructor's classroom policies and procedures make such an orientation seem both logical and reasonable for the student.

Students who adopt a grade orientation in a nonreflective way should be advised of some of the problematic implications of this orientation. For example, a common complaint voiced by many of today's college students is that they never received adequate training in how to study effectively, and therefore they earn poor grades. An extensive and comprehensive review of the voluminous study-skills literature (including both empirical research studies and books of the self-help variety), and many years experience in conducting study-skills improvement workshops for college students of all ages, led us to the conclusion that these students often lack clear answers to two interrelated questions: (1) "Why study?" and (2) "How can one study effectively and efficiently?" The second question can be answered directly in programs that employ group instruction and skill-building exercises; helping students confront the first question is far more difficult and problematic.

Formulating an answer to the question "Why study" causes many undergraduates great difficulty. For such individuals, several readily available, socially acceptable answers come to mind: "to get a good job," "to please my parents," or simply "to pass." After a closer and more critical analysis, many students recognize that they must confront a far deeper issue—namely, the personal meaning a college education has for them. For some students, course grades and a GPA provide prima facie evidence that they have done what should be done and accomplished satisfactorily what needed to be accomplished. For others, it is the sense of personal growth and enrichment that comes after learning something new that provides the reason for studying.

The constructs of learning- and grade-orientation and the use of the LOGO II instrument are meant to provide one means of helping students examine and question their educational values and goals. In this process, some students will recognize that they uncritically equate obtaining satisfactory course grades with educational growth and accomplishment. It was Mark Twain who humorously and pointedly remarked that he never let his schooling interfere with his education. In line with this sentiment, we might caution students to not let the pursuit of grades interfere with either their schooling or their education.

Looking beyond the years students spent in college, the Tennessee Higher Education Commission (1977) noted in a discussion booklet entitled "The Competent College Student" that "In a society of ceaseless and rapid change, it is essential to construe education as a continuing, self-directed, lifelong process. The individual should possess an increasing ability to take responsibility for his or her own learning" (p. 16). This observation is by no means new and few would argue against its validity. Unfortunately, adopting a grade-oriented attitude during undergraduate days ill prepares the individual to meet adult challenges.

Compare the following four items from LOGO II likely to be endorsed by a grade-oriented student with the next four likely to be endorsed by a learning-oriented student:

Grade-Oriented

- I think that without regularly scheduled exams I would not learn and remember very much.
- I do not find studying at home to be interesting or pleasant.
- I will withdraw from an interesting class rather than risk a poor grade.
- I get irritated by students who ask questions that go beyond what we need to know for exams.

Learning-Oriented

- I find the process of learning new material fun.
- I enjoy classes in which the instructor attempts to relate material to concerns beyond the classroom.
- I discuss interesting material that I've learned in class with my friends or family.
- I try to make time for outside reading despite the demands of my coursework.

If grade-oriented attitudes and actions have value for the student or society, that value appears limited strictly to the context of a traditional college classroom—in short, the orientation may have practical value only in directing the student's time and energies toward those activities that produce satisfactory grades. A larger and wiser view of the purposes and goals of higher education recommends that these same attitudes and actions are counterproductive and possibly detrimental.

Faculty. One profound implication of the difference between student orientations toward learning and grades can be seen in the types of students who enroll in a given class. For example, grade-oriented students tend to endorse the following statements:

- I try to find out how easy or hard an instructor grades before signing up for a course.
- When looking at a syllabus on the first day of class, I turn to the section on tests and grades first.
- I will withdraw from an interesting class rather than risk getting a poor grade.

Thus, the message carried indirectly by the student grapevine (or directly in the course syllabus) may well influence enrollment patterns. This will be true particularly if there are several faculty members with differing styles and reputations who all teach the same course.

Within their respective disciplines and particular subject areas, faculty members face the challenge of designing instructional programs and creating supportive classroom environments that maximize student learning. Among the many obstacles encountered in this pursuit is the inherent diversity of students. Recent research about student learning styles (see reviews by Claxton and Ralston, 1978; Fuhrmann and Grasha, 1983) suggests that efforts to explicitly acknowledge individual differences among learners and attempts to develop pedagogically appropriate instructional plans have just begun.

One pedagogical possibility is to make some attempt to match LO students with LO instructors and GO students with GO instructors. Although few instructors would ever admit publicly to having a strong grade orientation, it is possible to identify instructors who implicitly or explicitly structure and conduct their classes with a clear GO focus in mind. For example, such intructors might be expected to:

- Use frequent tests, and possibly surprise quizzes, strictly to enforce student reading
- Believe that students will not attend class regularly without coercion such as penalizing absences
- Post test grades without also reviewing correct answers

- Use elaborate point systems to monitor or reward student work
- Assign nongraded projects infrequently.

Efforts to develop a reliable way to assess the LO and GO preferences of faculty are currently being made by members of our research team.

　　While it is impossible to predict the extent to which such matches (or mismatches) between student and faculty orientations will influence student achievement and student satisfaction, personal anecdotal evidence suggests that the effect could be profound. This is borne out by the actions that characterize both the LO and GO student. How can we possibly expect a LO student ("I participate in out-of-class assignments even when extra credit is not given"; "I do optional reading even though it won't affect my grade") not to be affected adversely by a professor who believes that nongraded activities are a waste of time or who believes students will not do things unless coerced (or rewarded) by the threat (promise) of grades? Similarly, how can we possibly expect a GO student ("I will withdraw from an interesting class rather than risk getting a poor grade"; "I cut classes when confident that lecture material will not be on an exam") not to be irritated or upset by an instructor who frequently recommends optional assignments and who feels comfortable (even virtuous) in presenting material in class that goes well beyond the scope of examinations? While the possibilities of proper matches are intriguing, only future research will determine the relationship between student and instructor attitudes and actions in regard to learning- and grade-orientations. Until empirically derived recommendations for teaching these student groups can be made, we advise faculty to identify and consider very thoughtfully their own personal orientations (biases?) and to be alert to the impact these have for student orientation toward grades and learning.

　　It might be useful to reaffirm here the necessity for faculty to help students confront a question crucial for most young people, especially grade-oriented ones: Why study? The best illustration of a faculty effort in this regard is that of Penner (1984). Early in his speech classes, Penner attempts to show how the course will help students meet the economic, social, cultural, and political demands of their generation; and this is repeated periodically throughout the course. We are aware that there are courses and fields of study in which the advantages are not obvious to young people, but if a disciplinary specialist cannot fit subject matter into a broad context, who can? Providing such a perspective can be very enlightening to students.

Business People. Two findings were striking in the national survey results produced by our sample of business respondents: (1) Thirty-eight percent indicated that grades were of great or crucial importance in making initial hiring decisions—only 16 percent of the companies reported that grades were of little or slight importance; and (2) 37 percent indicated that when conducting inital employment interviews they often (or always) asked interviewees to explain their grades—22 percent reported rarely (or never). Ignoring the personal meanings that college grades have for individual job applicants may have important implications for personnel recruitment.

In an extensive literature review, Miller (1966) observed: "It seems reasonably clear that the grading system, at all levels including the graduate one, tends to reward the conforming plodder and to penalize the imaginative student who is likely to make a significant contribution in nearly any field" (p. 20). College recruiters would do well to determine, either empirically or even impressionistically, whether a particular job is better suited to a hard-working but traditional conformist or to an imaginative, self-motivated individual. If the latter is true, a High LO/Low GO student would be more likely to be successful in the job than would a Low LO/High GO student.

Three fourths of all groups in our national survey believe that one of the most important current purposes of grades is to supply information about students to business and industry. Business has a responsibility for assisting colleges and universities in attaining the desired ideal purpose of grading—that of promoting learning. A way business can help do this is to stop emphasizing the GPA during recruiting; if the school has certified that the student has graduated, such information should be enough.

Business leaders must consider the fact that there is slight relationship between grades and postgraduation achievements in industry.

General. One of the most important implications of the demonstrated differences between learning-oriented and grade-oriented students is that these two groups do not share the same criteria in judging the professoriate. As careful evaluation of faculty receives increasing attention (especially by students), it is crucial to the improvement of teaching and learning and to fair dealings with faculty that differences in evaluative criteria be considered.

Summary

We developed a questionnaire to explore college student orientations toward the pursuit of grades and toward the process of learning. Grade-oriented (GO) students view the college experience as a crucible in which they are tested and graded and which they endure on their way to getting a degree. Learning-oriented (LO) students view the college classroom as a context in which they encounter new information and ideas that will be both personally and professionally significant.

Administration of the resulting scale to hundreds of university and college students resulted in the identification of four types of LO/GO student orientations, and psychological tests revealed important differences among the four student groups. For example, High LO/Low GO students employ the most effective study methods and impress instructors as emotionally able, willing, and interested academically; Low LO/High GO students act in conventional ways, show the greatest respect for established ideas, and have poor study skills. Low LO/Low GO students are the most difficult to identify—their personal and educational patterns are less clear cut than those of students in the other groups. High LO/High GO students attribute great importance to luck and fate as powerful influences in their lives.

There were striking similarities in response to items in the National Grade Survey by students in the four groups; there were only clear cut differences for two of the items: Sixty-nine percent in the Low LO/High GO group reported having cheated in contrast to approximately half so reporting in each of the other groups, and more students in the Low LO/High GO group dropped courses because of fear of receiving a bad grade.

Several implications for improving the quality of college learning flow from the differences between GO and LO students. Perhaps the most important implication is that faculty must examine the extent to which they contribute to the development of GO students. The course requirements of many of these grade givers may encourage grubbing for grades. Complicating matters is the fact that many faculty are derisive of GO students. Faculty who hold positions in graduate and professional schools are also grade users. An issue for that group is the extent to which admission requirements influence the development of grade-oriented undergraduates. Still other grade users are leaders in business and industry. They should ponder the question "How do our recruitment policies influence the development of GO students?"

Above all, none of us in this society, which demands a modicum of success in higher education as a prerequisite for any sort of reasonable occupation, should be surprised at students who play the grade-getting game.

▓▓▓▓▓▓▓▓▓▓▓▓▓▓▓▓▓▓▓▓▓▓▓▓▓▓▓▓▓▓▓

SEVEN

What Grade- and Learning-Oriented Students Think About and Do in College Classes

One of the fundamental aspects of student reactions—whether or not the student is paying attention in class—is exceptionally difficult to determine. While students exhibit certain behaviors in class—such as looking at the lecturer or nodding at no one in particular during significant pauses—that suggest they are paying attention, these actions are not unfailing proof that the student is attending to the lecture. All of us can appear to pay attention even when we are not, and the problem of how to relate observations of one person's behavior to his or her unique experiences is both difficult and intriguing.

This problem is especially interesting when students are either grade oriented (GO) or learning oriented (LO); the logic of student types derived from LOGO II described in Chapter Six suggests that differences in attention level can be expected between LO and GO students. It is reasonable, for example, to propose that the standard classroom banter, "Now pay attention, this may be on the test," will more likely wake up the GO than the LO student. Similarly, when there is no clue given about the likelihood of information appearing on the exam, LO students may pay attention more frequently than their GO counterparts. Finally, students may appear attentive but actually be thinking about nonclass-related matters—how frequently would this circumstance occur for students in either the LO or GO group?

These questions so tantalized us that we developed methods to evaluate what students did and thought about during college lectures. We realized that it would not be easy to ask (or to answer) such questions in an experimentally rigorous way because there were few observational procedures appropriate to large lecture halls and no methods for eliciting student experiences as they listened to a lecture. Therefore, one of our first tasks required the development of an observational scheme and a self-report system.

The first half of this task was the easier of the two; we began by watching students as they sat in college lecture classes. A number of problems, initially unsuspected, arose. One was an ethical issue: Do we tell a student he or she is being observed or do we just go ahead and observe? Surreptitious observation has the advantage that the experimenter will not have to worry that the process of observation will affect what is being observed. Informed consent, however, helps build trust between student and observer and, more important, between the student and the professor who allows his or her classroom to be used for observations. Because trust is so significant to larger educational concerns, all observations were taken with the full and informed consent of both student and instructor.

Another problem involved the range and specificity of evidence to record. By employing some classroom observation systems presently used in elementary and high school environments (Sandargas and Creed-Murrah, 1980), evidence at two levels was recorded—one level requiring a slight degree of inference and the other almost no inference. The first level required the observer to decide the student's state of awareness—attentive or nonattentive. The second consisted of event categories such as taking notes, looking at one's watch, gazing out the window, asking a question, and so on. Some of these actions—taking notes, asking a question—are on-target to lecture content whereas others—gazing out the window, looking at one's watch—are off-target. Thus, each student observed received two separate entries: one a general estimate of his or her level of attention or nonattention, and the other a more detailed cataloging of specific actions.

Having handled the observational part of the situation, we wondered exactly how to ask students, "Tell us what you are aware of." The procedure we settled on was simple and direct. Early experiments with this procedure involved all students in a single class. At the beginning of the hour, students were told that a bell would sound several times during the lecture. At the bell, they would be asked to write what they were aware of just before the bell rang. They were assured their answers would be treated anonymously, and they were asked to be as honest as possible. They were informed that the stream of human conscious experience is known to vary from individual to individual and from time to time with the same individual. Thus, they were not to expect there to be right or wrong answers but merely to report what they experienced.

In addition to our using students in psychology classes, colleagues in other departments volunteered lecture classes to our efforts in developing the self-report procedure. Not satisfied with only academic audiences, we took the show on the road; Civitan, Rotary, and other community organizations requesting speeches on psychological matters were subjected to the self-report procedure. As with students, members of these lecture audiences found the task of self-report meaningful and insisted on sharing reactions. In almost all cases, at least as many of the shared self-reports were off-target as were on-target.

The following self-reports given by individuals in different on-the-road groups provide some idea of early results:

1. Why do all Yankees [meaning the lecturer] wear sweaters this time of year [October]?
2. Wondering when the self-report bell would ring.
3. I was thinking that I hope my ex-boyfriend (who is a football coach) loses his ball game tonight by at least twenty points.
4. How many times have I interrupted my parents' lovemaking?
5. Wondering why the first marriage didn't work and afraid of a second.
6. What time is it now?
7. I was aware of dropping my pen cap on the floor and seeing the wonderful legs on the woman sitting next to me.

8. I'm thinking about cheese and crackers.
9. He doesn't look like the type to write a book. Must be smarter than he looks.

This condensed list is enough to strike terror in the heart of even the most well-prepared and well-meaning lecturer. Before one decides the situation is hopeless and stops lecturing, it is important to point out that these responses represent only nine of some nine hundred that have been gathered and that these responses were chosen for their conspicuous special qualities. They are not representative of all nine hundred responses nor are they as wounding as they might appear at first glance. Take, for example, items 3, 4, and 5. Each of these occurred in response to the same request, and since the speaker was discussing the vicissitudes of human love in contemporary society, all of these items were partially in tune with lecture content. They represent that category of reactions in which the listener actively tries to relate what the speaker is talking about to his or her life. Although this involvement is more likely in a history than a chemistry class, good lecturers in all disciplines regularly invite students to go beyond the information given and relate it to other material.

The substance of the remaining comments is also of interest. Comments 1, 7, and 9 all refer to other people in the lecture environment, 2 and 6 are about time, and 8 shows a healthy regard for the body if not for the speaker. All in all, these comments suggest in miniature what more precise results will document later —namely, when not directly aware of the lecture content, members of a lecture audience are aware of relatively significant aspects of the human world such as other people, time, and their own bodies.

Student Classroom Behavior

We are reporting our observational procedure in some detail for several reasons: (1) Attention of the learner is a fundamental feature of teaching and learning endeavors, yet it has tended to be ignored in investigations of learning; (2) lecturing is a major teaching approach throughout higher education and facile pronouncements are made about its wonders; (3) grades and grading (the focus of this book) must be considered and weighed in the context of the broader issues of teaching and learning; and (4) we hope others will be stimulated to extend these initial efforts.

With both methodological pieces of the plan now ready, let us turn to the behavioral and experiential procedures. In actual practice, a student is observed for a thirty-second period. The observer records all event categories—taking notes, checking watch, and so on—that occur during the remaining twenty-five seconds of the observational period. This means that for each thirty-second period there is one entry for level of attention and one entry for each different student action (if any) observed during that period. This procedure sets an upper limit of 100 entires for each event category for each fifty-minute class observed. In actuality, few event catgories exceed thirty or so entries per fifty-minute hour and many do not reach even five per hour. (Specific categories used to code student actions may be found in Appendix C.)

Given this observational procedure, what do students do in the classroom? Based on observations of fifty-two students for whom we have complete results, the answer is: mostly they take notes. Of the 15,600 total entries possible for each category (52 students × 100 entries per fifty-minute hour × 3 hours of observation per student), 57 percent of the intervals involved note taking of one kind or another. If lecturers feel good about this, we hasten to add that the second most frequently listed category was fidgeting (43 percent). This last figure is not as bad as it appears, since we soon discovered there is a special type of student who always seems to have his or her motor running (swinging a foot, tapping a hand, and so on), and this behavior does not seem connected to boredom, excitement, or, for that matter, anything else. Indeed, some of our most prolific notetakers were also some of our most fidgety students.

The set of categories in which the student makes eye contact with the instructor and laughs or smiles in response to his or her remarks occurred in 17 percent of the observation intervals, and these activities provide all of us who lecture with that wonderful feeling of being understood and even liked. The opposite group of actions, which we do not like—laughing, smiling, and talking with a peer—was recorded in only about 5 percent of the intervals.

Whether these activities please or dismay us, it is important to note that they were produced in classes presided over by instructors with reputations as being exceptionally good lecturers. Since these professors were willing to allow observers into their classrooms, it can be concluded that they were fairly confident of their abilities. Spontaneous comments by the researchers/observers suggested that students all agreed these were good lecturers and all values here noted should be viewed in this context.

We were not content simply to describe the frequency with which certain events occurred in certain situations; our next step was to look for patterns of co-occurrence among categories. That is, if a student frequently took notes, is it possible to determine if he or she also frequently laughed with the instructor, frequently fidgeted, and so on? By using the statistical techniques of correlation and factor analysis, we partitioned the present set of student classroom activities into a smaller number of categories of events that frequently co-occurred with one another during the course of normal classroom activity. Our analyses revealed which categories were negatively related (that is, did not co-occur with one another).

These analyses also indicated that student classroom actions can be classified into four major groupings. The first of these includes the positively-related actions of laughing, smiling, and talking with peers. A second group includes the following as positively-related actions: hand raising, laughing and smiling with the instructor, and looking at the instructor. A third involves relaxing, watch checking, sleeping, and reading nonclass-related materials as postively related, and consistent note taking as negatively related. The fourth grouping is composed of consistent note taking as postively related and noninterpersonal behavior as a negatively related.

To provide some life for these groupings, let us embody them in student form. The first grouping describes the well-recognized classroom type, "Chatty Charlie," a student most concerned with interacting with peers. The second group describes "Super Student," or "Imitation Super Student," and captures the seemingly interested, alert, and instructor-oriented student all of us love. Whether this pattern is sincere or strategic cannot be determined from lecture-room behavior alone. The third grouping presents a readily observable classroom type, "Bored Bob," who stays by himself in a never-never land located somewhere between his wristwatch and the Land of Nod. The fourth, "Sam Scribbler," describes a student who is in touch with his or her notes, and perhaps, even with the content of the lecture. Unfortunately, it also describes a student not in contact with the professor or, for that matter, with anyone else in the classroom.

A different and somewhat more analytic way to describe these four groupings is in terms of two lecture-related questions: (1) Is the student on-target with respect to the lecture content? and (2) Is the student primarily oriented toward other people (the instructor or peers) or toward him- or herself? If we use the answers to these questions as organizing principles, it is possible to produce a categorization of student lecture types that would depend on a "yes" or "no" answer to the first question and an "other" or "self" answer to the second. With the Super Student category, those students who were on-target to the lecture but not directed toward other people are Sam Scribblers. Those who were off-target to content while paying attention to other people in the class are Chatty Charlies. And those who were off-target to the lecture content and paying attention only to themselves are Bored Bobs. These characterizations should be familiar for they all emerged quite naturally from careful observations of students attending college lecture classes.

The Self-Report Questionnaires

Student overt behavior is only half the story; we still must look at what students report being aware of during college lectures. Although coding spontaneous self-reports is difficult, the categorization scheme used was reasonably straightforward and reliable. After responses from a few initial groups of students were collected, two major divisions became apparent: items related to the teaching event and items not related to the teaching event. (The major categories used to code student protocols, and the specific items comprising both the on-target and off-target categories, may be found in Appendix D.)

Of all the individual protocols collected to date, about 63 pecent of the responses fall into the on-target category and 37 percent fall into one of the off-target categories. An examination of the errant 37 percent proved interesting; when specific off-target responses were examined, the largest percentage of items (27 percent) related to a concern with time—that is, when the class would end, what the student was going to do later that afternoon, and so on. The second most frequent category (25 percent) concerned other people who were either in the present context or only imagined. It is gratifying to find that many of these remarks concerned the lecturer. What is not so gratifying is that they were concerned more with nonteaching matters ("I never noticed how much the instructor looks like a chipmunk") than with the lecturer's dynamic style, personal bearing, or clear articulation.

The third (18 percent) and fourth (13 percent) most frequently coded categories included a focus on the student's body (I'm tired, hot, hungry, so forth) and on the student's mood (happy, bored, so forth). Most of the remaining protocols concerned what was going on in the present situation—looking at a bird on the window sill, waiting for the bell to signal a request to give a self-report, and so on.

A good deal of time was devoted to preparing a training manual for teaching relatively unsophisticated raters to code protocols reliably into categories. This manual (Pollio and others, 1984) contains numerous examples and provides specific training in using the category system. When independent raters are trained, it is not unusual for them to agree on major category placements for 80 to 85 percent of the items. When three independent raters are used, almost all items can be unequivocally placed by a two-of-three or three-of-three vote into one of the nine major categories.

Although the categories used to code self-report protocols were derived from what students reported, these categories are informed by discussions in the psychological (Giorgi, 1970; Van Den Berg, 1961; Pollio, 1982), sociological (Berger and Luckmann, 1967), and philosophical literature (Heidegger, [1927]

1962; Merleau-Ponty, 1962; Ihde, 1977) dealing with the nature of human experience. In fact the four major off-target categories of time, body, other people, and mood represent significant categories used by many philosophical analyses of human consciousness. Within this larger context, the present study may be seen as a first attempt to map the everyday lecture world of the American college student or, in more philosophical terms, the student's self-world.

This excursion into the more remote regions of self can be redirected back to the lecture hall if we keep in mind that people experience events against the background of their own and the society's everyday reality. Within the context of teaching, this means that students come into our lecture halls not as disembodied minds eagerly waiting to be filled with knowledge but as human beings having a rich complement of experiences against which our lectures must compete for center stage. The structure of human experience, in the lecture hall and elsewhere, is always one in which some event stands out against some background within some larger social context.

What LO and GO Students Think About and Do in Lecture Classes

With one set of procedures designed to tap into the student's self-world and a second designed to describe what students do during college lecture classes, it became possible to deal with the intriguing question of how thinking and doing relate to one another in the college classroom. Six undergraduate and graduate student raters were trained to use both the behavioral observation and self-report procedures. Training was considered complete for behavioral observation when pairs of raters produced agreement values for the various categories at 80 percent or better. Training for the self-report procedure also was considered complete when an 80 percent or better level of agreement was reached. Actual overall agreement rates were well above 85 percent.

To secure a more representative sample of classes involving a wide variety of teaching styles and student groups, self-report and behavioral observations were secured at the same time in two introductory psychology classes, three advanced-level psychology classes, and one large lecture in communication science. Individual students were asked if they would serve as in-class subjects. None of the original contact people, who were also the in-class observers, had any information about the student other than name. About 70 percent of students contacted agreed to participate, for a total of fifty-two students. (These are the same students whose behavioral reactions were discussed earlier.) For purposes of balance, an equal number of males and females was included from each class. All observers talked with the student until they felt the student was convinced that we were interested in ordinary classroom activities and not "proper" behavior.

Although our initial plan was to take an equal number of self-reports for all students, the ongoing world of the classroom events frequently refused to cooperate and we were left with a slightly different number of protocols for each student. For this reason, all of our observations are reported in percentage form. Table 14 contains the average percentage of both the behavioral records and self-report protocols that were educationally on- and off-target for students in each of the four LO/GO groups. For a behavior to be scored on-target, the student had to be attending to the lecture, taking notes, asking or answering questions, and so on. Off-target behaviors included talking to one's neighbor, reading a newspaper, looking at one's watch. For self-report protocols, only codings concerned with lecture content were coded as on-target. With these definitions in mind, the values presented in Table 14 indicate that an average of 49 percent of all behavior observed was coded as on-target and that an average of 61 percent of all self-reports was coded as on-target.

An examination of values produced by students in each of the four groups revealed that both for behavior and self-report data, students in LO/GO groups High LO/Low GO and Low LO/ Low GO produced a greater proportion of on-target entries than was true for students in the High LO/High GO and Low LO/High GO groups. It seems clear that high grade-oriented students, regardless of their orientation toward learning, are more often off-target than is true for low grade-oriented ones. What is perhaps most surprising is the very high degree of on-target self-reports

Table 14. Percent On-Target Behaviors and Self-Reports for Students in the
Four LOGO Groups

LOGO II Group	Average Percent Behavior On-Target	Average Percent Self-Report On-Target
High LO/High GO	47	51
High LO/Low GO	53	69
Low LO/High GO	45	45
Low LO/Low GO	53	81
Average	49	61

given by students in the Low LO/Low GO group. These students, who are somewhat anxious in general, might alleviate their anxiety by careful attention in class.

Two final points must be made: First, the pattern obtained across all four groups was similar for the various instructors observed, although there were some differences in the absolute level of on-target codings obtained in response to different instructors. There were no differences between male and female students in each of the groups. Second, differences among the four groups were less variable for behavior than for self-report codings. Thus, while there were differences in on- and off-target behaviors, there were even greater differences in on- and off-target self-reports across the four LO/GO groups.

Since student self-reports were on-target about 60 percent of the time, it is important to determine what students reported when they were aware that they were not attending to the lecture. Students in all four LO/GO groups indicated that the major off-target categories (which we previously have identified with the "world of everyday student reality") include other people, time, body, and mood. Despite faculty preconceptions, a good deal of off-target awareness did not involve fantasy. Interestingly, students in the High LO/Low GO group gave only one instance of a fantasy response; students in the remaining groups gave 10 to 15 percent of fantasy responses, with Low LO/High GO students giving the greatest proportion of these responses. An examination of the content of all student fantasies revealed they primarily concerned other people in other situations.

A similar analysis was made of the four LO/GO groups for each of the behavioral categories. What was most surprising about this analysis was that only three of the categories showed statistically significant differences among groups: laughing with instructor, fidgeting, and reading material unrelated to the class. In the case of laughing with the instructor, there were clear differences among LO groups, with High LO students laughing less than Low LO ones; the same pattern prevailed for fidgeting, where High LO students fidgeted less than Low LO students. Results were a bit more complicated for the reading of nonclass related materials; here, both the High LO/High GO and the Low LO/Low GO groups engaged in this activity infrequently whereas students in the High LO/Low GO and Low LO/High GO groups engaged somewhat more frequently. Although it is possible to make sense of these differences, it is perhaps more important to note that the majority of categories (nineteen of twenty-two) showed no systematic differences among students in the four LO/GO groups. This result suggests that while there may be scattered differences due to learning- or grade-orientation, the constraints of the lecture hall affect all students' behavior in relatively similar ways. There are only so many things a student may do in class, and all of them seem to be done to the same degree by most students, learning- or grade-orientation notwithstanding.

A potentially more revealing way to look at present results concerns the degree of concordance between how frequently a student produced an on- or off-target self-report when his or her behavior was on- or off-target. The easiest way to evaluate this issue is to determine whether or not the student was rated as being on- or off-target just prior to each self-report. There are four possibilities:

Behavior On—Self-Report On   Behavior Off—Self Report On
Behavior On—Self-Report Off   Behavior Off—Self Report Off

In the best of all possible worlds (best, that is, for lecturers and researchers), On/On plus Off/Off would total close to 100 percent. If this occurred, it would mean that instructors would know which students were on- or off-target simply by looking at what they were doing. Unfortunately, this was true in only 67 percent of the cases; in 33 percent of them, what a student is doing tells little about what he or she is aware of and, it is important to note, vice versa. Being on-target in self-report does not unequivocally reflect what the student is doing.

Table 15. Percent Agreement Between On-Target and Off-Target Codings of Self-Report and Behavioral Protocols for Four LOGO Groups

	LOGO Group						
	High LO/ High GO Self-Report		High LO/ Low GO Self-Report		Low LO/ High GO Self-Report		Low LO/ Low GO Self-Report	
Behavioral Record								
	On[a]	Off[b]	On	Off	On	Off	On	Off
On-Target	53	41	77	15	45	18	83	14
Off-Target	3	3	4	4	4	13	1	1

[a]On = On-target
[b]Off = Off-target

This type of analysis was carried out separately for each of the four LO/GO groups, and findings are presented in Table 15. It can be seen that students in the High LO/High GO group tended to present the impression of being on-target 41 percent of the time when their self-reports indicated that they were otherwise occupied; they appeared off-target when their self-reports were on-target 3 percent of the time, producing a total incongruency score of 44 percent. While it may be going too far to view the On/Off value of 41 percent as indicating a calculated strategy, it does suggest that students in this group try to put their best behavioral foot forward in the classroom. Students in the High LO/Low GO group present a reasonable degree of congruence between on-target actions and self-reports, producing an incongruency value of only 19 percent (15 + 4). Students in the low LO/High GO group also reveal a fairly low incongruency value of 22 percent (18 + 4).

Finally, students in the Low LO/Low GO group are exemplary for their 15 percent degree of incongruence (14 + 1) and for their 83 percent value for being on-target both behaviorally and phenomenologically. This final set of figures will surely make most classroom instructors feel somewhat better in assuming that something can be learned from a student's actions about what a student is aware of. This is more than can be said for some of the other groups—most especially for students in the High LO/High GO group, whose behavior and self-report data conflicted in over 40 percent of the cases.

Testing Preferences of LO and GO Students

One of the more important events in any college class is the midterm examination; here, too, we should expect differences between learning- and grade-oriented students. Perhaps the obvious expectation is that learning-oriented students (more specifically, those students scoring high in LO and low in GO on LOGO II) would favor essay-type examinations and that grade-oriented students (Low LO/High GO) would prefer multiple-choice tests. These predictions are based on the assumption that students perceive essay tests as more related to the learning of concepts and multiple-choice tests as more related to the memorization of factual details, as suggested by studies of fifty years ago (Douglass and Talmadge, 1934; Terry, 1934; Class, 1935).

Since "facts" are more definite, easier to study, less demanding to express, and easier to predict in terms of which ones will appear on a test, GO students, given the opportunity, should select multiple-choice over essay examinations. Because these reasons might apply for LO students as well, some also might choose to take the multiple-choice test. In general, it is reasonable to expect that a greater proportion of LO students will select an essay test than will GO students.

To test these predictions and to learn about self-reported reasons for their choice, Eison, Pollio, and Cunningham (in press) asked students in two different undergraduate lecture classes in psychology to complete the LOGO II questionnaire and to designate either a multiple-choice or an essay test as their regular in-class midterm examination. Class One consisted of ninety-four students enrolled in a humanistically oriented developmental course called "The Psychology of the Person," which characteristically is taken by first- and second-year students. Class Two consisted of 107 students enrolled in a junior/senior level course entitled "Learning and Thinking."

On the basis of their answers to the LOGO II questionnaire, students were divided into the now familiar four-part classification of High LO/High GO, High LO/Low GO, Low LO/High GO, and Low LO/Low GO. Approximately one week before midterm exams, all participants were asked to answer these three questions: (1) "Which type of test, multiple-choice or essay, do you plan to take for your midterm?"; (2) "Could you please tell me why you chose the type of examination you did?"; and (3) "Do you study differently for a multiple-choice examination than for an essay examination? If the answer is yes, please describe these differences."

Table 16. Choice of Testing Procedures by Students in Each of the Four LOGO Groups in Two Different Classes

Test Type Chosen	Class	High LO/ High GO	High LO/ Low GO	Low LO/ High GO	Low LO/ Low GO	Total	Percent
Essay	Humanistic	1	8	3	6	18	19
	Learning/ Thinking	6	13	13	5	37	35
Multiple- Choice	Humanistic	12	13	35	16	76	81
	Learning/ Thinking	10	17	26	17	70	65

The first result of interest concerns the general test preferences of students irrespective of LO/GO groups (see Table 16). As can be seen in the lower half of the table, the multiple-choice test was preferred by 81 percent and 65 percent of the students in both classes; the remaining 19 percent and 35 percent selected the essay test. Of the relatively small number of students selecting essay tests, the greatest number across both classes was in the High LO/Low GO group. The largest number selecting the multiple-choice test, on the other hand, was in the Low LO/High GO group. A slightly different way in which to describe these results is by the total proportion of students in each of the four groups choosing the various test alternatives. Here we see that of the High LO/High GO students, only 24 percent (7 of 29) chose the essay test; comparable values were 41 percent (21 of 51) for the High LO/Low GO group, 21 percent (16 of 77) for the Low LO/ High GO group, and 25 percent (11 of 44) for the Low LO/Low GO group. These values indicate that students in the High LO/ Low GO group were the only ones to differ in their pattern of choices; they tended to select the essay test *more* frequently than did those in any of the remaining groups.

An examination of test scores earned by students in all four groups indicated that those taking essay examinations performed better than did those who took multiple-choice tests; this was true in both classes. Whether this difference was due to the fact that essay papers were graded less stringently or that students selecting this procedure were more effective learners cannot be determined from present information. What can be said with confidence is that considerable care was taken to score all papers impartially. Results indicated that, across both test types, High LO/Low GO students consistently obtained the highest test scores and High LO/High GO students consistently obtained the lowest ones. Students lowest in both learning-orientation and grade-orientation (Low LO/Low GO) ranked second, while students low in learning-orientation and high in grade-orientation (Low LO/High GO) ranked third.

Table 17. Reasons Given for Choosing Multiple-Choice and Essay Tests for Different Groups of LOGO Students

| | Examination Type | | | | | | | | | | | |
| | Multiple-Choice | | | | | Essay | | | | | | |
Reasons Given	H/L H/G	H/L L/G	L/L H/G	L/L L/G	Sum	H/L H/G	H/L L/G	L/L H/G	L/L L/G	Sum	Row Totals	%
1. Easier to study for	0	1	0	3	4	0	1	0	0	1	5	3
2. Easier to take	6	14	11	27	58	2	8	3	9	22	80	52
3. Personal history	3	10	8	18	39	1	5	2	7	15	54	35
4. Learning-related	0	0	0	0	0	5	6	3	2	16	16	10
Totals	9	25	19	48	101	8	20	8	18	54	155	100

Note: H/L = High/LO, L/L = Low/LO, H/G = High/GO, L/G = Low/GO

Insight into factors which students reported lead them to prefer one type of test format over another are found in Table 17, which presents a tabulation of the reasons given for choosing multiple-choice or essay tests. Although the first two reasons seem self-explanatory, the third and fourth require a word of clarification. The category Personal History was used primarily for replies of the type: "I have done/do better on this type of exam," "I get better grades on . . . ," and so forth. The category Learning-Related was used for replies of this sort: "This type of exam helps me to learn (retain) more information," "This type of exam gives a better indication of what I've learned," and so on.

There were strong differences in the reasons given by the two test types. Looking only at reasons given by students taking the multiple-choice test, such tests were generally preferred because they were viewed as being easier (58 of 101 reasons) or because students felt more likely to do better on them (39 of 101 reasons). Few students reported that multiple-choice tests were easier to study for (4 of 101 reasons), and none reported they were likely to facilitate learning.

The reasons given for preferring essay tests, on the other hand, reveal a different pattern. While many essay-test takers reported they found essay tests easier to take (22 of 54), or that they did better on them (15 of 54), 16 of 54 reported that essay tests were more likely "to help them learn and retain" more information. Only one student wrote that essay tests were easier to study for. Many of the students who take essay tests seem more concerned with learning than do students who choose multiple-choice tests.

An examination of the interior cells of Table 17 sheds some light on the question of whether students in the various LO/GO groups differed in the reasons given for choosing each type of examination. Of those taking the multiple-choice test, students in all four groups responded in a similar fashion (that is, reasons 2 and 3 were clearly the major ones given). An examination of reasons produced by students choosing the essay test indicated that five of eight reasons given by students in the High LO/High GO group concerned reason 4 (Learning-Related) and that only two of eighteen reasons given by students in the Low LO/Low GO group concerned this reason. (Some of the 201 students surveyed did not give reasons.) Although not comprising many cases, these results suggest that Low LO/Low GO students are less concerned with learning (even when selecting the essay test) than any of the remaining groups and that High LO/High GO students prefer essay examinations because they serve to enhance learning; however, both conclusions must be viewed as tentative.

An examination of study methods described by students in each of the four LO/GO groups failed to reveal systematic group differences; the major method used was the same for both multiple-choice and essay tests. Where specific differences in study methods were noted, the majority of students taking both test types stated they studied specific details for multiple-choice tests or general concepts for essay tests. Surprisingly, thirteen of 103 responses produced by multiple-choice students said they studied general concepts for multiple-choice tests while none of the fifty essay students offered this as a study method. Although there were some differences in study methods for the two types of tests, there were no obvious differences among the four LO/GO groups. These results suggest that the powerful effect examination type has on study methods may serve to obscure other differences, even those differentiating among the various learning- and grade-oriented groups.

The results of this investigation of testing preferences clearly indicate that students tend to prefer multiple-choice to essay tests. This may be true because essay tests are a rare phenomenon even in small colleges. For example, a recent study in five Nebraska schools (Trani, 1979)—Union College, Chadron and Kearney State Colleges, and the University of Nebraska at Omaha and at Lincoln—revealed that 47 percent of forty-five hundred students reported they had never or rarely written an essay exam. The percentages were essentially the same at the smallest school (with an enrollment of nine hundred) as at the largest (with an enrollment of twenty-two thousand). Furthermore, our inspection of many essay-test items, coupled with a study at the University of Illinois (Spencer and Stallings, 1970), suggest that the term *essay* is used ambiguously by faculty. Sometimes it means "list the causes of . . . ," "name the factors contributing to . . . ," and so on. These questions seek factual information much the same as do multiple-choice questions. The difference here is that in the essay items answers must be recalled or remembered while in multiple-choice items answers need only be recognized.

The label *essay question* cannot be taken at face value. Recall, too, that faculty at the University of Kansas (Chapter One) thought their test questions were complex but in actuality sought only factual details. While this striking and consistent preference for multiple-choice tests will come as no surprise to the experienced classroom instructor, what might be surprising are the reasons students offered for favoring each type of test. Of those students choosing multiple-choice, 58 percent reported they found it easier to answer multiple-choice questions than essay ones. For some students, multiple-choice items provide a recognizably correct answer: In the words of one student, "I like multiple-choice exams better because I can choose an answer better than tell an answer." A second group of students indicated that based on previous test experiences they do better on multiple-choice exams. One student candidly calculated, "Odds are in my favor. I'm a good guesser and very lucky." None of these students selected a multiple-choice test because they believed it facilitated or improved learning.

Many students favoring essay tests also offered reasons based on relative test ease. For example, one student reported, "I feel that I can express my answers better in an essay whereas in the multiple-choice you either get it wrong or right." Often students choosing essay tests reported that past experiences with both types of test influenced their selection. One undergraduate wrote: "I hate multiple-choice. I've never been able to take them. I can narrow the answer to the right answer and one other, and sure as hell I pick the wrong one." One third of all essay-test takers reported they felt essay items were more likely to help them learn and retain more information. Said one student: "I feel essay tests are an aid to learning. Learning doesn't stop with studying for the exam. The essay exam gives you an opportunity to express your ideas rather than just mimic information doled out." None of the students who selected the multiple-choice examination gave reasons of this sort.

Though previous literature (Balch, 1964; Class, 1935; Douglass and Talmadge, 1934; Terry, 1934) suggests that in the distant past college students typically employed different study methods when preparing for multiple-choice and essay tests, the largest number of students in the present sample reported using the same methods for both types of tests. Whether this is a wise or recommended practice cannot be determined, for if the primary educational goal is to understand and remember as much of the course material as possible, the particular type of examination being studied for should be of secondary importance. In such instances, nondifferential test preparation makes good sense. On the other hand, if the student is interested in finding the easiest way to earn the highest grade possible, more clearly differentiated study methods seem appropriate. For those students who study in different ways for each examination type, things have changed little in fifty years. That is to say, when studying for multiple-choice tests they focus on specific and isolated details; when studying for essay tests they focus more on general concepts and ideas. Many faculty talk about the latter but test the former.

Turning now to the four LO/GO groups, essay tests were more frequently preferred by High LO/Low GO students than by students in any of the other groups. As expected, the largest number of multiple-choice test takers was found in the Low LO/High GO group. Differences among the reasons offered for preferring one type of test over the other (across all four LO/GO groups) were less obvious. Test preferences appear to be determined by the individual student's answer to one of two possible questions: "Which type of test do I think is easier to take?" or "On which type of test do I typically do better?" While some evidence suggests that students in the High LO/High GO group prefer essay examinations because they enhance learning, such reasons were less important than ease of test taking or expected outcome.

A comparison of test scores obtained by students in each of the four LO/GO groups reveals that the highest test scores (within each class and also within each test type) were made by High LO/Low GO students, while the lowest scores were made by High LO/High GO students. Both findings are consistent with previously reported ones (see Chapter Six) concerning the educational and personal characteristic of students falling in each of these groups. Compared to students in other LO/GO groups, students in the High LO/Low GO group have greater abstract reasoning ability, are more self-motivated, show a greater interest in new ideas and intellectual matters, report the highest levels of facilitating test anxiety and the lowest levels of debilitating test anxiety, and employ the most effective study methods. Students in the High LO/High GO group score lowest on abstract reasoning, attribute the greatest importance to luck and fate as powerful influences in their lives, and report the highest levels of debilitating anxiety. With this pattern of skills and attitudes, High LO/Low GO students may be expected to outperform High LO/High GO students; present results indicate that this expectation was met as indicated by test scores received by students in the two groups on both multiple-choice and essay type examinations.

General Implications: Pedagogic and Otherwise

The implications to be drawn from this initial investigation fall into two major categories: (1) issues related to teaching, learning, testing, and grading; (2) issues related to the study of human experience, whether in the lecture hall or elsewhere.

Teaching/Learning/Testing/Grading. There is an old psychological adage that "what gets noticed is what gets learned," and this observation provides one good reason for determining when students are or are not aware of content during a college lecture. It is not so much a question of the lecturer needing to know how well he or she is lecturing as it is a question of knowing if students are or are not dealing with the content. The stream of student consciousness—like all streams of human conscious experience—is a highly varying and fickle one and this fact creates certain problems for the lecturer. Probably the most obvious problem is that no student (no ordinary student, at any rate) will follow the lecture content for an entire fifty-minute hour. As lecturers, we must be content with a 50 to 60 percent batting average and not be disappointed if we cannot entrance students for an entire fifty-minute hour. Whether we like it or not, students have more on their minds than our lecture, and we are refusing to face facts by expecting to be at the center of their worlds even during a college lecture.

A second pedagogic implication is that some redundancy is necessary in most lectures. Since no student is on-target all the time, it is wise to provide a good deal of additional support for lecture content; such support could come in the form of pertinent outside readings as well as by redundancy in the lecture itself. Within the classroom context, support might also come from a sensitivity to and encouragement of questions. If the lecturer is no longer required to be a spellbinder, he or she must still remain an orderly and nonthreatening question-answerer. In fact, student questions may serve to clarify the lecturer's as well as the student's thoughts on the topic.

Given that students and not disembodied minds enter our classrooms, we ought to try when possible to relate course content to their world. (There is nothing new about this advice.) This does not mean trying to make things pertinent in a pandering sort of way; rather it means trying to convey the sense of excitement and broader implications the lecturer sees in the subject matter. Gearing the lecture to the wider concerns of the student does not mean becoming an entertainer (not that there is anything wrong with that if the instructor can carry it off with style); rather it means sharing with students the lecturer's unique view of the topic. Lecturers who uniformly get high marks from students are those who have a contagious and vigorous enthusiasm about their discipline —not those who only entertain. Students come to learn as much about us as about what we teach, and we deprive them of our presence if only our notes, our voice, and our chalk appear at each lecture.

Careful and rigorous monitoring of one's lecturing by behavioral observations and student self-reports may teach the lecturer something about often unstated pedagogic aims. If a lecturer were to learn that self-reports scarcely if ever contained what he or she thought was the lecture content, such information should make a difference in how and what the lecturer did in future presentations. Within this context, the present methodology seems to provide useful and nonthreatening feedback to the concerned lecturer. Lecturers should never be too rigid to change, especially if feedback can be provided in the relatively nonjudgmental way offered by a careful analysis of student behavior and self-reports as these occur during the lecture. No colleague, especially not one sent to evaluate us for tenure, could do as constructive or as nonthreatening a job of evaluation as would be done by self-evaluation gained on the basis of careful in situ self-observation.

Whether we like it or not, the implications of this study are clear on the issue of classroom testing. From the student's perspective, there is a definite preference for multiple-choice over essay examinations, and this is largely unrelated to a desire to learn course material; the preference reflects a common belief that such tests are easier to take and to get good grades on. Since about 30 percent of undergraduate students might be expected to favor essay tests (with many of these students acknowledging that essay tests enhance learning), combining the both types of tests, or providing students the option to select the test format they prefer, seems preferable to using only one type of examination. The idea of allowing (teaching?) students to choose their own examination type seems a wise and useful educational procedure—after all, we are in the business of teaching students to make choices and this should apply no less to examinations than to courses. Whatever tests we use should be of good quality—currently many are not.

Human Conscious Experience in the Classroom and Elsewhere. The stream of human conscious experience has been necessary to an understanding of human nature since the time of William James ([1891] 1950) and to literature before then. Current psychological models of human cognitive activity, informed either by mechanistic psychology or by computer technology, have attempted to emphasize the goal-directed (on-target) nature of human thinking as desirable and, for our purposes, the only one worthy of encouraging in the college environment. Results of our analysis of classroom behavior and our experience suggest that the stream of human consciousness only approaches the totally directed and on-target state as a distant limit and that much of thinking occurs, to use James's words, in the dialectic between focal and fringe awareness. Even Einstein was recorded to have said that "full consciousness rarely if ever occurred and I only use conventional symbols once productive thinking has already been completed on the basis of 'combinatorial play'" (as cited in Hadamard, 1945).

The variability exhibited by our protocols only confirms what other investigators (Hadamard, 1945; Klinger, 1978; also see Pollio, 1980 and 1982 for a survey of work on this topic) have observed and should not be understood in a negative way. The stream of human consciousness, whether in the classroom or in the nonclassroom world, is a living and restless stream and, as such, joins in the more general adventure that is human life. In its more restricted form as directed thinking—one of the major intellectual activities at issue in education—it reveals an open-ended and variable texture that continuously enables thinking to go beyond its present limits by relating present ideas to the contemporary world of the student/learner/thinker. The variability of human experience provides us not only with a problem to be dealt with in the lecture hall but with a resource capable of leading our students and our society in new directions if we are not intimidated by an occasional seeming lack of focus. For this reason we should never attempt to reduce the possibilities of human consciousness by insisting on mechanical attention to each and every detail in each and every classroom lecture. To do so would deprive us, the student, and our society of the conceptual play necessary for that most precious of human activities—the creation of a new idea, a new invention, or a new work of art.

Summary

Grade- and learning-oriented students have been found to differ in many ways, and the purpose of the research in this chapter was to determine if they also differ in what they think about and do in college classes. What was firmly established is that GO and LO students differ not only in their educational and personal characteristics but also in the type of test they prefer to take and in what they pay attention to and do in the college or university classroom.

Methods were developed to determine both what students did and what they were aware of during college lectures. Results for both procedures were coded into the categories of on- and off-target, and comparisons were made among the four different LO and GO groups. For both behavior and self-report, results indicated that low GO students were more often on-target than high GO students; specific differences in learning orientation were found to have no effect.

Perhaps the most significant differences among LO/GO groups concerned the degree of concordance between being on- and off-target for behavior and for self-report. For this analysis, students in both of the High GO groups often were found to appear on-target when their self-reports suggested they were off-target, an incongruency far more frequent than with Low GO students. These differences, especially characteristic of the High LO/High GO student, suggest that such students are more calculating in their classroom behavior than is true for the other student groups.

In addition to observations made during classroom lectures, a second analysis concerned the testing preferences of students in all four LO/GO groups. In two separate undergraduate classes, students were allowed to choose either a multiple-choice or an essay test for their midterm examination. Results revealed that while students in both groups chose multiple-choice tests, GO students chose such tests far more frequently than did LO students. An examination of test scores revealed that the highest scores on both types of tests were earned by students in the High LO/Low GO group; lowest scores were obtained by students in the High LO/High GO group.

Insight into the factors governing student choice was gained through a tabulation of reasons given by all students for preferring one test type over the other. Across both types, the major reasons offered for selecting that type of test were that the student had a history of success in taking that type of test and that such a test was easier to take. Essay tests were frequently seen as prompting classroom learning; multiple-choice tests were never seen as serving this purpose. Although there was some tendency for LO students to offer this reason more frequently than GO students, the number of students in each group was sufficiently small so as to make this a possibility rather than a fact.

Put somewhat simply, students who are highly motivated by

grades tend to be more concerned about what impression they create on their instructor than with learning the content of the lecture. A concern for grades, thus, does not translate directly into a concern for better learning; rather it translates into the student's attempt to *appear* concerned about learning. For these students, the grade is more important than the learning supposedly symbolized by the grade.

▨◫▨◫▨◫▨◫▨◫▨◫▨◫▨◫▨◫▨◫▨◫▨◫▨◫▨◫▨◫▨◫▨◫▨◫▨◫

EIGHT

Different Students View the Same Grade Differently

Son: My grades are average, Dad. You can't complain about that.

Father: You're forgetting one thing, son. In this world, average is below average.

"Small Society" cartoon (Brickman, 1981)

Every four months or so, students attending American colleges and universities receive official grade reports, and if living room and dining room walls could talk, they undoubtedly would attest to the fact that similar father-son conversations about average grades are commonplace. The conflicting perspectives demonstrated by parents and their grade-receiving children originate in alternative assumptions made by each about the significance of an "average" grade. Then too, there are different connotations associated with each of the remaining grading symbols of A, B, D, and F. Grade meanings, in short, can be understood properly only when we recognize explicitly that they are context-dependent evaluations made by an instructor and understood by a student and a parent from within each individual's own unique frame of reference.

In many homes, a grade of A implies excellent or outstanding achievement; in others a grade of A connotes expected performance and anything less is viewed with disdain. Some college students (and their parents) look upon the educational accomplishment symbolized by the letter C as representing good or even very good work; still others view a grade of C as meaning failure. So it goes with each of the four nonfailing grades, thereby forcing any would-be grade giver, receiver, and user to recognize a concept that can be called "grade-value relativism."

Though countless classroom studies have used grades as indices of achievement, few have examined the meaning these grades have for the students receiving them. In one set of studies, Eizler and Stancato (1981) and Stancato and Eizler (1983) asked many different groups of students to rate letter grades on several different polar-opposite adjective scales. The overall purpose was to uncover the general structure of concepts students use in thinking about the meaning of their grades. These investigators looked at which pairs of rating went together, on the assumption that students who saw "good" grades as "rewarding" or "satisfying" were responding on the basis of an underlying factor common to all three adjectives.

When Eizler and Stancato examined the ways in which their adjectives fell into groups, they found four major clusters. The first included adjectives such as "good," "rewarding," "satisfying"; these were assumed to reflect the operation of an underlying factor that tended to answer the question, "How good is this grade?" A second group, consisting of such items as "accurate," "clear," "like me," was seen as an answer to the question, "How accurate is this grade as a description of my performance or of me?" The third group of adjectives—"important," "relevant," "concerned"— was viewed as an answer to the question, "How important is this grade to me?" The fourth group—"complicated," "difficult," "hard"—was seen as answering the question, "How hard was it to earn this grade?" The results suggest that the meaning an individual grade has for any student is a complicated and multidimensional matter. This approach is a promising one not only for describing what the authors term the structure of "connective meaning" associated with grades but also for determining how individual students understood their own unique grade meanings.

The approach suggested by Stancato and Eizler is an outgrowth of an analysis of linguistic responses (especially adjectives) to grades. As such, it has its proper ancestry in the psycholinguistic work of Osgood and his co-workers (Osgood, Suci, and Tannenbaum, 1957) concerned with more general aspects of the connotative meaning of words. While this work may be used to demonstrate grade-value relativism (see the beginning work by Stancato and Eizler, 1983, on the effects of course content on grade meanings), it usually has not been as sensitive to the role of context in human judgment as is true for work growing out of a concern for perceptual phenomena long associated with the concept of adaptation level (AL) originally proposed by Helson (1964). This approach to the investigation of grade meanings was proposed initially by Eison, Pollio, and Milton (1982), who from the beginning insisted on incorporating contextual factors—both situational and personal—into their analysis. Chapter Two employed this type of approach in evaluating the role of socio-historical, institutional, and disciplinary factors in affecting grade meanings.

What is Adaptation Level Theory and how does it relate to grades? Derived originally from research on perceptual processes, such as vision and hearing, AL theory provides a quantitative procedure for assessing the ways in which various contextual factors affect the definition of a neutral value for a particular individual in a particular situation. Consider, as one example, an early study in the judgment of height by Hinckley and Rethlingshafer (1951). Five hundred twenty one men were asked to rate twenty-eight different heights ranging from 4 feet 8 inches to 6 feet 11 inches on a nine-point scale. A rating of 1 was defined as very, very short; 5 was defined as neither tall nor short; and 9 was defined as very, very tall. When over 100 "short" judges (5 feet 8 inches and less) were asked to make judgments, the average value (neither tall nor short) was found to be 5 feet 8 ½ inches). When over 150 "tall" judges (6 feet and over) were asked to make the same judgment, they were found to consider 5 feet 9 ½ inches to be average.

In addition to this difference in the neutral height given by short and tall respondents, individual scale values were determined for each of the heights tested. The central portion of the curve produced by both short and tall respondents is presented as Figure 4. For the range of heights displayed in the graph (from 5 feet 8 inches to 6 feet 1 inch), men in the shorter group consistently rated each height taller than did men in the taller group. Both tall and short men judge heights tall or short relative to some neutral standard determined, in part, by their own personal height. Each person's neutral value serves as an anchor point around which other judgments are made.

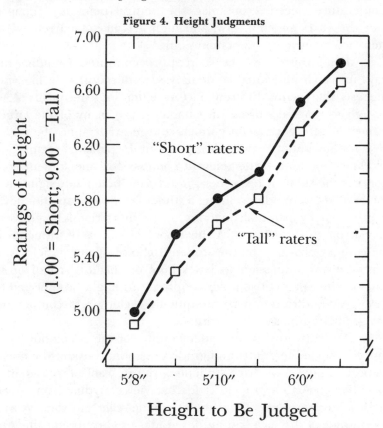

Figure 4. Height Judgments

Ratings of Height (1.00 = Short; 9.00 = Tall)

"Short" raters

"Tall" raters

Height to Be Judged

Further contextual effects on judgments are easy to document in many different aspects of human life. The meaning of a nice day—that is, one that is neither too hot nor too cold—will be greatly different for a person living in Florida and for one living in the upper Peninsula of Michigan. So, too, will the meaning of "fast" differ in track meets: Times close to 4:00 minutes for a mile were considered fast prior to 1956, when Roger Bannister broke that mark; now anything much more than 4:00 minutes is considered slow and runners have to beat 3:58 or less to be competitive. So as not to leave out the more sedentary among us, think about the value of 1,200 for the Dow-Jones Industrial Average. Prior to 1970, values of 1,000 were thought very high; now we talk about the market falling to the 1,000 level. In each of these cases, temperature, speed, economics, the neutral point has changed over the years and hot, fast, and high are all judged relative to their new neutral or adaptation point.

Using this same logic as an approach to understanding the ways in which individual students value college grades, likewise, suggests that many different factors enter into the picture. Although we have discussed (in Chapter Two) many of the larger frames of reference against which college grades must be evaluated for institutional purposes, other more personal factors are necessary to capture the relevant contexts for one student considering the value of his or her grades. One potentially significant frame of reference determining a student's grade adaptation level is provided by parental opinions. Peers and friends might also play a role in this process. A third possible source of influence is the context provided by the student's choice of major field; students seeking admission to law school or medical school or to other highly competitive graduate programs might be expected to view grades differently from students seeking less competitive postgraduation positions or careers.

To help provide an understanding of the adaptation level concept applied to grades and grade valuation, consider the hypothetical responses of three students given in Table 18. Student 1 considers an A to be a good grade but views anything less as bad grades. Student 2 uses the complete grade scale and views A as a good grade and F as a bad grade; grades of C represent this student's personal adaptation point. Finally, Student 3 views a C as a good grade and an F as a bad grade; the adaptation point here is the grade of D. If we add into the mix for each of our three students the adaptation level value ascribed to other members of their family, their friends, and their major—as well as the degree of importance the student attaches to each of these sources of influence—we are ready to compute each student's overall grade-value AL by the following formula:

Table 18. Adaptation Level Responses of Three Students

Question	Response		
	Student 1	Student 2	Student 3
1. What letter grade do you consider to be a good grade?	A	A	C
2. What letter grade do you consider to be a bad grade?	B	F	F
3. What was (or is) considered to be a good grade in your family?	A	A	C
4. What was (or is) considered to be a bad grade in your family?	B	F	F
5. How important (on a scale from 1 to 5) do you think your family's attitude toward grades is in determining your attitude toward grades?	5	3	1
6. What do your friends consider a good grade?	A	A	C
7. What do your friends consider a bad grade?	B	F	F
8. How important (on a scale from 1 to 5) do you think your friends' attitudes toward grades are in determining your attitude toward grades?	5	3	1
9. What do other people in your major consider a good grade?	A	A	C
10. What do other people in your major consider a bad grade?	B	F	F
11. How important (on a scale from 1 to 5) are the attitudes toward grades of people in your major in determining your attitude toward grades?	5	3	1
Adaptation Level	3.50	2.00	1.00

$$AL = \frac{W_1\,(ALself) + W_2\,(ALfamily) + W_3(ALfriends) + W_4\,(ALmajor)}{W_1 + W_2 + W_3 + W_4}$$

In this equation, the midpoint between (or average of) a good grade and a bad grade, as described by the student in response to Questions 1 and 2, is multiplied by the maximum weighting factor possible, 5. In addition, the midpoint between family estimations of good and bad grades (Q3 and Q4) is similarly multiplied by the weighting factor of "perceived importance of family opinion" giv-

en in response to Q5. The same applies to the midpoint between a
friend's estimation of good and bad grades (Q6 and Q7) and the
midpoint between good and bad grades in one's major field of
study (Q9 and Q10). Both of these latter components are weighted
by their appropriate weighting values (Q8 and Q11, respectively).
To determine each student's overall adaptation level (AL) for
grades, each of the four components (self, family, friends, and
major) is multiplied by its respective weighting value and averaged
over the sum of all weighting factors.

Applying this formula to each of the three students yields
the values shown at the bottom of Table 18. These values indicate
that Student 1 values only grades of A − or better, Student 2 values grades of C or better, and Student 3 values grades of D or better.
Student 1, thus, might be predicted to work for and only feel
satisfied with A's; Student 2 may be expected to view both A's and
B's as having positive incentive value; Student 3 would find grades
of C or better sufficient justification for feeling "good" about himself.

Theoretically, a letter grade of C represents the neutral
point in the grading scale presently used in higher education because it stands as the middle of the grade continuum that has A
and F as its endpoints. An AL value of 2.00 should provide the
theoretically neutral median value for student AL. This evaluation
is not the case for all or even most students. In fact, as will be
described, AL values observed in a large student sample span most
of the range from 1.00 to 3.50.

An adaptation level analysis of grade-incentive value suggests that the higher the AL the lower the person will value all
grades. Students whose AL is high would derive less satisfaction
from their accomplishment of receiving A's than would students
having lower ALs; for the first set of students, to earn anything
less represents poor performance. Students with lower ALs, on
the other hand, might be satisfied (or even pleased) with grades of
B and C; efforts to earn higher grades might be perceived as un-
necessary inconveniences. Classroom instructors will readily recognize at least one obvious implication: When given the opportunity
to improve one's final course grade by completing simple extra-
credit activities, some students (those with lower ALs) will let the

opportunity go by while others (with higher ALs) will rush to complete the added assignments.

Students for whom only high grades (A's and B's) have positive incentive value (high AL students) would be expected, all other things being equal, to work harder in classroom settings than peers with lower aspiration (adaptation) levels. To the extent that extra effort yields positive educational gains, one would anticipate that high AL students would earn higher course grades (have a higher overall GPA) than low AL students. A preliminary investigation of this prediction was reported in a study by Pollio, Eison, and Milton (in press). A group of 166 students enrolled in introductory psychology and biology courses at the University of Tennessee completed a brief questionnaire designed to assess each learner's adaptation level, to obtain their present GPA and ACT scores, and to have them note their degree of satisfaction with their GPAs. Students also rated each letter grade (A, B, C, D, and F) on a scale that ranged from "a very, very good grade" to "a very, very bad grade."

Results of this investigation are best described in two phases, the first describing the components of AL and the second describing the effects of AL on grade meanings. Table 19 gives the demographic properties of the student population studied. Values are provided for GPA and ACT. AL statistics indicate averaged AL values for the total sample; AL point values for self, family, friends, and field; and the average weights assigned by students to each of the major components. Also given for each value is the standard deviation, a statistical measure of some variability for the population studied.

In addition to showing that participants represented a relatively average sample of students found at a large state university (according to ACT and GPA scores), one of the more interesting aspects of these data is the specific weights assigned to each component of AL. Note especially, average weight given to family influences (3.77) was higher than that assigned to influences from the student's discipline (3.13) or than that related to attitudes held by friends (2.94).

These findings suggest family influences lead to significantly higher AL point values than those deriving from friends or

Table 19. Averages and Standard Deviations for Selected Indices

Index	Average	Standard Deviation
GPA	2.73	0.48
ACT	22.00	5.04
AL	2.22	0.33
AL Points:		
Self	2.34	0.48
Family	2.17	0.52
Friends	1.94	0.52
Field	2.25	0.51
AL Weights:		
Family	3.77	0.99
Friends	2.94	1.03
Field	3.13	1.04

discipline. The AL values associated with each of the four sources of influence reveal that AL points associated with both self and field are higher than those associated with family or friends. Thus, the strongest single component to a student's personal AL is provided by influences from family; such influences do not necessarily produce the highest AL values.

A second and perhaps more significant aspect concerns the relationship between AL and grade-incentive value. The graph in Figure 5 depicts the average value—on a scale of 1 to 7—of how "good" or "bad" students rated the grade categories A, B, C, D, and F. These values are shown for each of six different groups. The first of these, Group I, has an average AL value of 1.75 or lower; the last of the groups, Group VI, has an average AL of 2.75 or higher. The four intermediate groups all increase in steps of 0.25—Group II includes AL values from 1.76 to 2.00; Group III from 2.01 to 2.25; Group IV from 2.26 to 2.50; and Group V from 2.51 to 2.75. The number of students falling into each of these six groups is 11, 40, 27, 37, 15, and 14 for Groups I to VI, respectively. As should be clear, results for grade value shown in this figure are similar in meaning to the results for height presented earlier. Present results offer an evaluation of the way in which the grade-value frame of reference a student brings to college affects the value each grade category has for that student.

One feature of Figure 5 to note is the average scale value

Figure 5. Grade Value as a Function of Adaptation Level (AL)

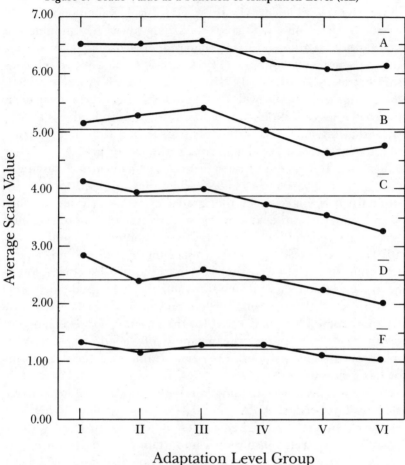

Adaptation Level Group

associated with each grade; this is indicated by the horizontal lines marked A, B, C, D, and F. For all grades except F, the average scale score is less than what might have been expected if subjects divided the seven-point rating scale equally into each of the five categories. More significant than average scale values are the mean values received by each grade for each of the six AL groups —in most cases the relationship is a decreasing one, with students in higher AL groups producing lower values than students in lower AL groups. For all grade categories, students with higher ALs

(IV, V, VI) valued the grades of A, B, C, and D less highly than did students with lower ALs (I, II, III). Grade valuation is clearly relative to AL value, with students having lower ALs judging the same grade as more valuable than students having higher ALs. Given these results, one possible expectation is a positive relationship between GPA and AL; that is, the less each grade is valued, the harder the student will work to get the higher grades needed to achieve a sense of personal accomplishment. Indeed, results did show that higher GPAs were clearly associated with higher ALs.

What does all of this mean for the use of grades in higher education? It suggests there are grave problems in assuming a cross-person invariance to grades when they are used to motivate students. It is not so much that grades are without value in motivating students; rather the problem is that they have little stability across different individual or educational contexts. As long ago as 1930, Crawford called grades "rubber micrometers," and the description is as apt now as then. Perhaps the clearest conclusion to be drawn is that different students value the same grade differently and that such differential valuation can be described easily by an AL theory. This implies that for the incentive value assigned to getting a "good" grade, the meaning of "good" depends very much on the given student's personal frame of reference, on his or her grade-value AL.

With this understanding, it is not surprising to find a strong relationship between GPA and AL—students having higher ALs work for and receive higher grades. Before we proceed with an analysis of this relationship, it is important to investigate one potential source of difficulty: How do we know that students having high GPAs do not also have high ACT or SAT scores and that this relationship is more important than that between grades and AL? The Pollio, Eison, and Milton study (in press) described earlier revealed that AL correlated with ACT at a value of 0.57 and that ACT correlated with GPA at a value of 0.33. If we control (statistically) for ACT score, the correlation between GPA and AL becomes 0.26 (a statistically significant value), suggesting that the relationship between GPA and ACT cannot account for all of the relationship observed between GPA and AL.

Since correlation does not imply causality—only covariation —it is necessary to develop some overall understanding of the pattern of relationships between GPA and AL, AL and ACT, and GPA and ACT. One description that might do the job runs as follows: High AL reflects the incentive value of grades to the student as derived from norms of family (and to a lesser extent, friends and academic discipline) as well as from a prior personal history of success in getting grades and a reasonably extensive fund of verbal and quantitative skills and information. Having a high grade-incentive AL and an extensive fund of knowledge will continue to lead to high grades. Since getting high grades requires the student continuously to acquire new information, this set of circumstances will lead to getting further good grades, thereby continuing the cycle and making sensible the triad of correlations just mentioned. What is suggested is not a causal relationship among variables but one of reciprocal and continuing influences over the course of a student's academic career.

If we enlarge this situation to students with different adaptation levels, there is the possibility of a pernicious educational cycle for the student with a relatively low grade AL. Assume two children of equal initial ability, one with an AL standard of 3.50 and the other with an AL standard of 2.00. Further assume that each child's family holds the same standard for grade value as does the child; this means that a grade of B will be met with approval from the family with the 2.00 standard and with disapproval from the family with 3.50 standard. In the lower AL family, there is no reason for the student to do any more than is required for grades of B or C. Under these conditions, a progressive decrease in what will be learned is to be expected for the low AL child vis-à-vis the child with the higher family standard. Following this line of argument further suggests that by the time the child from a low AL family reaches high school or college, not only will his or her grade-incentive AL be lower than it might be, so too will his or her GPA and SAT scores.

We must not ignore the fact that the incentive value of a grade is relative to the familial AL for grades; that is, getting good grades (A's and B's) does not motivate young people of lower socioeconomic classes as powerfully as it does young people from middle and upper socioeconomic classes (obviously there are exceptions to this generalization). Ignoring this fact will penalize the young people we, as a society, want to help by providing financial aid. Cross (1971) has studied these new students (as she calls them) extensively, and she writes, too, about how many of their educational values are different from those of their middle- and upper-class peers.

For many of the new students, a grade of D or C has the same incentive value as one of B or A has for some other students. Thus, to tie financial aid to getting good grades with these new students is just plain wrong; it is a misdirected impulse of society's. Newman (1985) also argues against financial aid being tied to grades. There are no quick fixes for this complex problem, but we believe that our suggestions (see Chapter 9) promoting a reduction in the number of grade categories—and most importantly, a redefinition of each one—will help ameliorate the effects of the unfair use of traditional good grades. "We must think anew, act anew."

The situation for the high AL family is somewhat more complex, and we may expect one of two outcomes. For the positive outcome, the script will be exactly opposite to that described above—the child will be motivated by family expectations and will learn and perform well throughout an entire academic career. Unfortunately, there may be a negative side effect to having an exceptionally high family AL—the student may be unable to achieve to family expectations, thereby making school a matter of avoiding failure rather than one of achieving success. If family expectations set AL at 4.00, the student will never be able to exceed (or often even reach) what is expected and will have to work extraordinarily hard merely to stay even with self and family AL.

Too demanding a parental (and later a personal) grade AL may lead to a second negative outcome. The student may reject the educational values producing such a grade AL in the first place and repudiate the educational context. While such students often return to college and come to a proper valuation of GPAs, ACTs, and the like, some talented students never achieve such an accommodation and their talents are thereby lost to society.

Grade Meanings in the National Grade Survey: Total
Population Results

Largely because the initial Pollio, Eison, and Milton (in press) study produced such clear findings, a section of the National Grade Survey was devoted to replicating and extending them. Students completing the national survey were asked to provide the following information: (1) GPA; (2) ACT or SAT; (3) AL points for self, family, friends and discipline; (4) weighting values for AL points deriving from family, friends, and discipline; and (5) 1 to 7 ratings for each of the grade categories, A to F. These procedures are identical to those used in dealing with the more limited sample studied at the University of Tennessee reported earlier in this chapter.

With the exception of ACT and SAT scores, results in the national sample are based on responses by over 80 percent of the total group. Average scores on ACT (23) and SAT (1,138), which were from only 25 percent of the sample, were somewhat higher than would be expected on the basis of demographic data obtained from institutional records. The average SAT score derived from college statistics reported in Chapter Three was about 1,035; the average ACT score was 20. Our national sample values exceed these averages, suggesting that students reporting their SAT or ACT scores were those who had done well on these tests. Such results imply that care should be taken in interpreting any analysis involving either SAT or ACT scores.

Perhaps the most significant data for purposes of comparison with our earlier sample are the various AL points and the weighting factors assigned to each. Results indicated that influences derived from the student's family continue to be weighted more strongly (mean value = 3.76) than influences from the student's field of study (3.06) and from the student's friends (2.92). Comparable values derived from the earlier University of Tennessee investigation duplicate these values both in selective order and absolute value.

AL points for each source of influence were derived from results in the national survey; average values were 2.27 for self, 2.24 for family, 2.06 for friends, and 2.32 for field of study. Examination of these values indicates a small difference between earlier and present results—self AL is lower than field AL for subjects in the national sample whereas the reverse was true for students in the Tennessee group. For both samples family AL is lower than self or field AL and higher than friend AL. In general, present values are quite similar to those derived from the smaller and more local sample.

To complete the picture, it is necessary to consider the pattern of correlations between AL points derived from each of the various sources of influence. Results of the national survey reveal that the strongest correlations are between self and family AL values ($r = 0.43$) and that the smallest correlations are between AL points derived from family and friends ($r = 0.23$). The remaining correlations for the components of AL all fell in the 0.29 to 0.38 range, with values as follows: self with friends = 0.30; self with major = 0.38; family with major = 0.29; friends with major = 0.38. The conclusion to be drawn is that the single most significant influence on student AL again is the student's family and that this influence is relatively independent of those of friends or major field of study.

A second and more critical analysis is that of the relationship between the rated incentive value of grade categories A through F and student AL. Figure 6 gives values produced by over thirty-five hundred students divided into five AL groups of approximately seven hundred students each. AL values increase from Group I through Group V. As predicted, there is a downward trend for ratings involving each of the grade categories; that is, each category was rated as less "good" by students having higher ALs. A careful inspection of each of the curves reveals that the difference in scale value between Group I and Group V was larger for the grades of C and D than for the grades of A and B. This suggests that students in the highest AL groups undervalue lower grades more than higher grades, and that students in the lowest AL groups overvalue lower grades more than higher grades. This means that C's and D's are felt to be "OK" for students in the lowest AL group (Group I) and, relatively speaking, "catastrophic" for students in the highest AL group (Group V). Students in Groups II through IV all fall neatly between these two extremes.

Figure 6. Average Value (All Grades) as a Function of Adaptation Level (AL) for the Five Groups in the National Grade Survey

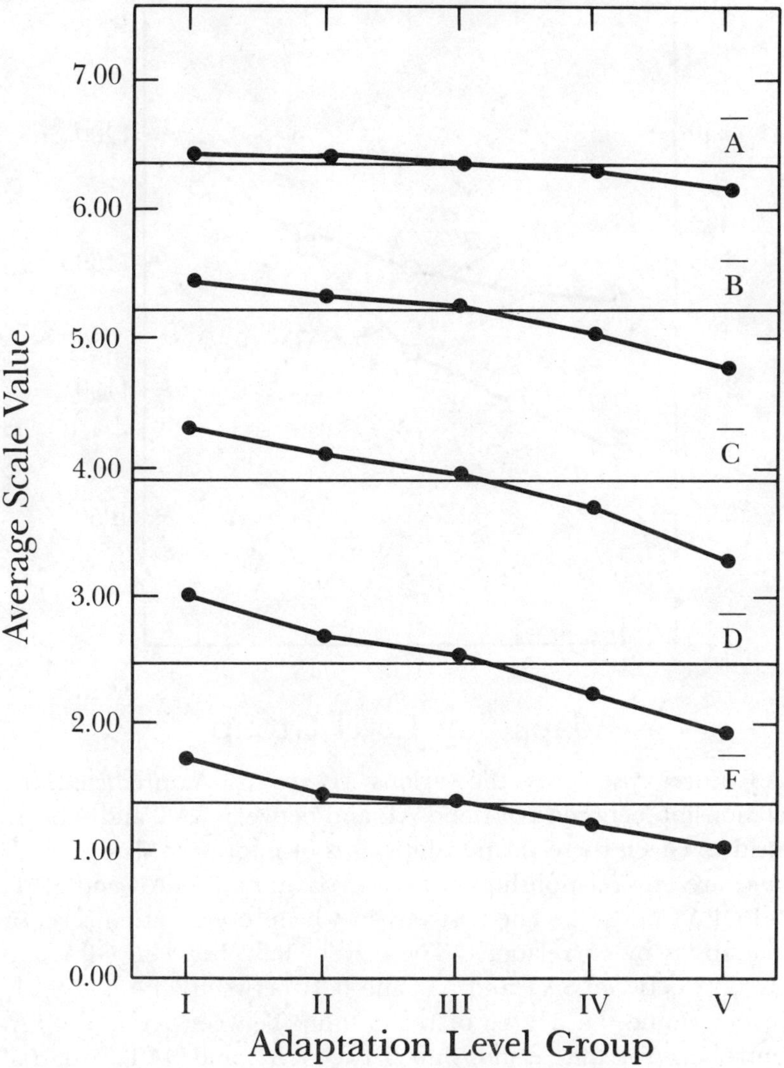

A final prediction of AL theory as applied to grades suggests positive relationships between AL and both GPA and SAT. For purposes of comparison, the data for SAT and GPA have been plotted on the same set of axes in Figure 7; the left axis represents GPA, the right SAT. As can be seen, both GPA and

Figure 7. Average GPAs and SAT Scores for the Five Adaptation Level (AL)
Groups in the National Grave Survey

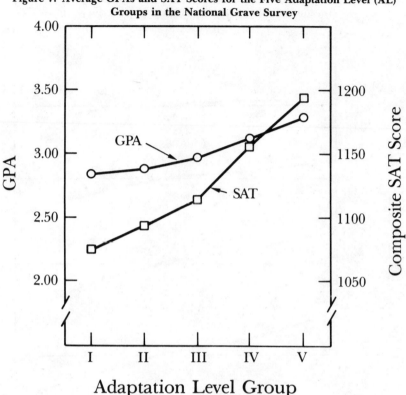

Adaptation Level Group

SAT scores rose across the various AL groups. As predicted, the
relationship between GPA and AL and between SAT and AL was
positive. Given these relationships, it is of interest to determine if
there are any relationships between AL and GPA, AL and SAT,
and GPA and SAT. The best way in which to evaluate this set of
relations is by correlations. These were 0.32 between GPA and
AL, 0.28 between SAT and AL, and 0.31 between GPA and SAT.
To determine the degree of relationship between AL and GPA,
controlling for the relationship between AL and SAT, a partial
correlation was calculated. The procedure gave a value of 0.27,
indicating that GPA is predicted by AL even when the possibly
confounding effects of SAT score are taken into account. A partial
correlation between GPA and SAT taking AL into account was not
performed since SAT scores were available only for a small por-

tion of the sample. The partial correlation must be interpreted with care because of this circumstance.

These results thus support and extend almost all of the conclusions reached on the basis of the earlier and more limited study. The value a grade has for a student depends on that student's AL, and this conclusion is as true for college students at over twenty different campuses as it was for students at the University of Tennessee. Grade values are never independent of the student who receives them no matter how much one might hope this to be the case for purposes of cross-situation use and presumed objective assessment.

Cross-Institutional Comparisons of AL Values

As noted in Chapter Two, one of the major frames of reference affecting the meaning and significance of a given letter grade is that of the institution the student attends. Five different institutional types were sampled in the national survey: community colleges, four-year colleges with relatively open admissions requirements, four-year colleges with relatively competitive requirements, comprehensive universities with relatively open requirements, and comprehensive universities with relatively competitive requirements. Because of the context-dependent nature of grades and grading practices, it is reasonable to expect different ALs for the five types of institutions, with competitive colleges and universities having relatively higher grade ALs than open admissions institutions, and all four of these institutional types having higher grade values than junior colleges.

Table 20 offers the results of AL computations performed across the five institutional types. The overall AL value for each institutional type is exactly as predicted, with community colleges producing the lowest AL values and the competitive college and universities producing the highest ALs.

This table presents data for each of the AL components. Almost without exception, the overall order for each component is identical to that for the total institutional AL. Similarly, the absolute level of AL points follows this order: self and field higher than family and friends. The weights assigned to each of these AL

Table 20. Relevant Adaptation Level Values for Five Different Types of
Institutions

| | | | AL Points | | | AL Weights | | | |
Institutional Type	N	Self	Family	Friends	Field	Family	Friends	Field	Overall AL
Community College	574	2.16	2.13	1.95	2.15	3.63	2.81	3.05	2.13
College, Open	1007	2.29	2.23	2.08	2.37	3.74	2.99	3.17	2.27
College, Competitive	502	2.42	2.39	2.15	2.47	3.77	2.82	2.83	2.37
University, Open	1005	2.22	2.22	2.03	2.25	3.72	2.92	3.05	2.20
University, Competitive	327	2.40	2.36	2.10	2.43	3.87	2.96	3.09	2.35

components indicate that for all students the largest weighting factors were assigned to influences arising from family and the lowest to influences deriving from friends.

If we now turn to the relation of weighting value to institutional type, some suggestive differences appear. For family influences, students at competitive schools produced weighting factors (3.87 and 3.77) larger than those produced by students at less competitive schools (3.72 and 3.74) or at junior colleges (3.63). For weighting values assigned to influences provided by friends, there was no clear pattern across the various schools; open institutions presented slightly higher values (2.99 and 2.92) than competitive ones (2.96 and 2.82). In addition, there was an insignificant difference between competitive colleges (2.82) and community college values (2.81). Influences arising from the student's field of interest indicated that open admissions colleges produced far and away, the largest value (3.17), followed in close order by competitive and open universities (3.09 and 3.05) and, finally, by community colleges (3.05). Students at competitive colleges, on the other hand, produced the smallest values (2.83).

What can be said to summarize these findings about student perceptions of the relative significance of family, friends, and discipline in determining how they value college grades? The most significant source of valuation is provided by the family and the least significant by friends. For certain types of institutions, such as an open admissions college, friends exert a strong influence;

for other types of institutions (competitive college) friends exert relatively little influence. Perhaps the most unexpected finding is that family influences are strongest in the most competitive institutions and that this pattern does not apply to any of the other sources of influence. In competitive schools, student AL seems to reflect parental values more strongly than any other source of influence.

With this last analysis we have moved to a new type of analysis: a study of factors that might be influential in the development and composition of a student's personal valuation of grades. Strictly speaking, this description belongs more to a history of individual development than to a discussion of college grading. Such a description testifies to the profound difference in personal significance of the grade categories as a consequence of values in the student's family. These results reinforce the view that grade meanings and the control they exert on individual student learning are likely to be different for different students. Grades are never independent of specific students, and specific students are never independent of their cultural, historical, familial, or personal contexts.

Toward a More Psychological Understanding of Grades

Chapters Two and Eight both provide a clear-cut description of the way in which grade meanings are affected by factors such as the socio-historical era in which they are given to factors as small as the value one student attaches to a single grade category. If we add to this the results from the national survey showing that business, parental, and professorial groups all view grades in quite different ways as well as the fact that learning- and grade-oriented students all view grades in their own unique ways, we are led to the conclusion that a grade is not necessarily the same grade for the giver, the receiver, or the user.

This suggests, in turn, that grade meanings constantly vary and that such variation almost always relates to one or more contexts. This chapter has tried to document that for at least one of these contexts—that produced by the student—such variation may be described nicely by a single value, the AL. It is reasonable to wonder what results would be obtained if the theory of adaptation level were applied to other contexts found to influence the meaning and value of grades.

If we move from the level of the student to that of the discipline, such an analysis has been offered already. As may be remembered, the outcome of cross-field comparisons made by Goldman and others (1974) revealed that higher grades often are given in disciplines involving students of lesser ability. The logic of adaptation level theory adequately deals with this finding: Grades are relative partly to the quality of students usually seen by the instructor. If generally lackluster students are seen by a particular professor, a relatively low level of brilliance will be required for the student to shine and thereby receive a grade of A or B. If, on the other hand, the discipline enrolls a large number of good to excellent students (however defined), the grade of A or B will emerge from a different standard leading to the results obtained; disciplines with brighter and more well-prepared students give lower grades than disciplines with less able and less motivated students. This result is not shocking—it is simply a fact of life that human judgments are contextual, and no matter how much we might like them to function as thermometers do, they resolutely continue to function as human judgment directed toward other human beings.

Moving now to the level of historical era (we skip a few levels, such as year in school or selectivity of school, largely because a similar analysis would apply), we run into the issue of so-called grade inflation. As may be remembered, grade inflation (or grade deflation) is inferred whenever grades do not increase or decrease in tandem with some measure of student quality such as that provided by SAT or ACT scores. Grades follow a trajectory quite in contrast to that defined by aptitude test scores—when SATs go down, grades go up (inflation); when SATs go up, grades go down (deflation). Such contrasting effects can be understood simply as adaptation level effects: When instructors see lots of able students, grading standards become more demanding; on the other hand, when the number of able students decreases, the general level of expectation decreases and weaker students get better grades.

The psychological process at work in all of these (and other) grade effects is neither a random nor a capricious one; rather, it can be made sense of by the psychological processes involved in producing an adaptation level appropriate to a given judgment. Foremost among these processes is the phenomenon of figure/ ground. This phenomenon refers to the fact that any event—perceptual, conceptual, judgmental, whatever—never stands alone but always appears within some context or other that moderates how it will be experienced. The psychological world is not a collection of separable elements but a coherent system in which less complex events always emerge against the full, rich background provided by the rest of the system. The meaning for a student of any event—grades included—always is part of an ever-widening context which at its extreme includes the total system known as the socio-cultural-historical era in which the event occurs.

Returning now to the more narrow precincts of an individual, be it student, professor, parent, or business person, we must always be aware that judgments have a temporal aspect. Because of this, judgments (such as those made about grade meanings) always are changing, always are subject to new influences. Here the relevant principles of change are those of pooling, assimilation, and contrast. By pooling we mean that every judgment includes a continuously updated summary of all relevant past judgments as well as a sensitivity to the present context. The nature of the pooling process is largely an unreflective one that is done in an automatic and unconscious way. To be sure, such judgments can become self-reflected; in most cases, however, they just happen and thus create a standard that directly applies to the present situation.

Assimilation and contrast refer to contemporary judgments made to both the present situation and the personal standard used by the individual making the judgment. Assimilation means the tendency of the person evaluating a grade to judge that there is no difference between the personal standard and the event. So, for example, if a student wants a good grade and his internal standard for such a judgment in the present context is that of B, it is possible that grades of B+ and B− will be reacted to as if they were equal to B, with the standard equally satisifed since both grades were assimilated (made equal) to the standard. Contrast could be exhibited with the same set of standards and grades—that is, the B + will be experienced as clearly better than good and the B − as clearly less than good. Under what circumstances might we expect assimilation and under what circumstances might we expect contrast? A university or college that does not differentially weigh B, B +, and B − is promoting assimilation, whereas one that differentially weights each is promoting contrast. If the highest grade in the class is a B −, a student will feel better about a grade of B − than if everyone else in the class earned an A and B − was the lowest grade. In the former case assimilation, in the latter case contrast.

The same sorts of judgmental effects exist in each of the other constituencies concerned with grades. Consider the professor and, by analogy, the business recruiter. (The case of the parent seems most similar to that of the student and need not be dealt with here.) Suppose Professor X only teaches courses that are attempted by the best students in the university. His or her standard of what constitutes B or C or A performance will be based on a standard derived from the best and the brightest. Further suppose that University L (where Professor X teaches) becomes an open admissions university. The first group of students after open admissions likely will be dealt with more severely (contrast) than the eighth, tenth, or twentieth group taught and graded by the good professor (assimilation).

What this analysis demonstrates is that there is nothing sinister or even unreasonable about the vicissitudes of grade meaning. Rather these effects may be accounted for by well-known and relatively straightforward psychological principles common to a wide variety of judgmental processes. This analysis has the virtue of suggesting that similar processes are at work in the several constituencies involved in the receiving, disseminating, and using of college and university grades. If there is anything sinister about grades and grading, it must be that the present commonsense analysis has been overlooked for so long. Who knows the number of minor and major tragedies that could have been averted had we not held to the myth that grades have a single value that endures across succeeding generations of students. Having posed the human problem in this way, it is reasonable to ask that some sort of remedies be undertaken. This in fact is exactly the task that the next and final chapter addresses. We provide some beginning answers to the question, "What can be done about the great GPA machine now grinding out both students and grades in contemporary American colleges and universities?"

Summary

If there is one fundamental assumption to hold about grades, it must be that they represent the outcome of a judgment. Adaptation Level Theory provides a way of understanding the factors and forces that influence all judgments, whether these are about temperature, height, the stock market, track records, or college grades. We have discussed the role of contextual factors in grade practices that as are as extensive as the socio-historical era in which a grade is given or as limited as the number of years a professor has been teaching. We have examined the incentive value of college grades for students currently enrolled in our colleges and universities.

What sorts of factors affect the AL a student uses to determine the value of his or her grades? There are at least four major sources of influence: family attitudes and values, disciplinary attitudes and values, peer attitudes and values, and the student's own personal attitudes and values. Using values derived from each of these sources, a single value—the student grade AL—was derived from a number of students attending many different colleges and universities.

One of the more important results yielded by considering grades as an adaptation level phenomenon is that students having different ALs value the same grade differently. This was true for each of the grade categories as well as for the complete system. Students with higher ALs were found to have higher GPAs, and this was true even when SAT or ACT score was taken into account. This means that for some students a grade of C is probably no less valued than a grade of A is by other students.

Cross-institutional comparisons clearly reveal that competitive admissions colleges and universities are attended by students having higher grade ALs than is true for students attending less competitive institutions of higher education. Across all institutions, the strongest nonself component to student AL is provided by the student's family. In combination with results from Chapter Two, we are led to conclude that grade meanings constantly vary and that a grade is not necessarily the same grade for the grade giver, the grade receiver, or the grade user. Although there is nothing sinister to this conclusion, it does suggest that our society should take a new and focused look at the ways in which grades are used in contemporary business practice as well as in contemporary higher education.

NINE

What to Do About Grading Practices

There is certainly no single recommendation for improving the grading game; the magnitude of the grading system, the complexities of subject matter, smugly recalcitrant faculties, and the varying aims of colleges and universities signal the necessity for several approaches if we hope to even make dents in the academic armor surrounding the grade issue. We insist that a central theme or purpose for grades is crucial. In our opinion, despite all the resistances, the differences, and the variations, the central theme should be that of influencing learning. All instructional activities must be directed toward that one end. Testing and grading form one corner of the learning pyramid, but for entirely too long both have been considered as independent of learning. Recall that even in the early days of American higher education, college grades were used primarily for ranking students, and tests were thought to waste valuable teaching time. Recall also that graduate teaching assistants have sole responsibility for testing and grading in many courses in many universities today.

The suggestions offered in this chapter represent our answer to the question, "What changes do you recommend once we decide to employ grades in the service of learning?" Two of these changes concern classroom testing and propose that we not only recognize the nonranking functions of tests but that we use tests and their feedback to students as positive procedures to promote learning. The remaining suggestions concern institutional changes designed to have the grading system relax its hold on classroom educational practices. If we reduce the institutional demand for differentiation and suggest reasonable alternatives for summarizing student learning patterns, we will have removed some of the needless paraphernalia serving to reinforce the notion of grades as ranking rather than teaching and learning devices.

In none of this is our intention to reduce standards; our only aim is to bring to bear the enormous resources of the academic community in considering a vital issue that has seldom been approached in a scholarly (let alone rational) way. If, on the basis of considered opinion and analysis, the reader's purpose in grading students is simply to rank them, then there is little reason to read the remainder of this chapter. If, however, you are willing to consider other possibilities that include teaching, learning, or simply finding out what students do or do not know, then perhaps our suggestions will make sense.

We make five recommendations that, if implemented properly, will improve college learning; they are supported by research evidence, for the most part, and just plain common sense.

1. We must clarify what we want grades to do: Are they to serve the purpose of promoting learning and teaching, or are they to serve the purpose of rank ordering students? If we select the former purpose, test and grades are in the service of teaching and learning. If we select the latter, tests and grades will continue as exercises in ranking, not teaching and learning.

2. Let us improve the quality of classroom tests so that whatever purpose tests and grades serve for us will be fairly and properly implemented. Test questions should be written more clearly than many are and should seek more than isolated factual information.

3. We must supply considerable information to students (far more than the letter symbol) about their performance on course tests and other academic exercises.

4. Let us use less, rather than more, differentiated grading systems and let us not reify grades or any other metric used to describe academic performance. The perspective should be that grades are not more precise than the techniques used to create them; as it now stands, such techniques are rela-

tively less precise than the metrics by which they are quantified.

5. Let us abolish the GPA; it is a useless and misleading statistic for either teaching or research purposes. If administrators or researchers feel the need for an overall summary of student college learning, we should redesign transcripts so they show patterns in a student's academic career; let us never condone or condemn a student on the basis of a single number, artificially significant to two decimal places.

Clarify What We Want Grades to Do

The life force of higher education is good, clear thinking followed by good, clear decisions. We seldom have done good, clear thinking when it comes to grades, and about the only decision we seem to make is whether to change the grading system from five to twelve units or from twelve to five units. In short, we tinker without ever examining seriously what we are trying to do. There are at least two major purposes potentially served by grades: to promote learning or to provide a ranking system for other social purposes. A critic immediately might ask, "Can't they do both?" We believe the answer to this question is "No," for if the ranking purpose is important to instructors they will design tests that are aimed to rank order students. This means that grades, and the tests from which they are derived, will be focused more on differentiating among students than on determining if students know significant course content.

We believe grades and grading practices should be in the service of learning and teaching, not ranking. Once we take this decisive turn the whole quality of classroom life should change, as should a number of well-established academic practices. When students in our National Grade Survey reported that grades "put instructors in a position of power over me" and serve to "interfere with our being friends," they simply were expressing their perceptions of the nonintellectual consequences brought about by grading. Faculty members who do not want to be friends with students or who do want to have power over them would still have these choices available; what they would not have available is support for these personal choices in institutional policies that encourage the use of grades as devices for rank ordering and thereby controlling students.

We are aware that certain national survey findings are contrary to some of our recommendations; two items indicate that all groups prefer numerically quantifiable differentiations among students (Chapter Three). This is true for grade-reporting systems and for grade-assigning procedures. Quantification presumably serves to inform students about their academic performance and to rank order them for personnel selection purposes. These quantification arrangements are preferred for at least two reasons: (1) The great majority of students and former students (representing millions of people) are or were graded primarily on these bases and most have accepted uncritically the serious associated limitations because the arrangements are familiar to them; and (2) this nation is on an objectivity "kick" and tends to equate quantification with objectivity.

Our reactions against the presumed quantification preciseness of grades are scattered throughout this book. Quantification does not necessarily or automatically indicate objectivity, especially if the quantities (numbers) have been determined carelessly (a point so elementary that we are embarrassed to mention it, but it is ignored routinely in the testing and grading enterprise). Also, a letter grade is a judgment and *all* judgments are context dependent. This means that numerous factors and forces must enter into the interpretation of a grade, whatever its purpose. Each of us subjectively weighs and judges these factors and their contributions to the end product, the symbols A, B, C, D, or F. It is not a matter, then, of being objective in the testing and grading enterprise; it is a matter of recognizing our contribution in choosing the test, deciding on the evaluation plan, selecting the content to be tested, and so on, that gives the evaluation procedure its unique flavor and requirements. Although we may be fair and precise in saying what we expect students to know, we must not lose sight of the fact that judgment and choice—our judgment and choice—lie behind both the testing procedure developed and the evaluative symbol given. Tests and grades do not just happen; we create them out of our personal values.

Misunderstandings and confusion about these issues are illustrated by the following statements gathered in the national survey. The first is from a student: "The fairest way to grade is the straight percentage. This way I understand exactly where I stand and there is less room for faculty subjectivity." A parent stated: "Subjective grading is relatively worthless. Grades somehow need to be divorced from personalities and based on objective criteria." While efforts should be made to correct such confusion, cause for alarm exists because of the belief expressed in this faculty member's statement: "Grades serve as objective measures of success and ability." Just why this nation disparages judgment and choice in human actions we do not know, although its fascination with numbers (even for assessing such complex affairs as student learning) is surely part of the answer.

One reason for the current extensive use of multiple-choice tests is that many, both inside and outside the academy, think they are objective. In reality, they are not objective. How do questions get selected in the first place, and how are correct and incorrect answers decided?—by an act of human choice. Textbook publishers are beginning to supply tests for introductory courses that are composed of multiple-choice questions selected (sometimes randomly) by a computer and scored by a machine; in a sense, such testing is objective since once this procedure is chosen by the professor he or she has little further to do with it, but by choosing this route our instructor has indicated a belief. Testing and grading are not integral features of instruction. We are emphatically opposed to such arrangements and beliefs. The contemporary rage for computer technology suggests it will be used increasingly and thoughtlessly for course testing purposes. As Bob (in press) recently noted: "If we are ever to de-massify education we need to get away from methods which are mechanical, even if they are easy. Until we do, students will correctly perceive that educators regard them to be graded, sorted, labelled, and moved along the educational assembly line."

There are further and seldom-considered ill effects from this emphasis on the ranking of students; some are reflected in the observations of one faculty member in the national survey: "The mean-spirited competition for grades among bright students appalls me. In some ways, good grades become palliative for bright students whose needs (for stimulation and support) go unmet year after year. The waste is atrocious." These insights remind us of the Davis (1964a) and Thistlethwaite (1965) investigations mentioned in Chapter One, showing that large numbers of capable students with less than B+ averages did not feel capable of further formal study.

To us the most significant and encouraging results from the entire national survey are those for two items concerning the central purpose of influencing learning: (1) *When a college faculty member assigns a final course grade, to whom do you think the grade is addressed primarily?* and (2) *Discussions of grades and grading practices suggest that grades serve several purposes. Indicate the relative importance each purpose currently has and the degree of importance you would like each purpose to have.* The findings bear repeating.

For the first item, all groups reported that the main audience is students; for the second, all groups agreed that they would *like* the most important purpose of grades to be that of communicating to students how much learning was achieved. But there was equally strong agreement across groups that the most important current purpose of grades is to provide "other educational institutions, such as graduate or professional schools, with information for making decisions about the student." The striking discrepancy between the primary present purpose of grades and the primary desired purpose indicates that something is awry and changes are in order. It was heartening to learn that the two chief participant groups in the learning endeavor—students and faculty —agree that grades and grading practices are not communicating about learning to the extent they would like them to. Unfortunately, the faculty group is out of step with the other three groups regarding one desired purpose of grades as providing information about students to other educational institutions; the faculty group ranks it third in importance among fourteen, while all the others rank it in the middle, or much less important.

Statistics about the current purpose of grades are buttressed even more tellingly by questions, answers, and comments heard repeatedly on all campuses by those who listen, "What did you get out of English lit [or psych, or p-chem, or zo]?"—"I got a

C." "I'm going into the poly sci [or econ, or double-e, or western civ] final with an 84 average; if I can pull an A, I'll have a 3.00." If testing and grading communicated better, learning would be enhanced and students might not have such narrow views of their courses; tests and grades as we now know them do not serve the purpose of promoting student learning very well.

Improve Classroom Tests

The feature of instruction with which to start influencing learning for the better is classroom tests. Course tests help determine how many students study and what they learn (Milton, 1982a), as revealed by the familiar questions "Will that be on the final?" and "Will the test be objective or essay?" College and university professors should not be surprised that tests influence learning; it is but another illustration of the well-known fact that the act of measurement influences the phenomenon being measured, which in physics is called the Heisenberg Uncertainty Principle. A prime example is the act of taking a blood-pressure reading. Any number of factors, some subtle and some not, associated with the procedure (measurement) alter the value of the reading (score) obtained. These factors include the physician entering the examining room, the place of the test (office, hospital, or elsewhere), the very thought of the procedure, and the pressure of the inflated cuff; the good physician weighs or judges these influences—subjectivity. We wonder if many faculty and educational researchers are aware of test influences upon learning. In a recent article entitled "Learning Improvement Programs: A Review of Controllable Influences" (Sherman, 1985), classroom tests are not even mentioned!

In the national survey, results regarding how long the difference in knowledge represented by an A and a C will last suggest that faculty members, much more so than the other three groups, put unwarranted faith in the quality of classroom tests as measurement devices. Knowing what we now know about a significant number of course tests (and what we know about students), we doubt very much that the difference lasts as long as is believed. (We make allowances, also, for what we know about the laws of

forgetting.) It is our guess that the faculty answered this item solely on the basis of their own remembered experiences, either as a
student or more recently as a faculty member.

As we indicated in Chapter One, entirely too many test
questions ask for nothing but isolated factual information. We do
not mean to condemn the notion that students should know factual information—sound basic factual information is indeed a sine
qua non for higher-order mental processes such as comprehension. But factual information is not enough. While this is not the
place for an extensive discussion of the dynamics of learning, a
few comments are necessary to bring to the fore once again our
insistence that the chief purpose of the grading game must be that
of influencing learning.

In almost all courses there is a desire by faculty—and by
many students—that the material learned be utilized later and in
other contexts. This may mean using what has been learned in the
very next course, applying a concept to the world of work, or
using course content as a citizen in understanding events in society. These are all instances of what has been called "transfer of
learning." Now, transfer does not occur automatically (as has been
demonstrated by extensive research), but for hundreds of years it
has been believed that it does, and the notion is believed today by
many faculty "without observation or reasoning." This belief is
found especially for the field of mathematics. For example, John
Locke (Fowler, 1890) admonished: "Would you have a man reason
well? . . . Nothing does this better than mathematics, which therefore I think should be taught to all who have the time and opportunity, not so much to make them mathematicians as to make
them reasonable creatures" (p. 20). A not-too-distant endorsement
came from Robert Maynard Hutchins (1936): "Correctness in
thinking may be more directly and impressively taught through
mathematics than in any other way" (p. 84).

We asked samples of faculty in five universities (Milton,
1972) to respond to this statement: "The study of mathematics is
especially important in helping students learn to think logically."
Forty-three percent of almost six hundred agreed; almost two-
thirds of the "hard" scientists in the sample did so. The fact that so
many of this group supported the notion without having seen the
kinds of research results they would demand in their disciplines

(only one respondent asked about research) is presumptive evidence against automatic subject-matter transfer; observe a faculty meeting for more direct evidence!

While it is not our mission to talk about the curriculum, it is important to emphasize the issue of transfer in this context because efforts are being made all around the nation to increase high school and college mathematics so as to make "reasonable creatures" and to develop "correctness in thinking." Algebra, geometry, and trigonometry will not do the trick. Adding these to the curriculum represents just one more attempt at a quick and somewhat unscholarly solution to a complex problem. Kline (1980) declares in his preface: "We know today that mathematics does not possess the qualities that in the past earned for it universal respect and admiration. Mathematics was regarded as the acme of exact reasoning, a body of truth in itself."

The chances of transfer of learning occurring for any subject matter are increased if applied examples are discussed in class and if applied questions are asked on exams. The first question below about the statistical median is more likely to aid students in applying or using correctly what they have learned than is the second question:

1. Given the scores 10, 6, 4, 8, 2, the value of the median is:
   a. 4   b. 5   c. 6   d. 8
2. The median is defined as the:
   a. most frequently occurring score in a distribution
   b. middle score in a distribution
   c. sum of all scores divided by the number of scores
   d. square root of the sum of the scores

Other desired manifestations of learning include comprehension or understanding (transfer is one indication of this), analysis, synthesis, and evaluation; these are oft-stated course objectives. Few questions relative to any of these objectives appear on classroom tests; at least one study (Milton, 1982b) suggests that many faculty are not very concerned about these deficiencies. Analyses were made of the sorts of statements almost nine thousand faculty chose to submit via questionnaires to their students in order to learn their reactions to instruction. Around sixty-five hundred or three fourths chose items such as "My instructor displays enthusiasm when teaching." This is laudable. However, only eight hundred instructors or one tenth of the sample chose to submit for student reactions "Exams are coordinated with course objectives." If students know higher-order questions are coming they will be more likely to exercise higher-order mental processes while studying rather than merely memorizing isolated facts.

In this connection, Newman (1985) in his very thoughtful and comprehensive book *Higher Education and the American Resurgence* deplores the fact that "Students ... take safe courses, are discouraged from risky or interdisciplinary research projects, and are discouraged from challenging the ideas presented to them" (p. 54). There are few who will disagree with those criticisms. We must insist, again, that the limited nature of so many course tests coupled with the rank-ordering purpose of tests and grades are largely responsible for those student characteristics. Corrective actions must include improved classroom tests and grading systems.

Another deficiency of course tests is that many questions are poorly written. The major sin seems to be a lack of clarity and ambiguity; at least this is the charge usually leveled by students. (Read a few test items used by your colleagues.) Poorly written questions arouse resentment and detract attention from the basic issue of learning, and they produce false scores for many students. We are inclined largely to agree with student complaints because we have had such justified ones many times. Also, the English language is a difficult one in which to write (let they who have published disagree) because it is replete with words and phrases that are used ambiguously. For example:

Seeded: something having been *added*—caraway seeds added to bread

Seeded: something having been *removed*—seeds removed from raisins

Seeded: *ranking* of players or teams in sports tournaments

Think better of a project: cast it aside

Think better of a person: admire more

According to the previously mentioned study describing the self-evaluative interests of nine thousand faculty, not many faculty seem concerned about ambiguity or clarity of test questions. Only some two hundred selected the item "Exams are free from ambiguity" to submit to their students for judgments. Poorly written items are one explanation of the unreliability of test scores. Many readers will become defensive now and insist that students cannot judge such matters. Some faculty will argue that ambiguous test items are useful in helping students learn to live in a world of ambiguity! These same faculty ignore the fact that the loss of a few points for an incorrect answer does not help students live in the world of a grade-ranked reality.

The individual test question is the starting point for classroom tests of better quality. Test questions can be improved immeasurably by the simple expedient of having each question edited by a colleague prior to administering the test; the colleague should be asked to judge "Are the questions clearly written?" and "What facet of learning does each item tap—factual information, application, evaluation, and so on?" Of course, faculty need to know much more about the measurement of achievement than many currently do.

If a college or university is serious about improving course tests, evaluation of the tests should become part of the evaluation process of faculty members. This would make classroom tests an integral part of instruction. This is not the place to provide the details of such an arrangement, but in essence a committee of an instructor's peers would examine the tests used in conjunction with the objectives or goals of that course. Three ratings should be sufficient—excellent, adequate, and inadequate. (Several guidelines for how to test for achievement are available; some are inexpensive paperbacks.)

Faculties complain about many faculty evaluation systems, and rightly they should because many of the schemes are similar to grading arrangements for students. For example, if Professor X has an overall rating of 3.19 and Professor Y an overall rating of 2.59, there are those in the academy who think that useful evaluation has occurred. The interesting thing here is that faculties or administrators do not transfer their knowledge (see the connection?) of the deficiencies of arrangements for evaluating them to those arrangements for grading students when in fact there are often remarkable similarities.

More and Better Information to Students

To further realize the goal that grades communicate more fully to students (as expressed in the national survey), it is well to remember Dressel's (1983) definition of a grade: "An inadequate report of an inaccurate judgment by a biased and variable judge of the extent to which a student has attained an undefined level of mastery of an unknown proportion of an indefinite material." Another definition that might be more palatable and is almost impossible to challenge substantively is this: A grade is a unidimensional symbol into which multidimensional phenomena have been incorporated, a true salmagundi. Translated this means a given grade can reflect level of information, attitudes, procrastination, errors or misconceptions, cheating, and mixtures of all of these plus other ingredients; all of this was noted in the literature over fifty years ago (Odell, 1928) as well as today (Duke, 1983) and is well known but ignored. The lone letter symbol is a conglomerate which specifies none of its contents. How is a student to know what the symbol reveals or hides? Furthermore, a symbol discloses nothing about the quality of the tests through which it was derived. To complicate matters, most students are unable to judge all the features of test quality, and sadly many faculty are not either.

So, what do grades communicate to students? "I got a B," and "After finals I'll have a 3.01." More effective communication must include more than isolated numbers or mere letter symbols. It is well known that the essential route to communicating with students and influencing their learning positively is done on the basis of feedback. Research evidence for at least half a century provides the message of how important feedback is for learning; so, too, does common sense. For example, one early study by Curtis and Woods (1929) compared four methods of marking examination papers in seventh- and eighth-grade general science, tenth-grade biology, and eleventh-grade chemistry. The method, which included discussions of test results was found to produce the highest scores on both an immediate retest and one six weeks later. In a different study, involving seventy-four teachers and over twenty-one hundred students in grades 7 through 12 from three school districts, Page (1958) demonstrated that students receiving appropriate comments on test papers did better on the next test—regardless of type—than did students who received no comments or mechanical ones specified by the experimenter. Sassenrath and Garverick (1965) found that discussions of multiple-choice questions with college students two days after midterms facilitated performance on the final exam on both repeated questions as well as new ones. A second group of students received no feedback, members of a third group compared their answers with correct ones placed on the blackboard, and the fourth group reread the material from which the questions had come. In another investigation with both day and evening college students, Wexley and Thornton (1972) demonstrated that giving the answer along with explanations by the instructor facilitated learning. The day undergraduates ranged in age from eighteen to thirty-one and the evening students, all of whom held jobs, ranged in age from seventeen to forty-eight.

These illustrative studies by no means exhaust the relevant literature. They do indicate that the usefulness of feedback is not restricted to students of certain ages or to those in college. Moreover, parents know the role feedback plays in helping young children learn, and feedback is what good editors provide to authors of books and journal articles. As might be expected, the national report *Involvement in Learning* (U.S. Department of Education, 1984) stresses that improvement in learning is more likely to occur following both written and oral critiques of student work.

Be that as it may, there is no way of knowing the number of returned examination papers that contain only a lone symbol, such as a B or 78 percent, and no other marks—not even those noting incorrect answers. There is also no way of knowing the number of tests which are never returned to students—this occurs especially with final examination papers and surely numbers into the millions. (Not returning test papers is consistent with the current primary purpose of grades providing "other educational institutions with information for making decisions about the student.") A significant approach to improving the grading game, then, is to supply much more information to each student than the lone number or letter symbol on a test paper. Feedback can range from noting student errors to detailed criticisms to lengthy discussions and explanations of test material. In any case feedback, not grade ciphers, serve to promote student learning. If we put only a letter or number grade on the student's examination paper we may be fulfilling the ranking function of the test, but we certainly are not fulfilling its learning function.

Reduce the Number of Grade Categories

Another feature of the grading game that needs substantial altering is the number of symbol categories into which student evaluations are coded. To reiterate, the national survey shows that all groups prefer grading systems that have the greatest number of categories—that is, those that are supposedly the most highly differentiating. The recording system of A+, A, A−, and so on, was ranked first by all groups in overall preference. This system gives the illusion of precision; the desire for it may be based on measurement myopia, simple lack of thought, or ignorance. Because a central task of college faculties is that of combating ignorance through teaching and research, we should be the first to admit the personal void. Such action might set a good example for students—many of whom resist vigorously being deprived of their ignorance.

The thirteen points from A+ to F (why not F+ and F−?) are inexact ones. As a matter of fact, it is known that the distance between B− and C+ is psychologically much larger than between any other pair of adjacent categories (Stancato and Eizler, 1983). Comments by two of our informants during initial interviews for the national survey also illustrate the misunderstandings about quantitative grading system. One said, "Using percentages tells me right on the line what they think of me." The other said, "I'll go with the A+, A, A−, and so forth; it is a system of communication everyone understands." In the first case, a lone percentage cannot do that; in the second, the problem is it is a system which many think they understand but do not. How many people—including faculty and administrators—are properly aware of all or even most of the factors affecting the assignment of a grade as detailed in Chapter Two? Recall that a current Harvard faculty member declared, "The grade conveys a relatively unambiguous message . . . in a universally understood system of academic notation." Wow!

The caricature of exactness by those who should know better is not only unfair to students but it communicates false information to any would-be grade user. Many faculty know very little about how to measure learning or how to construct classroom tests. (In one of our local faculty surveys, 28 percent said their knowledge was based on intuition.) Many of these same faculty are "hard" scientists who know about the measurement of phenomena in their fields and its attendant difficulties but who somehow do not transfer the principles—which are the same—to measuring student learning. Are these faculty of today much like those of Harvard of 100 years ago who in grading students insisted that they "could distinguish between fractions of one percent" and who "sometimes assigned marks of less than zero"?

One of the basic features of measurement that needs to be better known concerns the number of letter symbols used to categorize students. This need was pointed out by McCall (1939), one of the early educational measurement specialists, in this manner: "Every pupil, teacher, and patron needs to learn—and the sooner the better—that every measurement made in the world is not a point but a probable-error blur—narrow with micrometer measurements and wide with mental measurements" (p. 45). Note the date of that warning—almost half a century ago. Judging by our national survey results and the current presumed wonders of grades (many of which are based on restricted measurements), the warning has not been heeded. One explanation is the belief in the soundness and virtues of numbers—not only in higher education but in other fields as well—no matter whether they have been derived carefully or carelessly. This insight by Richard Hofstadter (1966) is ignored repeatedly: "The American mind seems extremely vulnerable to the belief that any alleged notion which can be expressed in figures is in fact as final and exact as the figures in which it is expressed" (p. 339).

A careful examination of the metric properties of grades, such as that undertaken in Chapter Two, indicates that grades are context-dependent phenomena subject to an enormous number of identifiable factors. As such their exactness must be very much in doubt, and any attempt to equate the number derived from classroom grading and testing practices with that derived from physical measurement procedures is doomed to failure. College grades are metrically inexact phenomena and, while they are not without meaning in an individual class, they certainly are neither precise nor rigorous enough to resist distortions brought about by different disciplines, classrooms, students, and so on. A proper role for grading then is to provide a student (and the society) with feedback certifying that the student knows the relevant content in a certain course area. Each faculty member would have to specify what constituted an acceptable level of knowledge and when and where the student fell short (that is, could not be certified as having command of the relevant course content). With this understanding, grades would let both the student and the society know that a given level of learning had been attained and the student and the public might be spared a lot of imprecise argumentation about the precise meaning of a grade. The grade would become a communication between the professor and the student that would refer to learning and not to ranking.

As a starting point, we recommend that the grading system have two major units: Credit and No Credit. Research studies cited in Chapter One show that P/F systems, embedded within the context of traditional thirteen-unit systems, have not worked too well. We believe they would work if the overriding thirteen-unit system were abolished. Because we feel that colleges and universities do have a social and personal responsibility to the obviously superior student, we would like a separate category, sparingly used, of Honors. Although other schools in the recent past have had the same idea, we are disappointed in the decreasing use of the three-category grading systems. We understand that 1985 is not 1970, but we realize that a good idea is a good idea and that the present historical moment is more concerned with rank ordering than with learning. As should be clear, we prefer a less differentiated system that stresses learning and course mastery to one that stresses differentiation and precise positioning for each and every student.

Because of this admitted emphasis, we feel that the category of Honors should be received by very few students. One of these students comes along only occasionally and is recognized by all as being decidedly more able than the rest. As such, the grade of H would mean that the student displayed exemplary knowledge and skill in dealing with course content. Credit would be received by most students, indicating they had performed to some acceptable level on course tests of good quality and on other assignments. The number of students not receiving credit would vary from course to course and would be few, we hope. Three levels should suffice for necessary institutional record-keeping purposes and, in contrast to a greater number, would help to shift the focus from tests and grades to a proper perspective—that is, away from differentiating among students for personnel selection purposes to a focus on command of knowledge.

This shift should appeal to many faculty because, according to the national survey results, almost half of them wish students would emphasize grades less. It should have certain appeal also because many faculty seek to help students learn such intangibles as respect for honest differences of opinion; those intangibles cannot be assessed on written tests, but they can be judged by observation. The three levels eliminate the need for presumed preciseness. Those faculty who find grading unpleasant should welcome this change. One stated in the national survey: "I still find assigning grades the most distasteful part of my teaching," and another commented: "The more I have had to try to establish and execute fair systems of grading, the more trouble I have had about achieving that goal. I give them now only because of administrative edict and because students are so conditioned to receiving them."

Using the system would necessitate a change in the nature of course tests. Under present circumstances, where differentiating among students is the goal, grading determines test content. Under the model we advocate, testing is determined by an instructor's beliefs about important knowledge in the field. This means that nit-picking questions will disappear from testing endeavors, to be replaced by questions about significant content, issues, transfer of learning, reasoning, and so on. Both learning and society will be served.

The use of only three symbols will mean that arguments about grading on the curve will fade into insignificance; as results of the national survey reveal, no one seemed to like the curve anyway. We are not sure that the following story about the curve is apocryphal (Grose, 1975). Five students were assigned to an advanced seminar in a university that remains nameless. The instructor announced that since grades in that school were curved there would probably be one A, one B, one C, one D, and one F. After a few weeks the general ranking of the five students was clear; the low man announced he was dropping the course to avoid failure. The others said they would pay his tuition if he would continue so that all four of them would pass. So much for the bell-shaped curve.

As we have suggested, students would benefit from an altered grading scheme that changes the focus of classroom testing from ranking to learning. This would be reflected to some extent by a decrease in the number who drop courses to avoid receiving bad grades. Recall that almost half of the national survey student respondents indicated having dropped courses for this reason. It should be reflected also in a decrease in the number of students reacting as did one faculty member now teaching at a highly regarded university: "I used to get scared about getting good grades and did not explore as many fields as I'd have liked to in college because of it."

At the same time, the hundreds of thousands of older people who are returning to college have no need to be ranked by grades. It has been predicted (Brazziel, 1985) that by 1988 there will be more than four million college students twenty-five years and older and almost one million thirty-five years and older. It seems better to certify that such students know course material than to subject them to the inane machinations of having to run against a twenty-year-old for a higher place in the rank order.

Abolish the GPA

The fifth and final suggestion for improving the grade game is to abolish the grade-point-average, the meaningless mean.

It is meaningless for several reasons. Ask several people, "What is the meaning of a GPA of 3.00?" Almost all will say with little hesitation, "the student has a B average." And therein is one reason for the numbers being so meaningless. A GPA is an abstraction that has become reified in defiance of the fact that to have meaning any number must have some reference—the name of the school of origin being a simple starting point. In some schools a GPA of 3.00 means an A average. Few people seem to ask for any details before jumping to interpretations or conclusions. It is our guess that when viewing a transcript many people look first at the overall GPA; their reactions to the remaining information are then colored—rightly or wrongly—by this initial reaction. As a business recruiter remarked during one of the early interviews for the national survey, "When I first look at the data sheet, I look at the overall grade-point."

A second reason is the varied and sundry contents comprising the GPA from school to school—grades from easy courses, grades from hard courses, all grades being used, some grades being used, and so on. Add into the mix the finding that large numbers of students cheat on tests and the meaninglessness gets worse. Most important, the details of the mixtures and their calculations are not always described, so the reader of a transcript cannot know the permutations. The reader is forced to interpret the numbers. ("Objectively" a student with GPA of 3.49 is superior to and more capable than another with a GPA of 3.01.) With computers we might revive that calculation procedure of Yale around 1800, mentioned in Chapter One: "Multiply each annual average by the divisor used in obtaining it, and divide the sum of the products by the sum of the multipliers." There may well be equally bizarre calculations already in operation.

And tinkering with numbers brings us to a third reason for the GPA being meaningless. Generally speaking, a GPA is calculated by taking less-differentiated metrics (A B C D F) and recasting them into the more-differentiated metrics of decimals. While it is arithmetically quite proper to go from a more differentiated metric (percent correct on a test) to a less differentiated one (A B C D F), it is much less defensible to go from a less differentiated metric to a more differentiated one—the GPA number calculated to one, two, three, or more (watch the computer!) decimal places.

Aside from the perspective of administrative convenience, several students commented about GPAs from the perspective of influences on them personally. This statement reflects the halo that GPAs have attained: "Problems arise when someone outside the university looks at the GPA and judges a person on that basis. For instance, one can get a 25 percent reduction in car insurance if she or he has a GPA of 3.00. But a 2.50 in one college does not make the same student a less responsible driver than 3.00 in another with lower standards." A vivid statement comes from this student enrolled in a highly selective college: "As a freshman, my first time ever to be away from home, I made a 1.30. The following semester, after having learned many lessons and self-discipline, I made a 2.60. I am a junior now and my cumulative GPA is only 2.00—which looks awful. My first semester will hinder me until my days' end. I wish first-semester grades were not treated as though you are either dumb or smart."

Our recommendation is either do not calculate GPAs or, if a school just must have them for internal purposes, delete them when transcripts are sent to outsiders. In the words of Erickson (1971): "Communicating what a student has accomplished to agencies beyond the classroom is *not* a legitimate educational purpose and does *not* serve the instructional (that is, evaluative) needs of the student. The institution needs to forsake its role as quality controller for society" (p. 6).

What we propose as a positive replacement for the GPA is a redesigned version of the academic transcript. As they now stand, transcripts are organized chronologically (when the student took what course) and by little else. It would seem a relatively simple matter to redesign transcripts so they would reveal patterns in a student's academic career rather than simply that "such and such a course was taken at such and such time." Obviously, the term-by-term GPA and the cumulative GPA would not be needed if the pertinent information would be immediately accessible to the reader. Although none of us is an expert in the design of transcripts, the results of our efforts to produce a more usable transcript for a liberal arts student are presented in Figure 8. This figure can serve as a guideline for areas such as engineering, business administration, nursing, and others. We have grouped

Figure 8. Proposed Revision of College Transcript For Liberal Arts Majors Only (Additional Years Could Be Added as Needed)

Content Area	Year 1			Year 2			Cumulative $Y_1 + Y_2$			Year 3			Cumulative $Y_1 + Y_2 + Y_3$			Year 4			Cumulative $Y_1 + Y_2 + Y_3 + Y_4$		
	C	NC	H	C	NC	H	C	NC	H	C	NC	H	C	NC	H	C	NC	H	C	NC	H
Humanities and the Arts																					
Natural Sciences, Math, and Statistics																					
English																					
Studio and Performing Arts																					
Foreign Languages																					
Social Sciences																					
Independent Study																					
Extra-College Study																					
Totals																					

Note: Under each letter—C, NC, and H—a numerical value would be entered to indicate the number of course hours evaluated under that category.

courses into content areas that are usually used to describe meaningful curricular divisions. Numerical values will be entered in
pertinent locations to indicate the number of credit hours the student has completed successfully in any given content area.
Cumulative summaries, requiring nothing more than simple addition of course credits, are provided at the end of years 2, 3, and 4.
Obviously an examination of the entire transcript will be required;
this will force any would-be user to look at cross-year and cross-
content patterns. While we think this type of transcript represents
an improvement over those currently in use, it is not meant to be
the final word. Rather it is meant as a suggestion in the direction
of providing a more useful summary of college work than that
currently provided either by GPAs or by chronologically, and not
educationally, arranged transcripts.

We do not believe that there will be a mad rush to implement many (if any) of our suggestions. We do believe that to begin
improving the grading game, formal arrangements to reconcile
testing and grading grievances should be established on all campuses. Averill (1983) has declared that methods and standards of
evaluation "should be openly acknowledged as arbitrary, not in
the sense that they have been carelessly crafted . . . but in the sense
they might have been otherwise" (p. 88). He asserts further, "Examinations and their evaluations are always arbitrary, but almost
never acknowledged as such" (p. 89). We must add that sometimes
faculty thoughtlessness or capriciousness enters the testing and
grading enterprise.

Students should be able to fight back in such instances and
to have the balance of power on their side. This presumes an
American system of justice designed to protect the rights of the
weak against those of the strong. Such fairness should exist in
colleges and universities. Indeed, several important organizations,
including the American Association of University Professors and
the Association of American Colleges, issued a joint statement
some twenty-five years ago declaring that students should have
protection through orderly procedures against prejudiced or capricious academic evaluation (Milton and Edgerly, 1976).

We believe that in all institutions a final judge or judges
should have the authority to change a grade; this is true presently

for some of the campus grievance committees but not for others (Milton and Edgerly, 1976). The authority to alter a grade is necessary because in some cases the offending faculty member (and other officials) does not respond to reason; there is refusal to follow a recommendation or even a directive of a grievance committee. At Southern Oregon State College, for example, students sought redress in the courts (*McBeth* v. *Elliot*, 1978) because two faculty members, joined by the president and registrar, refused to obey the order to change grades issued by the school's duly authorized grievance committee. Such is the power of grades and of those who bestow them. The letter symbols A, B, C, D, F must symbolically signify omnipotence to their wielders. Apparently the power or authority of the disciplinary knowledge possessed by a faculty member is insufficiently gratifying.

We are quite cognizant of the cries about violations of academic freedom that will resound. What we must recognize is that all of us are capable of making mistakes in judgment, and having them corrected has nothing to do with academic freedom. Some of us can be carelessly arbitrary and cockily capricious when it comes to dealing with students. Colleges and universities have an obligation to abide by the avowals they utter and to set examples for the large society of which they are a part.

A Summary in the Form of a Final Polemic

Although the National Grade Survey produced a considerable amount of new information, one of its main conclusions has been known by many but denied in practice for a long time. In his article on "Marking Systems" in *The Encyclopedia of Educational Research*, Geisinger (1982) repeatedly points out the role contextual factors play in grading and even concludes one of his sections: "Thus, one must be extremely cautious when comparing grades from two or more instructors, GPAs of individuals who major in different disciplines, or GPAs from different colleges" (p. 1147). By this comment, Geisinger clearly and explicitly recognizes grades as a context-dependent phenomenon. We wonder why this insight—so easily documented and understood—has made so little impression on either graders, grading systems, or grade users.

One reason for not accepting Geisinger's conclusion must be that to accept it, and the implications that follow from it, would require a radical reconceptualization of the role of grades in contemporary society. As a nation we are just not ready to do that. Another reason militating against acceptance of grade reforms is that we are a quantitatively oriented and highly competitive society and the notion of tampering with (abolishing) a well-established metric ranking procedure can be seen only as a type of societal heresy of the first order. While both of these reasons undoubtedly have merit, what is of greater importance is that the various imperfections in current grading systems are regarded as problems to be fixed, not as fatal flaws. This is one explanation for the more or less constant tinkering with grading arrangements throughout the academy. What is missing from the nation's evaluation of grades is a proper frame of reference for conceptualizing the magnitude of the problem (and the difficulty of its resolution) if certain known pieces of information are viewed as of central and not of peripheral importance.

The relativistic nature of grades and grade meanings, in both their evaluative and incentive functions, is well recognized by some (for example, Duke, 1983). What is not well recognized is that grades have come to influence educational practice in ways that are detrimental not only to the educational endeavor but to society as a whole. Consider classroom tests. Entirely too few citizens know that many of these tests are not designed to test knowledge but to sort students into presumably socially useful groups. Since sorting is one purpose of testing, we ask trivial questions and rarely ask what it is the student knows. To ask questions that deal with the major facts or concepts in a field and to tell students what these are in advance would do violence to the ranking functions of grades. Instead of telling students what we want them to know and then asking them to show us they know it, we ask them questions better suited to obsessive nitpicking than to critical or creative thinking. Faculties seem not to know that their chief instructional role is to promote learning and not to serve as personnel selection agents for society. We have often wondered why so many instructors will devalue with bad tests what they perceive as the excellence of their teaching.

It is most encouraging that all four groups surveyed want the chief purposes of grades to be that of communicating to students and of serving the cause of teaching and learning. The question, "What do grades presently communicate to students?" must be investigated. In entirely too many instances grades are seen as communicating only self-worth. Speaking from personal experience, it is shattering to have a student who received a B in a course become depressed because to that student the grade of B meant failure as a person. Recall the studies cited in Chapter One concerning the large number of students in high-ranking schools who did not feel capable of pursuing graduate or professional study.

What we need to remember is that students who go to college represent a special subpopulation; to assume that a normal distribution describes their abilities is just flat out wrong. Even if this were valid for some institutions, it says little for the teaching skills of instructors if they make no effort to modify the distribution. It is not a symbol of rigor to have grades fall into a "normal" distribution; rather, it is a symbol of failure—failure to teach well, failure to test well, and failure to have any influence at all on the intellectual lives of students. We should not be adversaries to our students in the educational endeavor; rather we are colleagues at levels of development different from theirs. While it may be an unfortunate fact that we are not all of equal intellect, it is downright absurd to believe that proper teaching can do so little. The notion of a "normal" distribution (or of some other unchanging description of the ability to know new material) is a kind of biological determinism that has little place in institutions oriented toward the continuity of change rather than the immutability of human nature.

It is almost impossible to treat the topic of grades without being impressed by the welter of conflicting attitudes that surround them. Take for example two findings uncovered by our national survey: Some 38 percent of faculty believe that the difference in learning represented by a grade of A and one of C lasts for five years or more, whereas their colleagues in business—and their students—believe that opinion, if not exactly nonsense, is not exactly truth either. Business respondents are not immune to inconsistency: They report that grades provide "a very good indication of ability to get grades" and at the same time are "measures of academic achievement." Although promotions, fortunately, are not often tied to college grades, business recruiters continue to use grades for selection purposes despite the fact that only 11 percent of companies have conducted predictive studies addressing this issue. (We are confident they have not read the research literature or, to use one of their favorite expressions, "the bottom line.")

While it would be possible, at this point, to reemphasize results for learning- and grade-oriented students, or those involving an assessment of grade-incentive values by students having different adaptation levels it seems clear that we are not dealing with a phenomenon amenable to ordinary rational (or even ordinary) analysis. For this reason we must recognize that when it comes to grades, we all tend to choose sides in an either/or manner. In one sense, this is the way we poor mortals do all sorts of things. In another sense, it means that fundamental changes in grade practices will be won only on the basis of extensive and careful research work. College professors are opinionated but they are not witless, and the ultimate confrontation between the yea and nay sayers will be decided by facts and informed opinion rather than by personal opinion alone. Our hope is that the present work will stimulate a reemergence of concern over grades and grading practices on our college and university campuses. We further hope that such a reemergence of concern will be undertaken with an open and not a closed mind.

We will conclude with an additional line to President Lincoln's quotation used in the Preface: "The dogmas of the quiet past are inadequate to the stormy present. . . . We must think anew, act anew. We must disenthrall ourselves."

Appendix A
The National Grade
Survey Questionnaires

There are four questionnaires. Pages 1 through 7 and page 11 of each are identical. The remaining pages of each one are directed to a specific group: students, faculty, parents, business people. (All of the questions for all four groups appear in Appendix B.)

Only the faculty questionnaire is reproduced as Appendix A. Copies of any of the questionnaires may be obtained by contacting: Learning Research Center, University of Tennessee, 1819 Andy Holt Avenue, Knoxville, Tenn. 37996.

ATTITUDES TOWARD GRADES
IN
CONTEMPORARY HIGHER EDUCATION

Ohmer Milton, Ph.D.
James A. Eison, Ph.D.
Howard R. Pollio, Ph.D.

The Learning Research Center, University of Tennessee
Knoxville, Tennessee

One of the most prominent aspects of classroom instruction, at all grade levels, is the assignment of course grades. Though grades and grading practices provide the basis for frequent discussions among students, parents, faculty members, and business people, they seldom have been studied on a large scale or systematically. We invite you now to participate in the first national study of attitudes towards grades in contemporary higher education.

This booklet contains a series of questions designed to explore your personal understanding of, and experiences with, grades. Your help and cooperation, by completing this survey in a careful and candid manner, will assist in developing a clearer picture of the meaning and significance of grades in our society.

Great care has been taken to assure that participants selected for this project represent an accurate national sample. It is therefore extremely important that we receive a completed response from you. We might note that earlier participants reported that completing this survey was both interesting and thought provoking.

Now for a few brief directions:

(1) All answers are to be marked directly in this booklet with a NUMBER 2 PENCIL.
(2) FILL IN BUBBLES COMPLETELY — PLEASE MAKE NO STRAY MARKS.
(3) Allow yourself 30 minutes to complete this survey.
(4) Please return this material promptly following the instructions that appear on the last page of the booklet.

Thank you very much. Should you have any questions regarding this research project, we can be reached at the following address:

Grade Project
Learning Research Center
The University of Tennessee
Knoxville, TN 37996

This research is supported with financial assistance by The Lilly Endowment Inc.

IN ORDER TO CODE THE DATA FROM THESE QUESTIONNAIRES PLEASE PROVIDE
THE FOLLOWING INFORMATION.

Name _____

Sex   ○ Female   ○ Male

Age   ○ 10-19   ○ 20-29   ○ 30-39   ○ 40-49   ○ 50 and greater

EXAMPLES	IMPORTANT DIRECTIONS FOR MARKING ANSWERS
WRONG 1 ① ⊠ ③ ④ ⑤ WRONG 2 ① ② ⊘ ④ ⑤ WRONG 3 ① ② ③ ⬤ ⑤ RIGHT 4 ① ② ③ ⬤ ⑤	• Use black lead pencil only (No. 2 or softer). • Do NOT use ink or ballpoint pens. • Make heavy black marks that fill the circle completely. • Erase cleanly any answer you wish to change. • Make no stray marks on the answer sheet.

PAGE 3

When a college faculty member assigns a final course grade, to whom do you think the grade is addressed primarily? **Please rank order each of the following five audiences with number 1 indicating the primary audience and number 5 indicating the least important audience.**
(PLEASE USE EACH NUMBER ONLY ONCE)

① ② ③ ④ ⑤ the student
① ② ③ ④ ⑤ the student's parent(s)
① ② ③ ④ ⑤ other faculty members
① ② ③ ④ ⑤ prospective employers
① ② ③ ④ ⑤ the official school record

Please rank order each of the following grade reporting systems with number 1 indicating your most preferred choice and number 7 indicating your least preferred choice.
(PLEASE USE EACH NUMBER ONLY ONCE)

① ② ③ ④ ⑤ ⑥ ⑦ percentages (0-100%)
① ② ③ ④ ⑤ ⑥ ⑦ letters with pluses and minuses (A+, A, A-, B+, B, B-, etc.)
① ② ③ ④ ⑤ ⑥ ⑦ letters without pluses and minuses (A, B, C, etc.)
① ② ③ ④ ⑤ ⑥ ⑦ Honors, Satisfactory, Unsatisfactory
① ② ③ ④ ⑤ ⑥ ⑦ Pass/Fail
① ② ③ ④ ⑤ ⑥ ⑦ Pass/No Credit
① ② ③ ④ ⑤ ⑥ ⑦ written narratives

Please indicate how strong a relationship you personally feel there is between the grades a college student receives and how well s/he will do in life. (MARK ONLY ONE)

○ very high   ○ high   ○ moderate   ○ slight   ○ very slight or none

Two students in the same class got different grades from their instructor — one received an A while the other received a C. How long do you think the difference in knowledge (achievement, learning, performance, etc.) represented by the grades A and C will last?

○ 0-3 months   ○ 1-2 years   ○ greater than 5 years
○ 3-12 months   ○ 2-5 years   ○ no real initial difference

Discussions of grades and grading practices suggest that grades serve several purposes. Using the five-point rating scale below, indicate in the <u>LEFT-HAND</u> column the relative importance you believe each purpose currently has in higher education. Then please indicate in the <u>RIGHT-HAND</u> column the degree of importance you would like each purpose to have.

1) of no importance   3) of some (i.e., average) importance   5) of major importance
2) of slight importance   4) of moderate importance

Currently has	Purposes	Should have
① ② ③ ④ ⑤	Communicates to the student how much learning was achieved	① ② ③ ④ ⑤
① ② ③ ④ ⑤	Provides reward (or warning) for outstanding (or unsatisfactory) performance	① ② ③ ④ ⑤
① ② ③ ④ ⑤	Provides student with information for making educational or vocational decisions	① ② ③ ④ ⑤
① ② ③ ④ ⑤	Provides other educational institutions, such as graduate or professional schools, with information for making decisions about the student	① ② ③ ④ ⑤
① ② ③ ④ ⑤	Provides potential employers with information for making decisions about the student	① ② ③ ④ ⑤
① ② ③ ④ ⑤	Provides the instructor information about teaching effectiveness	① ② ③ ④ ⑤
① ② ③ ④ ⑤	Reflects academic standards of a department, college, or university	① ② ③ ④ ⑤
① ② ③ ④ ⑤	Helps maintain academic standards	① ② ③ ④ ⑤
① ② ③ ④ ⑤	Provides historical record of a student's educational experiences and achievement	① ② ③ ④ ⑤

<u>This question continued</u>

PAGE 4

Currently has	Purposes	Should have
① ② ③ ④ ⑤	Helps prepare students for the competitive nature of adult life	① ② ③ ④ ⑤
① ② ③ ④ ⑤	Helps students learn to discipline themselves for later work or job requirements	① ② ③ ④ ⑤
① ② ③ ④ ⑤	Helps remind students that school is really work, not fun	① ② ③ ④ ⑤
① ② ③ ④ ⑤	Provides a way of pleasing parents and meeting their demands	① ② ③ ④ ⑤
① ② ③ ④ ⑤	Affords an accounting to society of how well the university or college is educating its students	① ② ③ ④ ⑤
① ② ③ ④ ⑤	Other, please describe _____	① ② ③ ④ ⑤
① ② ③ ④ ⑤	Other, please describe _____	① ② ③ ④ ⑤

Faculty members employ different procedures for assigning grades. Using this 1-6 scale, please indicate your preference for **each** of the following grading procedures.

1 — I strongly prefer this procedure   4 — I oppose this procedure
2 — I prefer this procedure   5 — I strongly oppose this procedure
3 — I neither prefer nor oppose this procedure   6 — I do not understand the meaning of this procedure

① ② ③ ④ ⑤ ⑥   Fixed Levels — there are fixed levels for each grade category, i.e., 90-100=A; 80-89=B; etc.

① ② ③ ④ ⑤ ⑥   Normal Distribution — a designated percentage of each grade category is based on the bell-shaped curve

① ② ③ ④ ⑤ ⑥   Inspection — instructor reviews scores made by students on each test and then decides about cut-off scores for each letter grade

① ② ③ ④ ⑤ ⑥   Personal Change — a change in the performance of a student is used as the basis for grades. The extent of change is decided by instructor

① ② ③ ④ ⑤ ⑥   Amount of Work Completed — grade is determined by number of tasks completed under a pre-arranged contract system

① ② ③ ④ ⑤ ⑥   Student Self-Grading

① ② ③ ④ ⑤ ⑥   Students Grade Other Students' Work

① ② ③ ④ ⑤ ⑥   Combinations of Two of the Above — please describe _____

① ② ③ ④ ⑤ ⑥   Other Approaches — please describe _____

Please use this 7-point rating scale to describe your personal feeling about each of the grades A through F.

1 — a very, very good grade   5 — a bad grade
2 — a very good grade   6 — a very bad grade
3 — a good grade   7 — a very, very bad grade
4 — a neutral grade (i.e., neither good nor bad)

To me a college grade of: A is   ① ② ③ ④ ⑤ ⑥ ⑦
                              B is   ① ② ③ ④ ⑤ ⑥ ⑦
                              C is   ① ② ③ ④ ⑤ ⑥ ⑦
                              D is   ① ② ③ ④ ⑤ ⑥ ⑦
                              F is   ① ② ③ ④ ⑤ ⑥ ⑦

PAGE 5

Fill in the appropriate bubble to indicate the degree to which you feel _each_ of the following groups should consider changing its emphasis on grades.

Groups	emphasize much more	emphasize somewhat more	No change needed	emphasize somewhat less	emphasize much less
College professors	○	○	○	○	○
Students	○	○	○	○	○
Parents	○	○	○	○	○
Business people	○	○	○	○	○

Indicate the level of schooling you completed:
- ○ less than high school
- ○ high school graduate
- ○ 1-3 years college
- ○ college graduate
- ○ some post graduate work
- ○ M.A.
- ○ M.D., D.D.S.
- ○ Ph.D., Ed.D., J.D.

In general, what type of grades did you receive in each of the following grade levels?

Elementary School
- ○ mostly A's
- ○ mostly B's
- ○ mostly C's
- ○ mostly D's and F's

High School
- ○ mostly A's
- ○ mostly B's
- ○ mostly C's
- ○ mostly D's and F's

Junior High School
- ○ mostly A's
- ○ mostly B's
- ○ mostly C's
- ○ mostly D's and F's

College
- ○ mostly A's
- ○ mostly B's
- ○ mostly C's
- ○ mostly D's and F's

Using the following 5-point scale, please indicate how important grades were to you at each of the educational levels listed below:

1 — of little or no importance
2 — of slight importance
3 — of moderate importance

4 — of great importance
5 — of crucial importance

Educational Levels	Importance	Educational Levels	Importance
Grades 1-6	①②③④⑤	College	①②③④⑤
Grades 7-9	①②③④⑤	Post graduate	①②③④⑤
Grades 10-12	①②③④⑤		

Students report they work for grades to satisfy or please different groups of people. For each of the following grade levels, use the five-point scale below to rate the relative importance each of the following groups of people had (has) _for you._

1 — of little importance
2 — of slight importance
3 — of moderate importance

4 — of great importance
5 — or crucial importance

	Grades 1-6	Grades 7-9	Grades 10-12	College	Post Graduate
Self	①②③④⑤	①②③④⑤	①②③④⑤	①②③④⑤	①②③④⑤
Parents	①②③④⑤	①②③④⑤	①②③④⑤	①②③④⑤	①②③④⑤
Teachers	①②③④⑤	①②③④⑤	①②③④⑤	①②③④⑤	①②③④⑤
Friends	①②③④⑤	①②③④⑤	①②③④⑤	①②③④⑤	①②③④⑤
Future Educational Institution	①②③④⑤	①②③④⑤	①②③④⑤	①②③④⑤	①②③④⑤
Future Employers	①②③④⑤	①②③④⑤	①②③④⑤	①②③④⑤	①②③④⑤

PAGE 6

For each grade level, please fill in the bubble to indicate which of the following action(s) describes <u>your parents'</u> typical response to any <u>good</u> grades or report cards you received. (<u>MARK ALL WHICH APPLY</u>).

	Grade Level			
	1-6	7-9	10-12	College
made no mention of it	○	○	○	○
joked and/or made other appreciative comments	○	○	○	○
remarked that good grades were expected	○	○	○	○
praised and encouraged	○	○	○	○
gave monetary (or other tangible) rewards	○	○	○	○
were supportive, proud	○	○	○	○
said "grades were not worth killing oneself over"	○	○	○	○
discussed the general importance of grades	○	○	○	○
said "You're doing better than I did"	○	○	○	○
asked if I were "turning into a bookworm"	○	○	○	○
reminded that "there is more to life than just good grades"	○	○	○	○
cautioned against getting a "swelled head"	○	○	○	○
said "What is important is that you do your best."	○	○	○	○
other (please specify) _____	○	○	○	○

For each grade level, please fill in the bubble to indicate which of the following action(s) describes <u>your parents'</u> typical response to any <u>bad</u> grades or report cards you received. (<u>MARK ALL WHICH APPLY</u>).

	Grade Level			
	1-6	7-9	10-12	College
made no mention of it	○	○	○	○
asked for an explanation	○	○	○	○
made demeaning jokes	○	○	○	○
gave me "the cold shoulder"	○	○	○	○
expected even less from me in the future	○	○	○	○
were sarcastic	○	○	○	○
accused me of laziness	○	○	○	○
nagged	○	○	○	○
showed anger	○	○	○	○
withdrew privileges	○	○	○	○
lectured to or verbally scolded me	○	○	○	○
administered physical punishment	○	○	○	○
said "What is important is that you do your best"	○	○	○	○
helped me study afterwards	○	○	○	○
told me not to worry	○	○	○	○
other (please specify) _____	○	○	○	○

Did you ever cheat because you wanted a better grade?   ○ yes   ○ no

If "yes" how frequently?   ○ once only   ○ 1-5 times   ○ 6-10 times   ○ 11 or more times

Did you ever drop (or audit) a course because you were afraid of a poor grade?   ○ yes
                                                                                        ○ no

If "yes" how frequently?   ○ once only   ○ 1-5 times   ○ 6-10 times   ○ 11 or more times

PAGE 7

To what extent have you either read about (in magazines, newspapers, etc.) or discussed with others the issues of grade inflation?

- ○ not at all
- ○ a little
- ○ a great deal

How strongly does the issue of grade inflation trouble or concern you?

- ○ Not at all
- ○ Only slightly
- ○ Moderately
- ○ Strongly
- ○ Very strongly

Using this five-point scale (1 — excellent; 2 — good; 3 — fair; 4 — poor; 5 — not at all) please indicate the usefulness of a student's grades or grade point average as an indicator of:

general intelligence	① ② ③ ④ ⑤
academic achievement	① ② ③ ④ ⑤
motivation	① ② ③ ④ ⑤
creativity	① ② ③ ④ ⑤
psychological adjustment	① ② ③ ④ ⑤
communication skill	① ② ③ ④ ⑤
interpersonal skill	① ② ③ ④ ⑤
self-discipline	① ② ③ ④ ⑤
conformity	① ② ③ ④ ⑤
ability to get grades	① ② ③ ④ ⑤
ability to cope with stress	① ② ③ ④ ⑤
ability to work within a system	① ② ③ ④ ⑤
ability to compete	① ② ③ ④ ⑤

In your own words, please describe the manner in which you feel grades have had the greatest impact on your school career or life. (You may want to describe a specific incident, share a general impression, or relate something that came to mind while answering earlier sections of the questionnaire.) Your reactions may be either positive, negative, or both.

DO

NOT

WRITE

IN

THIS

AREA

PAGE 8

How strongly does the fact that you assign grades influence your relationship with students? (MARK ONE)
- ○ little or no influence
- ○ some influence
- ○ moderate influence
- ○ strong influence
- ○ very strong influence

Mark **all** of the following consequences which seem to result from the fact that you assign grades:
- ○ puts me in a position of power over students
- ○ causes students to take my class more seriously
- ○ causes students to put pressure on me to give higher grades
- ○ helps define our roles — mine as an instructor and theirs as students
- ○ makes the student try to meet my requirements
- ○ reminds the student that I must judge (assess) him/her
- ○ helps create a reputation for fairness
- ○ helps create a reputation for having high standards
- ○ helps create a reputation for unfairness
- ○ prevents me from viewing student as friends
- ○ prevents student from viewing me as a friend
- ○ other (please specify) _____

If you were reviewing materials of undergraduate students for admission to graduate school, how strongly would you value each of the following pieces of information. Assign a number from 1 through 7 indicating the degree of importance you place on each with 1 representing minimum value and 7 representing maximum value.

standard test scores (ACT, SAT, GRE, etc.)	①②③④⑤⑥⑦
overall grade point average	①②③④⑤⑥⑦
grades in major courses	①②③④⑤⑥⑦
breadth of courses taken	①②③④⑤⑥⑦
number of difficult courses completed	①②③④⑤⑥⑦
letters of recommendation	①②③④⑤⑥⑦
samples of student writing	①②③④⑤⑥⑦
participation in extra curricular activities	①②③④⑤⑥⑦
nature of non-college jobs held	①②③④⑤⑥⑦
breadth of personal life experiences	①②③④⑤⑥⑦
publications, awards, honors	①②③④⑤⑥⑦
contributions to school	①②③④⑤⑥⑦
personality of student	①②③④⑤⑥⑦
affirmative action needs	①②③④⑤⑥⑦
reputation of previous school attended or of recommenders	①②③④⑤⑥⑦

other (please specify) _____

other (please specify) _____

PAGE 9

In the following list please mark the <u>THREE</u> most important factors which you believe have led to grade inflation.

- ○ faculty wanting to maintain high student enrollments
- ○ faculty showing less concern for maintaining standards
- ○ students being more competitive for grades
- ○ use of pass/fail grading systems
- ○ liberalization in course-withdrawal policies
- ○ students repeating courses more often to raise their grades
- ○ faculty expecting less of students
- ○ students on the whole not being as bright as they used to be
- ○ declining quality of education in elementary and secondary schools
- ○ overcrowded classes forcing a change in grading standards (i.e., lowering standards or giving more F's)
- ○ product of the student movement of the 60's
- ○ other (please specify) _____

_____

Do you think it is necessary to attempt to control grade inflation?
         ○ yes   ○ no

A. — If "yes" for which of the following reasons? (MARK ALL WHICH APPLY)

- ○ because grade inflation dilutes the value of the only reward/feedback system we have for students
- ○ because grade inflation gives students a false concept of their ability and/or performance
- ○ because grade inflation is just another example of lowered standards
- ○ because grade inflation lessens the ability of graduate schools and business to make knowledgeable decisions
- ○ because grade inflation reduces the value of a college degree
- ○ other (please specify) _____

_____

B. — If "no" for which of the following reasons? (MARK ALL WHICH APPLY)

- ○ because nothing can be done
- ○ because grades are detrimental to students anyway
- ○ because there is no real standard against which alleged inflation can be compared
- ○ because grades do not necessarily reflect student ability and/or performance
- ○ because the system will ultimately correct itself
- ○ other (please specify) _____

_____

Do you feel colleges should allow a "forgiveness policy" that enables students to retake failed courses and thus remove F's from their records?
         ○ yes   ○ no

PAGE 10

Have you ever given a student a final course grade on the basis of some information or criterion not used for the remainder of the class?

    ○ yes   ○ no

A. — If "yes", approximately how often? (MARK ONE)

○ only once or twice in several years
○ once or twice per year
○ once or twice per term
○ several times per term

B. — If "yes", for which of the following reasons? (MARK ALL OF WHICH APPLY)

○ physical illness
○ personal crisis (i.e., divorce, death in family, psychological problems, etc.)
○ grade needed for graduation or certification
○ grade needed to maintain athletic eligibility
○ language disability (i.e., foreign language student)
○ other knowledge of student suggested grade did not reflect student's ability
○ knowledge of student's other responsibilities (i.e., student is the sole provider for family)
○ progressive improvement from an exceptionally poor start (i.e., 3 grades of F, C, & C might result in a grade of C)
○ other (please describe) _____

_____

_____

○ other (please describe) _____

_____

_____

Print Name: _____

Rank: _____

Number of years teaching: _____

Department: _____

School Affiliation: _____

PAGE 11

In accordance with Federal Guidelines concerning human research, please read and sign the following statement.

I grant permission to use my answers for research purposes.
I understand that all information will be used anonymously.

Date: _____   Signature: _____

PLEASE PRINT: Name _____

Street Address _____

City _____ State _____ Zip Code _____

Instructions for returning completed questionnaires:

At your earliest convenience, please return your completed questionnaire to:

Grade Project
Learning Research Center
The University of Tennessee
Knoxville, TN 37996

Use the enclosed envelope.

Appendix B
Percent of Responses to Each Feature of Each Item in the National Grade Survey

Common Items:	N = 6,165 respondents
Faculty Items:	N = 854 respondents
Student Items:	N = 4,365 respondents
Parents Items:	N = 584 respondents
Business Items:	N = 362 respondents

When a college faculty member assigns a final course grade, to whom do you think the grade is addressed primarily? Please rank order each of the following five audiences with number 1 indicating the primary audience and number 5 indicating the least important audience.

	Faculty					Students					Parents					Business				
	1	2	3	4	5	1	2	3	4	5	1	2	3	4	5	1	2	3	4	5
	%	%	%	%	%	%	%	%	%	%	%	%	%	%	%	%	%	%	%	%
the student	91	5	1	1	2	83	9	4	2	3	87	10	2	0	1	86	8	1	1	4
student's parents	1	14	18	31	36	3	23	24	25	25	4	38	25	20	14	2	26	24	26	23
other faculty	1	8	20	27	46	2	9	16	25	48	1	7	15	25	53	1	9	19	26	44
prospective employers	3	31	39	19	8	4	25	31	25	15	2	15	28	32	23	1	13	34	31	21
official records	6	40	20	17	17	10	33	25	20	13	10	30	30	19	11	11	40	21	15	13

Please rank order each of the following grade reporting systems with number 1 indicating your most preferred choice and number 7 indicating your least preferred choice.

	Faculty							Students							Parents							Business						
	1	2	3	4	5	6	7	1	2	3	4	5	6	7	1	2	3	4	5	6	7	1	2	3	4	5	6	7
	%	%	%	%	%	%	%	%	%	%	%	%	%	%	%	%	%	%	%	%	%	%	%	%	%	%	%	%
percentages	26	18	29	9	5	6	9	37	23	22	7	4	3	4	43	17	27	6	3	2	4	35	16	34	5	5	2	3
letters with +,-	44	33	10	4	3	5	1	32	37	16	5	4	4	2	37	41	12	4	2	3	2	33	46	11	3	2	2	1
letters no +,-	16	32	34	7	5	2	3	16	23	37	12	5	4	3	12	29	41	10	5	1	3	20	24	37	9	5	4	2
Honors, Sat., Unsat.	5	5	12	49	17	7	5	4	4	8	40	27	11	6	4	5	9	48	26	4	6	5	3	7	52	25	5	3
Pass/Fail	1	2	6	12	43	24	11	3	4	6	15	31	27	14	1	3	3	9	35	35	14	1	3	5	5	40	35	12
Pass/No Credit	2	4	3	5	15	46	25	2	4	4	6	16	40	28	1	1	2	4	11	44	37	2	4	2	2	7	42	42
Written Narrative	7	4	3	10	10	7	59	8	5	6	14	11	9	48	6	3	5	18	15	7	45	7	3	3	22	15	7	44

Please indicate how strong a relationship you personally feel there is between the grades a college student receives and how well s/he will do in life. (MARK ONLY ONE)

	Faculty	Students	Parents	Business
	%	%	%	%
Very High	3	3	7	2
High	34	22	32	33
Moderate	53	54	52	56
Slight	8	17	7	7
Very slight or none	2	4	2	2

Two students in the same class got different grades from their instructor -- one received an A while the other received a C. How long do you think the difference in knowledge (achievement, learning, performance) represented by the grades A and C will last?

	Faculty	Students	Parents	Business
	%	%	%	%
0-3 months	6	21	8	8
3-12 months	15	25	18	23
1-2 years	20	16	15	25
2-5 years	19	7	11	19
greater than 5 yrs.	34	7	22	13
no real initial diff.	8	24	26	11

Discussion of grades and grading practices suggest that grades serve several purposes. Using the five-point rating scale below, indicate in the LEFT-HAND column the relative importance you believe each purpose currently has in higher education. Then please indicate in the RIGHT-HAND column the degree of importance you would like each purpose to have.

1) of no importance
2) of slight importance
3) of some (average) importance
4) of moderate importance
5) of major importance

Currently has

Purposes	Faculty					Students					Parents					Business				
	1	2	3	4	5	1	2	3	4	5	1	2	3	4	5	1	2	3	4	5
	%	%	%	%	%	%	%	%	%	%	%	%	%	%	%	%	%	%	%	%
Communicates to students	2	8	25	32	33	3	12	33	32	20	4	5	26	28	36	3	6	29	32	30
Provides rewards	2	4	13	36	44	3	9	21	33	33	3	6	15	27	50	2	5	16	34	42
Information to students	2	11	36	36	14	5	18	34	28	15	4	15	33	27	22	5	19	32	31	13
Information to educ. inst.	2	4	9	32	53	2	6	14	25	53	4	3	13	25	55	3	4	11	28	54
Information to employers	2	10	30	40	18	3	10	25	38	24	3	10	24	38	25	2	9	25	44	20
Feedback to instructor	12	26	38	18	7	7	21	35	26	11	7	19	34	22	18	9	28	35	21	8
Reflects academic standards	6	18	36	30	11	5	13	30	33	20	5	14	32	26	22	5	21	29	28	18
Maintains academic standards	5	16	34	32	13	3	9	28	38	22	4	10	26	35	26	2	16	31	34	16
Provides historical records	3	7	25	39	27	3	8	23	35	32	5	5	25	32	33	4	6	16	42	33
Prepares students for compet.	6	16	37	29	13	7	17	33	31	13	6	13	35	31	15	6	23	34	27	9
Students learn discipline	3	16	37	34	11	3	13	29	35	20	3	14	31	34	19	3	16	40	32	11
Reminds students	17	18	32	23	10	8	15	29	29	19	10	17	35	23	16	14	22	34	21	9
Pleases parents	22	21	28	20	10	12	16	26	26	20	16	16	27	22	19	11	22	24	29	15
Accounting to society	19	26	31	17	6	6	14	32	32	16	11	17	28	27	17	11	22	32	22	13

Should have

Purposes	Faculty					Students					Parents					Business				
	1	2	3	4	5	1	2	3	4	5	1	2	3	4	5	1	2	3	4	5
Communicates to students	5	3	7	21	65	4	5	15	28	48	5	3	10	23	58	5	5	8	20	62
Provides rewards	4	6	16	32	42	5	8	21	33	34	6	5	14	26	50	3	5	14	28	50
Information to students	3	6	24	40	27	4	8	23	32	34	3	7	21	30	40	3	9	18	38	32
Information to educ. inst.	2	6	21	45	27	3	9	29	40	20	3	6	27	39	25	2	7	28	43	21
Information to employers	3	11	37	36	13	5	14	38	30	13	5	10	36	35	14	3	10	34	38	15
Feedback to Instructor	9	14	31	27	19	4	7	17	32	40	5	5	12	26	53	6	8	18	39	29
Reflects academic standards	7	15	28	28	22	5	11	27	33	24	8	11	22	29	31	6	15	28	30	21
Maintains academic standards	6	10	25	34	26	4	9	24	37	26	6	8	19	33	34	5	12	27	31	25
Provides historical records	4	9	26	36	26	4	10	28	34	24	7	7	23	33	30	3	7	22	37	31
Prepares students for compet.	13	17	30	29	12	7	11	26	31	25	6	11	21	33	28	5	12	27	34	23
Students learn discipline	5	8	20	36	31	3	5	15	35	43	4	5	11	35	45	2	5	14	40	40
Reminds students	36	18	22	17	8	15	15	27	27	16	14	14	25	24	23	18	18	25	27	13
Pleases parents	52	23	17	6	3	31	25	27	12	5	32	22	27	13	7	31	28	29	7	4
Accounting to society	28	23	24	17	8	11	17	31	26	16	16	19	24	24	17	17	22	30	21	10

Facutly members employ different procedures for assigning grades. Using this 1-6 scale, please indicate your preference for each of the following grading procedures.

1 - I stongly prefer this procedure
2 - I prefer this procedure
3 - I neither prefer nor oppose this procedure
4 - I oppose this procedure
5 - I stongly oppose this procedure
6 - I do not understand the meaning of this procedure

Faculty

Procedure	1 %	2 %	3 %	4 %	5 %	6 %
Fixed levels	28	27	21	15	9	1
Normal Distribution	4	14	25	29	27	2
Inspection	15	28	28	15	11	3
Personal Change	4	20	36	24	13	4
Amt. of work completed	6	22	37	21	12	2
Student self-grading	1	4	16	28	45	7
Students grade other students	1	2	13	25	53	7
Combinations of two above	1	4	16	28	45	7
Other approaches	79	13	1	1	6	0

Students

Procedure	1 %	2 %	3 %	4 %	5 %	6 %
Fixed levels	19	37	23	16	6	1
Normal Distribution	16	29	24	16	12	4
Inspection	15	30	29	16	8	3
Personal Change	10	25	29	21	11	4
Amt. of work completed	8	27	36	18	10	2
Student self-grading	3	8	26	31	26	6
Students grade other students	2	5	15	28	45	5
Combinations of two above	3	8	26	31	26	6
Other approaches	54	18	6	3	9	10

Parents

Procedure	1 %	2 %	3 %	4 %	5 %	6 %
Fixed levels	29	37	20	11	3	1
Normal Distribution	14	24	26	17	14	6
Inspection	9	25	32	21	10	4
Personal Change	3	16	32	28	15	6
Amt. of work completed	8	28	39	18	4	3
Student self-grading	1	3	13	39	39	6
Students grade other students	1	2	12	31	49	6
Combinations of two above	1	3	13	39	39	6
Other approaches	47	19	6	8	8	11

Business

Procedure	1 %	2 %	3 %	4 %	5 %	6 %
Fixed levels	26	44	15	10	5	0
Normal Distribution	11	28	26	26	8	1
Inspection	11	19	30	23	14	3
Personal Change	2	16	32	27	17	6
Amt. of work completed	6	28	39	17	7	2
Student self-grading	1	2	14	33	45	4
Students grade other students	0	3	13	32	50	3
Combinations of two above	1	2	14	33	45	4
Other approaches	50	27	14	0	0	9

Please use this 7-point rating scale to describe your personal feeling about each of the grades A through F.

1 - a very, very good grade
2 - a very good grade
3 - a good grade
4 - a neutral grade (neither good or bad)
5 - a bad grade
6 - a very bad grade
7 - a very, very bad grade

Faculty

To me a college grade of	1 %	2 %	3 %	4 %	5 %	6 %	7 %
A is:	46	50	3	1	0	0	0
B is:	1	29	68	3	0	0	0
C is:	0	0	16	73	10	0	0
D is:	0	0	0	3	73	22	1
F is:	0	0	0	1	6	44	49

Students

To me a college grade of	1 %	2 %	3 %	4 %	5 %	6 %	7 %
A is:	55	37	7	0	0	0	0
B is:	3	33	56	8	0	0	0
C is:	0	1	20	55	22	1	0
D is:	0	0	1	8	50	32	10
F is:	0	0	0	1	10	25	64

Parents

To me a college grade of	1 %	2 %	3 %	4 %	5 %	6 %	7 %
A is:	61	36	3	0	0	0	0
B is:	3	46	51	1	0	0	0
C is:	0	1	29	62	7	1	0
D is:	0	0	1	13	63	19	4
F is:	0	0	0	1	13	31	55

Business

To me a college grade of	1 %	2 %	3 %	4 %	5 %	6 %	7 %
A is:	52	45	3	0	0	0	0
B is:	1	35	61	3	0	0	0
C is:	0	0	21	70	8	0	0
D is:	0	0	0	7	69	21	4
F is:	0	0	0	1	12	32	55

Fill in the appropriate bubble to indicate the degree to which you feel each of the following groups should consider changing its emphasis on grades.

Groups	Emphasize Much More				Emphasize Somewhat More				No Change Needed				Emphasize Somewhat less				Emphasize Much Less			
	Fac. %	Stud. %	Par. %	Bus. %	Fac. %	Stud. %	Par. %	Bus. %	Fac. %	Stud. %	Par. %	Bus. %	Fac. %	Stud. %	Par. %	Bus. %	Fac. %	Stud. %	Par. %	Bus. %
Faculty	5	6	6	10	27	19	25	31	47	47	47	36	19	26	20	21	2	3	3	2
Students	9	15	16	18	29	41	43	46	21	22	28	22	33	17	12	13	9	4	2	1
Parents	3	3	5	5	11	9	19	13	30	35	32	36	42	39	36	37	14	13	9	9
Business	3	3	3	3	16	14	15	15	44	37	37	37	30	38	38	41	6	8	8	5

Indicate the level of schooling you completed:

	Faculty %	Students %	Parents %	Business %
Less than H. S.	0	0	1	0
High Sch. Grad.	0	13	22	1
1-3 yr. College	1	74	26	8
College Grad.	0	8	15	32
Some post-grad.	2	3	13	28
M.A.	27	1	17	29
M.D./D.D.S.	1	0	3	0
Ph.D., Ed.D., J.D.	70	0	4	3

In general, what type of grades did you receive in each of the following grade levels?

	Elementary School				Junior High School				High School				College			
	Fac. %	Stud. %	Par. %	Bus. %	Fac. %	Stud. %	Par. %	Bus. %	Fac. %	Stud. %	Par. %	Bus. %	Fac. %	Stud. %	Par. %	Bus. %
Mostly A's	68	57	58	57	60	48	50	45	61	43	42	39	61	23	32	25
Mostly B's	26	34	32	34	31	40	37	45	31	45	46	46	37	54	54	61
Mostly C's	6	9	10	8	8	11	12	10	8	12	13	14	3	23	13	14
Mostly D's and F's	0	0	0	1	1	0	1	0	1	1	0	0	0	1	1	0

Using the following 5-point scale, please indicate how important grades were to you at each of the educational levels listed below:

1 - of little or no importance
2 - of slight importance
3 - of moderate importance
4 - of great importance
5 - of crucial importance

Education Level	Faculty					Students					Parents					Business				
	1 %	2 %	3 %	4 %	5 %	1 %	2 %	3 %	4 %	5 %	1 %	2 %	3 %	4 %	5 %	1 %	2 %	3 %	4 %	5 %
Grades 1-6	17	35	25	17	6	18	21	31	22	9	13	13	33	32	9	16	16	27	30	11
Grades 7-9	7	14	40	33	7	5	15	44	29	7	3	12	40	37	8	2	13	44	32	10
Grades 10-12	4	9	33	40	14	4	8	31	42	16	2	5	39	42	12	1	7	36	43	12
College	1	4	27	50	18	1	4	19	45	31	3	3	33	50	11	1	5	31	52	11
Post-Grad.	5	8	22	40	26	4	4	17	34	41	6	8	25	42	20	3	7	27	42	22

Students report they work for grades to satisfy or please different groups of people. For each of the following grade levels, use the five-point scale below to rate the relative importance each of the following groups of people had (has) for you.

1 - of little importance
2 - of slight importance
3 - of moderate importance
4 - of great importance
5 - of crucial importance

Grades 1-6

	Faculty					Students					Parents					Business				
	1%	2%	3%	4%	5%	1%	2%	3%	4%	5%	1%	2%	3%	4%	5%	1%	2%	3%	4%	5%
Self	14	14	37	27	8	16	19	35	21	9	8	14	35	35	8	16	17	32	25	10
Parents	5	8	30	44	14	4	7	25	42	22	4	9	29	43	14	3	6	25	42	23
Teachers	8	8	35	39	11	9	13	35	34	10	4	11	36	40	9	4	7	34	39	15
Friends	32	26	30	10	2	27	25	30	15	4	24	26	32	16	2	23	27	29	15	6
Future Ed. Inst.	62	15	12	8	2	53	19	16	8	4	52	14	19	12	2	60	15	12	8	5
Future Employment	77	10	9	3	1	67	14	12	5	3	66	10	16	6	2	80	10	5	3	2

Grades 7-9

	Faculty					Students					Parents					Business				
	1%	2%	3%	4%	5%	1%	2%	3%	4%	5%	1%	2%	3%	4%	5%	1%	2%	3%	4%	5%
Self	4	13	39	35	9	5	12	42	31	10	1	10	39	40	9	3	12	45	32	9
Parents	3	7	35	43	13	2	5	28	46	19	4	5	34	45	11	1	5	28	47	19
Teachers	5	9	38	38	10	8	14	40	31	7	5	9	42	38	6	2	10	38	39	12
Friends	25	25	35	12	3	19	24	36	17	4	17	28	38	15	2	14	26	36	19	4
Future Ed. Inst.	46	19	20	11	3	30	23	27	15	6	35	21	24	17	3	40	21	23	10	5
Future Employment	68	14	13	5	1	47	21	21	8	3	54	17	18	9	2	71	16	9	3	2

continued on next page

Grades 10-12

	Faculty					Students					Parents					Business				
	1	2	3	4	5	1	2	3	4	5	1	2	3	4	5	1	2	3	4	5
Self	3	7	29	45	17	3	6	28	44	20	1	4	31	51	14	1	6	35	47	12
Parents	3	8	33	44	12	3	6	29	44	18	3	6	34	48	10	1	4	29	49	16
Teachers	6	10	35	39	10	8	14	39	31	8	4	13	38	39	7	3	10	37	41	9
Friends	22	21	37	17	4	17	22	37	20	5	17	24	40	18	2	8	22	47	19	4
Future Ed. Inst.	13	8	22	37	20	7	7	23	39	25	11	8	26	41	16	7	6	21	43	22
Future Employment	38	15	30	15	2	19	14	31	27	9	25	14	33	22	5	31	19	31	16	4

College

	Faculty					Students					Parents					Business				
	1	2	3	4	5	1	2	3	4	5	1	2	3	4	5	1	2	3	4	5
Self	1	3	20	51	25	1	2	14	46	37	2	1	23	56	18	0	4	27	52	17
Parents	9	13	38	29	6	7	11	30	35	18	9	13	38	34	6	8	12	33	37	9
Teachers	8	14	36	35	7	14	20	34	26	8	10	17	40	28	6	8	18	41	27	6
Friends	24	22	37	16	2	20	22	34	19	5	22	29	33	15	1	14	31	39	15	1
Future Ed. Inst.	7	6	18	42	28	5	5	17	39	35	12	10	20	38	19	11	9	24	37	20
Future Employment	13	8	25	41	13	5	4	20	41	31	10	7	30	39	14	6	7	24	49	14

Post-Graduate

	Faculty					Students					Parents					Business				
	1	2	3	4	5	1	2	3	4	5	1	2	3	4	5	1	2	3	4	5
Self	2	4	16	42	35	3	3	12	35	47	3	5	18	44	30	1	5	19	45	30
Parents	31	24	27	15	4	12	13	26	28	21	29	21	29	18	5	28	24	29	12	7
Teachers	11	13	30	33	12	12	17	30	26	15	15	19	31	22	10	17	21	33	21	9
Friends	33	27	27	15	4	22	18	34	17	9	33	27	27	10	4	37	26	21	13	3
Future Ed. Inst.	23	9	16	30	22	10	7	13	30	39	20	12	16	31	21	30	12	20	17	20
Future Employment	11	7	22	36	24	5	3	15	31	46	11	8	25	38	19	13	6	20	38	22

For each grade level, please fill in the bubble to indicate which of the following action(s) describes your parents' typical response to any bad grades or report cards you recieved. (MARK ALL WHICH APPLY.)

	Grades 1-6				Grades 7-9				Grades 10-12				College			
	Fac. %	Stud. %	Par. %	Bus. %	Fac. %	Stud. %	Par. %	Bus. %	Fac. %	Stud. %	Par. %	Bus. %	Fac. %	Stud. %	Par. %	Bus. %
no mention	13	9	10	5	13	6	10	4	14	8	12	6	23	11	14	16
explanation	31	42	36	47	35	53	39	56	34	53	39	54	14	35	17	31
demeaning jokes	0	2	1	0	1	3	1	0	—	3	1	0	—	2	0	0
"cold shoulder"	0	2	1	0	1	3	1	—	—	3	1	—	—	2	0	—
expected less	1	1	0	0	1	2	1	0	0	3	1	—	0	2	0	0
sarcastic	1	3	1	2	1	4	2	—	—	6	2	2	—	3	0	—
accused of lazy	4	12	5	8	6	18	7	10	6	21	8	11	2	13	2	7
nagged	3	8	2	4	5	13	3	6	5	15	3	6	2	9	2	3
showed anger	3	10	6	5	5	13	7	8	5	13	6	9	2	6	2	4
withdrew privileges	3	12	6	11	5	14	7	15	4	12	8	9	0	3	—	1
lectured to	8	16	12	18	11	20	16	23	11	20	16	18	2	10	4	8
physical punish.	1	4	2	2	1	3	2	—	—	2	1	—	0	2	0	—
"do your best"	23	33	29	31	25	36	31	33	27	41	33	35	22	43	22	30
helped me study	16	23	22	26	1	3	1	—	—	3	1	—	—	2	0	—
don't worry	7	11	8	10	7	12	7	10	6	15	8	11	7	19	7	16

For each grade level, please fill in the bubble to indicate which of the following action(s) describes your parents' typical response to any good grade or report cards you recieved. (MARK ALL WHICH APPLY).

	Grades 1-6				Grades 7-9				Grades 10-12				College			
	Fac. %	Stud. %	Par. %	Bus. %	Fac. %	Stud. %	Par. %	Bus. %	Fac. %	Stud. %	Par. %	Bus. %	Fac. %	Stud. %	Par. %	Bus. %
no mention	8	9	9	7	6	6	7	4	7	7	8	4	16	9	12	10
joked	19	24	17	18	21	26	19	19	20	27	18	22	16	22	9	16
good grades expected	29	31	30	35	32	37	30	38	33	40	30	37	19	28	14	22
praised	69	69	65	74	69	67	59	71	64	66	57	67	49	61	37	56
rewards	14	28	13	20	12	22	10	14	11	16	9	11	7	9	4	5
supportive	58	61	55	62	60	62	59	66	62	65	58	69	58	63	43	62
"grades not worth"	2	6	1	3	4	8	2	3	5	12	2	5	6	20	3	11
general importance	11	20	15	21	17	26	18	29	18	34	21	32	10	26	9	17
"You're doing better"	5	8	6	6	5	10	7	9	8	16	9	11	7	14	6	9
"bookworm"	1	2	1	1	1	2	1	1	2	4	2	1	3	5	1	3
"more to life"	1	3	1	2	1	4	2	2	3	9	4	4	6	16	4	8
"swelled head"	3	3	1	3	3	4	2	2	5	6	2	4	3	5	1	3
"do your best"	31	42	35	41	32	44	37	44	33	50	41	46	29	53	27	42

Did you ever drop (or audit) a course because you were afraid of a poor grade?

	Faculty %	Students %	Parents %	Business %
Yes	30	47	18	40
No	70	53	82	60

If "yes", how frequently?

	Faculty %	Students %	Parents %	Business %
once only	51	53	74	46
1-5 times	48	45	26	53
6-10 times	1	2	0	1
11 +	0	1	0	1

How strongly does the issue of grade inflation trouble or concern you?

	Faculty %	Students %	Parents %	Business %
not at all	6	22	15	8
only slightly	16	21	17	20
moderately	36	35	39	38
strongly	30	18	23	25
very strongly	12	4	6	9

Did you ever cheat because you wanted a better grade?

	Faculty %	Students %	Parents %	Business %
Yes	36	56	34	42
No	64	44	66	58

If "yes", how frequently?

	Faculty %	Students %	Parents %	Business %
once only	34	14	29	19
1-5 times	57	61	58	61
6-10 times	4	13	10	14
11 +	5	12	3	6

To what extent have you either read about (in magazines, newspapers, etc.) or discussed with others the issues of grade inflation?

	Faculty %	Students %	Parents %	Business %
not at all	3	42	32	16
a little	51	48	52	60
a great deal	46	9	16	24

Using this five point scale (1 - excellent; 2 - good; 3 - fair; 4 - poor; 5 - not at all) please indicate the usefulness of a student's grades or grade point average as an indicator of:

	Faculty					Students					Parents					Business				
	1 %	2 %	3 %	4 %	5 %	1 %	2 %	3 %	4 %	5 %	1 %	2 %	3 %	4 %	5 %	1 %	2 %	3 %	4 %	5 %
general intelligence	5	41	39	12	3	5	29	39	20	7	13	40	32	10	5	4	41	41	12	3
academic achievement	35	48	12	3	2	31	43	19	6	2	39	45	12	3	1	39	45	12	3	1
motivation	24	47	20	4	3	21	39	25	11	4	27	43	23	5	2	16	44	27	9	4
creativity	2	12	37	33	17	3	14	31	32	20	5	18	35	24	19	1	9	32	39	18
psychological adjustment	3	16	39	29	15	4	16	37	27	16	4	19	40	22	15	2	12	33	33	20
communication skill	9	37	36	13	5	5	26	39	21	10	9	37	34	14	6	5	22	39	24	12
interper. skill	2	13	34	30	21	3	18	35	29	16	5	22	36	22	15	1	8	29	37	26
self-discipline	22	47	21	7	2	23	42	23	9	4	26	47	21	5	1	17	49	27	5	2
conformity	9	29	36	18	9	9	25	40	17	9	11	33	35	15	6	9	28	39	16	8
to get grades	40	36	17	5	2	31	35	22	8	4	36	36	18	7	3	42	38	14	5	2
to cope with stress	5	30	37	21	8	8	27	34	20	11	7	28	30	23	12	4	14	41	25	15
to work within system	17	47	25	9	2	15	40	30	11	5	20	44	27	6	4	12	42	35	8	3
to compete	16	43	30	9	2	17	35	30	12	6	20	42	27	8	4	12	40	35	10	4

Faculty

Have you ever given a student a final course grade on the basis of some information or criterion not used for the remainder of the class?

    Yes=52%   No=48%

    If Yes, approximately how often? (mark one)

        only once or twice in several years 66%

        once or twice per year   26

        once or twice per term   6

        several times per term   3

    If Yes, for which of the following reasons? (MARK ALL THAT APPLY)

        personal crisis (divorce, death in the family,
          psychological problems, so on)   27%

        physical illness   19

        grade needed for graduation or certification   6

        grade needed to maintain athletic eligibility   1

        other knowledge of student suggested grade did not
          reflect student's ability   15

        language disability (foreign language student)   13

        knowledge of student's other responsibilities
          (student is sole provider for family)   4

        progressive improvement from an exceptionally poor
          start (3 grades of F, C, & C might result
          in a grade of C)   28

        other   7

Do you feel colleges should allow a "forgiveness policy" that enables students to retake failed courses and thus remove Fs from their records?

    Yes=66%   No=34%

Business

When comparing the grade point averages of interviewees from different
schools, how much importance do you place on the reputation of each
educational institution?

little=7%; slight=8%; moderate=41%; great=42%; crucial=2%

In general is there a minimum grade point average or cutoff score used
by your company for initial hiring of recent college graduates?

If "yes," please indicate which one (assume A=4.0, B=3.0, etc.)
3.50=0.5%, 3.25=2%; 3.00=26%; 2.75=19%; 2.50=28%; 2.25=7%; 2.00=19%
less than 2.0=0.5.

When conducting employment interviews, do you ever ask interviewees to
explain their grades to you?

Always-9%; Often=28%; Sometimes=41%; Rarely=15%; Never=7%

How would you react to an interviewee who said that his/her grades did
not give a good indication of ability?

accept the explanation with reservations	21%
accept the explanation with some reservations	33
accept the explanation with moderate reservations	29
accept the explanation with strong reservations	15
dismiss the explanation totally	3

Has your company conducted any studies relating college grades to on-
the-job performance?

Yes=11%   No=89%

If "yes," what did you find?

grades were excellent predictors of job performance	24%
grades were good predictors of job performance	42
grades were fair predictors of job performance	24
grades did not predict job performance at all	10

Please fill in the appropriate bubbles to indicate the extent to which
college grades and grade point averages influence the following decisions
made by your company.

Decisions	Extent of Influence				
	of little imp.	of slight imp.	of moderate imp.	of great imp.	of crucial imp.
initial hiring	4%	12%	46%	35%	3%
initial salary	37	20	28	14	2
selection for special training programs	37	27	21	13	2
subsequent promotions	59	26	13	2	0

Business-Faculty

In the following list, please mark the THREE most important factors which you believe have led to grade inflation.

	B	F
faculty wanting to maintain high student enrollments	38%	41%
faculty showing less concern for maintaining standards	40	32
students being more competitive for grades	23	23
use of pass/fail grading systems	14	13
liberalization of course-withdrawal policies	14	34
students repeating courses more often to raise grades	10	11
faculty expecting less of students	41	53
students on the whole not being as bright	2	4
declining quality of education in elem. & sec. schools	43	41
overcrowded classes forcing a change in grading standards	16	6
product of the student movement of the 60s	16	22

Do you think it necessary to attempt to control grade inflation?

	B	F
Yes	75	79
No	11	15

If "yes," for which of the following reasons? (MARK ALL THAT APPLY)

	B	F
because grade inflation dilutes the value of the only reward/feedback system we have for students	56%	51%
because grade inflation gives students a false concept of their ability and/or performance	64	51
because grade inflation is another example of lowered standards	46	40
because grade inflation lessens the ability of graduate schools and businesses to make knowledgeable decisions	67	47
because grade inflation reduces the value of a college degree	48	46

If "no," for which of the following reasons? (MARK ALL THAT APPLY)

	B	F
because nothing can be done	2%	2%
because grades are detrimental to students anyway	2	2
because there is no real standard against which alleged inflation can be compared	9	11
because grades do not necessarily reflect student ability and/or performance	16	8
because the system will ultimately correct itself	7	2

When you are reviewing materials of recent college graduates for employment in your firm (If you were reviewing materials fo undergraduate students for admission to graduate school), how strongly would you value each of the following pieces of information? Assign a number from 1 to 7 indicating the degree of importance you place on each with 1 representing minimum value and 7 representing maximum value.

		1	2	3	4	5	6	7
standard test scores (ACT, GRE, etc)	B	40%	13%	12%	17%	13%	5%	2%
	F	3	5	8	19	33	24	9
overall grade point average	B	5	3	10	20	30	23	10
	F	1	4	7	15	38	29	6
grades in major courses	B	6	2	6	10	25	38	14
	F	2	3	4	5	21	42	23
breadth of courses taken	B	3	4	14	24	28	23	5

		1	2	3	4	5	6	7
	F	2	3	8	15	32	29	11
number of difficult courses completed	B	6	9	13	25	24	18	5
	F	3	3	6	14	28	33	14
letters of recommendation	B	11	17	21	22	18	9	3
	F	3	6	10	18	24	24	15
samples of student writing	B	10	16	16	24	16	14	4
	F	4	5	9	14	25	26	18
participation in extra curricular act.	B	5	6	11	22	30	21	5
	F	12	13	22	23	20	8	2
nature of non-college jobs held	B	1	5	6	17	33	28	11
	F	9	17	22	23	19	8	3
breadth of personal life experiences	B	1	6	14	21	31	20	8
	F	7	11	16	27	22	13	5
publications, awards, honors	B	2	3	12	17	41	21	5
	F	2	5	9	18	31	26	9
.ontributions to the school	B	9	11	15	26	25	12	3
	F	11	13	17	26	20	11	2
personality of student	B	1	3	3	10	24	40	20
	F	7	9	16	21	28	14	5
affirmative action needs	B	8	8	15	31	23	13	3
	F	23	13	19	24	14	6	3
reputation of school attended or of recommenders	B	3	4	10	21	33	21	8
	F	2	5	10	20	30	23	10

Faculty-Students

How strongly does the fact that you assign grades influence your relationship
with students (MARK ONE). How strongly does the fact that faculty members
are required to grade students influence your relationship with them? (MARK ONE)

little or no influence	some influence	moderate influence	strong influence	very strong influence
F 14%	30%	32%	20%	4%
S 25	23	32	17	3

Mark all of the following consequences which seem to result from the fact that you assign grades (you feel result from the fact that faculty members grade students)

	F	S
puts me in a position of power over students	43%	
puts faculty in a position of power over students		64%
causes students to take my class more seriously	56	
causes students to take classes more seriously		59
causes students to put pressure on me to give higher grades	33	
causes students to put pressure on faculty to give higher grades		17
helps define our roles--mine as inst., theirs as students	46	
helps define our roles--mine as a student, theirs as faculty		48
makes the student try to meet my requirements	71	
makes the student try to meet the instructor's requirements		73
reminds the student that I must judge (assess) him/her	55	
reminds the student that faculty must judge (assess) him/her		50
helps create a reputation for fairness	49	
creates a reputation of fairness for the faculty member		23
helps create a reputation for having high standards	52	
creates a reputation of having high standards for the f. m.		24
helps create a reputation for unfairness	7	
created a reputation of unfairness for the faculty member		20
prevents me from viewing students as friends	12	
prevents students from viewing faculty members as friends		25
prevents students from viewing me as a friend	18	
prevents faculty members from viewing students as friends		19

Students

What year are you in school?

Fr.=28%; Soph.=25%; Jr.=21%; Senior=19%; Other=7%

What is your present (or future major?)

Social Science. . . .11%		Nursing. 7%	
Natural Science. . . 13		Communications. . .3	
Humanities. 5		Agriculture. . . . 1	
Fine Arts. 2		Home Economics. . .1	
Business. 23		Undecided. 5	
Education 6		Other... 7	
Engineering.. 7			

To what degree are you satisfied/happy with your present grade point average?

Very, very unhappy=4%	Neutral=21%	Happy-29%
Very unhappy=7%		Very Happy=11%
Unhappy=27%		Very, very happy=3%

ACT (composite) mean = 23.29   SAT (composite) mean = 1137.40

What letter grade do you consider to be a good grade?

A= 48%; B=49%; C=3%; D=0; F=0

What letter grade do you consider to be a bad grade?

A=0; B=1%; C=27%; D=54%; F=18%

What was (or is) considered a good grade in your family?

A=45%; B=50%; C=5%; D=0; F=0

What was (or is) considered a bad grade in your family?

A=0; B-1%; C=25%; D=57%; F=18%

How important do you think your family's attitude toward grades is in determining your attitude toward grades?

extremely unimp.	unimp.	neither imp. nor unimp.	important	extremely imp.
4%	7%	18%	55%	16%

What do other people in your major consider a good grade?

A=51%; B=46%; C=4%; D=0; F=0

What do other people in your major consider a bad grade?

A=0; B=2%; C=29%; D=52%; F=17%

How important are the attitudes toward grades of people in your major in determining your attitudes toward grades?

extremely unimp.	unimp.	neither imp. nor unimp.	important	extremely imp.
8%	21%	33%	32%	6%

Parents-Students

Personal data given by parents about college-age student and data given by students:

Age:	P	S		P	S
Less than 18	1%	1%	22-25	20%	18%
18	10	13	26-35		10
19	24	20	26 and older	1	
20	24	19	36 and older		4
21	21	16			

Grade-point-averages: (Assume A=4.0, B=3.0, so forth; the two groups were provided different categories)

	P	S		P	S
less than 2.0	1%	2%	3.00-3.49	35%	32%
2.01-2.49	.9	14	3.50-4.00	28	23
2.50-2.99	23	26	I don't know	5	3

How closely did (do) you pay attention to your child's grades for each of the following grade levels? How closely did (do) your parent's pay attention to your grades for each of the following grade levels? (MARK ONE FOR EACH LEVEL)

Grade	Very Closely		Closely		Moderately		Slightly		Not at all	
	P	S	P	S	P	S	P	S	P	S
K-3	48%	32%	33%	31%	17%	25%	2%	9%	1%	3%
4-6	47	31	37	36	14	26	2	6	0	1
7-9	48	28	39	42	12	25	0	4	0	1
10-12	52	32	37	38	11	23	0	6	0	1
Coll.	39	26	33	30	24	25	4	12	1	7

For each of the following grade levels, how often did (do) you ask about the grades earned by his/her friends? For each of the following grade levels, how often did (do) your parents ask about grades earned by your friends. (MARK ONE FOR EACH LEVEL)

Grade Level	Never		Rarely		Sometimes		Often		Always	
	P	S	P	S	P	S	P	S	P	S
K-3	53%	53%	26%	28%	17%	13%	3%	4%	1%	2%
4-6	44	47	30	31	21	16	4	5	1	2
7-9	34	38	30	29	27	23	7	7	1	2
10-12	29	35	32	27	29	24	8	11	1	3
Coll.	48	44	25	25	20	20	6	8	1	3

Before your child was in college, did s/he ever tell you that s/he was graded unfairly? Before you were in college, did you ever tell your parents that you were graded unfairly? (MARK ONE)

	Parents	Students
Yes	79%	65%
No	21	35

If "yes," which of the following actions did you take? If "yes", which of the following actions did they take? (MARK ALL THAT APPLY)

	P	S
told the child (you) to discuss it with his/her (your) teacher	67%	42%
spoke to the child's (your) teacher	38	20
spoke to some other school personnel (counselor, principal)	17	9
told the child (you) the grade did not matter all that much	10	7

	P	S
told the child (you) the teacher is probably the best judge in such matters	9%	10%
ignored the (your) complaint	3	5
wrote a letter to the teacher	3	3
wrote a letter to the principal	2	1
wrote a letter to the school board	0	0
wrote a letter to the newspaper	0	0
spoke to an attorney	0	0
spoke to the parents of other students (children in the class)	13	6
told the child there was nothing she/he or I could do about it (you or they could do about it)	3	7
offered sympathy to the child (you sympathy)	30	19
contacted a public official (major, legislator, so forth)	1	0
other	5	4

Now that your child is in college has s/he ever told you that s/he was
graded unfairly? Now that you are in college, have you ever told your parents
that you were graded unfairly? (MARK ONE)

	Parents	Students
Yes	50%	39%
No	50	61

If "yes", how did you (they) handle it? (MARK ALL THAT APPLY)

	P	S
told the child (you) to discuss it with her/his teacher (with your instructor)	44%	29%
spoke to the student's (your) instructor	2	2
spoke to some other school personnel (advisor, dean, so forth)	3	1
told the student (you) the grade did not matter all that much	4	4
told the child (you) the instructor is probably the best judge in such matters	4	3

	P	S
ignored the (your) complaint	2%	2%
wrote a letter to the instructor	0	0
wrote a letter to the department head	1	0
wrote a letter to the governing board	0	0
spoke to an attorney	0	0
spoke to the parents of other students (in the class)	0	0
told the child (you) there was nothing she/he or I (they or you) could do about it	4	4
offered sympathy	17	13
contacted a public official (for example, a legislator)	0	0
other	2	3

Parents

Did you ever discuss your child's grades with his/her teacher?

Grade Level	a) Never	b) During regular conferences only	c) Only when bad grade received	Both b & c	b & c and more often
K-3	11%	69%	2%	11%	8%
4-6	9	66	3	15	8
7-9	13	57	5	17	8
10-12	25	45	8	17	5
College	85	11	2	2	1

For each of the following grade levels, how do (did) you typically react when your child received a good grade? (MARK ALL THAT APPLY)

	Grades 1-6	Grades 7-9	Grades 10-12	College years
made no mention of it	1%	1%	1%	2%
joked and/or made other appreciative comments	23	24	24	22
remarked that good grades were expected	19	21	22	19
praised and encouraged	87	86	83	79

	Grades 1-6	Grades 7-9	Grades 10-12	College years
gave monetary (or other tangible) rewards	22%	19%	16%	6%
was supportive, proud	76	75	77	74
said grades were not worth killing oneself over	1	2	3	4
discussed the general importance of grades	25	32	38	30
said, "You're doing better than I did"	6	8	13	12
asked if he/she were "turning into a bookworm"	0	1	2	1
reminded that there is more to life than just good grades	2	4	8	9
cautioned against getting a "swelled head"	2	2	3	2
said, "What is important is that you do your best"	51	51	51	58
other	2	2	3	3

For each of the following grade levels, how do (did) you react when your child received a _bad_ grade? (MARK ALL THAT APPLY)

	Grades 1-6	Grades 7-9	Grades 10-12	College years
made no mention of it	3%	2%	2%	3%
asked for an explanation	54	57	60	45
made demeaning jokes	0	1	1	1
gave my child "the cold shoulder"	0	0	0	0
expected even less in the future	0	0	1	0
was sarcastic	1	1	1	1
accused my child of laziness	5	8	8	4
nagged	2	5	6	3
showed anger	4	6	8	3
withdrew privileges	9	13	13	2

	Grades 1-6	Grades 7-9	Grades 10-12	College years
lectured to or verbally scolded my child	12%	17%	17%	8%
administered physical punishment	1	1	0	0
said, "What is important is that you do your best"	44	45	47	48
helped my child study afterwards	47	46	33	7
told my child not to worry	12	11	12	13
other	7	7	8	8

Appendix C
General Structure of Categories Used to Record Classroom Behavior

I. State categories
   Attentive
   Nonattentive
II. Event categories

A. *On-Target*

Note taking, consistent
Note taking, intermittent
Note taking, mirrored
Question, spontaneous
Answer, prompted
   by instructor
Answer, spontaneous

Hand raising (spontaneous
   and prompted)
Class-related material
   (reading)
Interpersonal behavior
   (with instructor)
Laughing (with instructor)
Smiling (at instructor)

B. *Off-Target*

Fidgeting
Conversing
Relaxing
Noninterpersonal behavior

Sleeping
Nonclass-related material
   (reading)

Watch checking

Eating/drinking

Laughing (with peer)
Smiling (at peer)
Doodling

Appendix D
Categories Used to Code
Self-Report Protocols

   I. Teaching event
  A.   1. Actively listening and absorbing
        2. Relating material to other material or own life
        3. Forming opinions, evaluations, ideas about materials
        4. Taking notes and understanding
        5. Participating in class discussion
        6. Rehearsing questions or comments about material
        7. Listening and attempting to understand
  B.   1. Listening, but so confused it makes no sense
        2. Listening, but passively—just hearing words
        3. Taking notes and not understanding
        4. Other
  C.   1. Teacher
  II. Other focused
     Observing or thinking about:
       1. Same sexed classmate
       2. Opposite sexed classmate
       3. Thinking about girlfriend/boyfriend
       4. Thinking about other class, school in general
       5. Thinking about this class
       6. Other person
 III. Time focused
     Thinking about:

    1. Something earlier today
    2. Something else later today
    3. Something later this week
    4. Something in the past week
    5. Something more than a week ago
    6. Another class
    7. Something in more distant future
    8. How much time is left
    9. Other

IV. Body/self focused
    1. Feeling hungry, thinking of food
    2. Feeling sleepy, fighting sleep
    3. Feeling need to go to bathroom
    4. Feeling sick, nauseated, and so on
    5. Meditating
    6. Sleeping
    7. Hearing music in head
    8. Totally spaced, nowhere, blank
    9. Feeling warm/cold
    10. Other

V. Fantasy focused (must include specific verb to indicate fantasy)
    1. Sports
    2. Achievement (being a star, president, and so on)
    3. Marital, male-female relationship
    4. Sex
    5. Food

VI. Activity focused (doing something)
    1. Studying
    2. Writing a letter
    3. Reading
    4. Drawing/doodling
    5. Making a list or schedule
    6. Talking to someone
    7. Calculating (money, calories, and so on)
    8. Other

VII. Mood focused
    1. Thinking bad things about class

       2. Being bored
       3. Worrying about this course, school in general
       4. Worrying about social relationship (boy/girlfriend, spouse, family, friend, and so on)
       5. Worrying about other
       6. Worrying about being called on
       7. Other mood content
VIII. Environmental event
       1. Something in the classroom environment
       2. Something else in environment (decor, scene outside, a sound, a smell)
  IX. Experimental event (waiting for the bell to sound)

References

Aiken, L. R. "The Grading Behavior of a College Faculty." *Educational and Psychological Measurement,* 1963, *23,* 319–322.

Alpert, R., and Haber, R. "Anxiety in Academic Achievement Situations." *Journal of Abnormal and Social Psychology,* 1960, *61,* 207–215.

American College Testing Program. *College Student Profiles: Norms for the ACT Assessment.* Iowa City: American College Testing Program, 1966.

Arreola, R. A. "Grading Practices and Grade Inflation at Florida State University." Unpublished paper, Florida State University, Tallahassee, 1978.

Astin, A. "Freshmen Characteristics and Attitudes." *Chronicle of Higher Education,* February 17, 1982, pp. 11–12.

Averill, L. *Learning to Be Human: A Vision for the Liberal Arts.* Port Washington, N. Y.: Associated Faculty Press, 1983.

Balch, J. "The Influence of the Evaluating Instrument on Students' Learning." *American Educational Research Journal,* 1964, *1,* 169–182.

Becker, H., Geer, E., and Hughes, E. *Making the Grade: The Academic Side of College Life.* N. Y.: Wiley, 1968.

Berger, P. I., and Luckmann, T. *The Social Construction of Reality.* N. Y.: Anchor Books, 1967.

Birnbaum, R. "Factors Related to University Grade Inflation." *Journal of Higher Education,* 1977, *48,* 519–539.

Bob, M. L. "Multiple Choice Is No Choice." *National Forum,* in press.

Bowers, W. J. *Student Dishonesty and Its Control in College.* Cooperative Research Project 1672, USOE. N. Y.: Bureau of Applied Social Research, Columbia University, 1964.

271

Brazziel, W. "Waiting for the Older Student." *AAHE Bulletin,* 1985, *37* (6), 8–9.

Brown, W., and Holtzman, W. *The Survey of Study Habits and Attitudes Manual.* N. Y.: The Psychological Corporation, 1967.

Burwen, L. S. *National Grading Survey.* San Francisco: Office of Institutional Research, San Francisco State University, 1971.

Cattell, R., Barton, K., and Dielman, T. "Prediction of School Achievement from Motivation, Personality, and Ability Measures." *Psychological Reports,* 1972, *30,* 35–43.

Cattell, R., Eber, H., and Tatsuoka, M. *Handbook for the Sixteen Personality Factor Questionnaire.* Champaign, Ill.: Institute for Personality and Ability Testing, 1974.

Chickering, A. W. "Grades: One More Tilt at the Windmill." *AAHE Bulletin,* 1983, *35* (8), 10–13.

Class, E. "The Effect of the Kind of Test Announcement on Students' Preparation." *Journal of Educational Research,* 1935, *28* (5), 358–361.

Claxton, E. S., and Ralston, Y. *Learning Styles: The Impact on Teaching and Administration.* Research report no. 10. Washington, D. C.: American Association of Higher Education, 1978.

Collins, J., and Nickel, K. *Grading Policies in Higher Education: The Kansas Study/The National Survey.* Wichita: Wichita State University Bulletin, University Studies, no. 103, 1975.

Cross, P. "Creativity." *Research Reporter, II,* no. 2. Berkeley: Center of Research and Development in Higher Education, University of California, 1967.

Cross, P. *Beyond the Open Door: New Students to Higher Education.* San Francisco: Jossey-Bass, 1971.

Cullen, F., and others. "The Effects of the Use of Grades as Incentive." *Journal of Educational Research,* 1975, *68* (7), 277–279.

Cureton, L. W. "The History of Grading Practices." *Measurement in Education,* 1971, *2* (4), 1–9.

Curtis, F., and Woods, G. "A Study of the Relative Teaching Values of Four Common Practices in Correcting Examination Papers." *School Review,* 1929, *37,* 615–623.

Davis, J. *Great Aspirations.* Chicago: Aldine, 1964a.

Davis, J. *Summary of Major Findings from the College Student Characteristics Study.* Princeton, N. J.: Educational Testing Service, 1964b.

Douglass, H. R., and Talmadge, M. "How University Students Prepare for New Types of Examinations." *School and Society*, 1934, *39*, 318–320.

Dressel, P. *Evaluation in Higher Education*. Boston: Houghton-Mifflin, 1961.

Dressel, P. "Grades: One More Tilt at the Windmill." In A. W. Chickering (Ed.), *Bulletin*. Memphis: Memphis State University, Center for the Study of Higher Education, Dec., 1983.

Duke, J. D. "Disparities in Grading Practice, Some Resulting Inequities, and a Proposed New Index of Academic Achievement." *Psychological Reports*, 1983, *53*, 1023–1080.

Eison, J. "The Development and Validation of a Scale to Assess Differing Student Orientations Toward Grades and Learning." Unpublished doctoral dissertation, Department of Psychology, University of Tennessee, Knoxville, 1979.

Eison, J. "A New Instrument for Assessing Students' Orientations Toward Grades and Learning." *Psychological Reports*, 1981, *48*, 919–924.

Eison, J. "Educational and Personal Dimensions of Learning-Grade Oriented Students." *Psychological Reports*, 1982, *51*, 867–870.

Eison, J., Pollio, H. R., and Cunningham, P. "Testing Preferences of Learning- and Grade-Oriented University Students." *Teaching of Psychology*, in press.

Eison, J., Pollio, H. R., and Milton, O. *LOGO II: A User's Manual*. Knoxville: Learning Research Center, University of Tennessee, 1982.

Eison, J., Pollio, H. R., and Milton, O. "Educational and Personal Characteristics of Four Different Types of Learning- and Grade-Oriented Students." *Contemporary Educational Psychology*, in press.

Eizler, C. "The Meaning of College Grades in Three Grading Systems." *Educational Research Quarterly*, 1983, *8*, 12–20.

Eizler, C., and Stancato, F. A. "Effects of Course Content and Intended Audience on the Affective Meaning of College Grades." *College Student Journal*, 1981, *15*, 8–21.

Entwistle, N. "Personality and Academic Attainment." *British Journal of Educational Psychology*, 1972, *42* (2), 137–151.

Erickson, S. "Grading Evaluation." *Memo to the Faculty,* no. 46. Ann Arbor: Center for Research on Learning and Teaching, University of Michigan, 1971.

Evans, E., Dodson, P., and Bailey, D. "Assessment of Psychology Instructors' Perceptions and Use of Textbook Test-Item Manuals for Measuring Student Achievement." *Teaching of Psychology,* 1981, *8* (2), 88–90.

Fowler, T. (Ed.). *Locke's Conduct of the Understanding.* N. Y.: Macmillan, 1890.

Frederiksen, N. "The Real Test Bias: Influences of Testing on Teaching and Learning." *American Psychologist,* 1984, *39* (3), 193–202.

Fuhrmann, B., and Grasha, A. *A Practical Handbook for College Teachers.* Boston: Little, Brown, 1983.

Geisinger, K. F. "Who Are Giving All Those A's?" *Journal of Teacher Education,* 1980, *31* (2), 11–15.

Geisinger, K. F. "Marking Systems." *Encyclopedia of Educational Research,* 1982, *3,* 1139–1149.

Geisinger, K. F., and Rabinowitz, W. "Individual Differences Among College Faculty in Grading." *Journal of Instructional Psychology,* 1982, *1,* 20–27.

Geisinger, K. F., Wilson, A. N., and Naumann, J. J. "A Construct Validation of Faculty Orientations Toward Grading Comparative Data from Three Institutions." *Educational and Psychological Measurement,* 1980, *40,* 413–417.

Giorgi, A. *Psychology as a Human Science.* N. Y.: Harper & Row, 1970.

Goldberg, L. "Grades as Motivants." *Psychology in the Schools,* 1965, *2,* 17–23.

Goldman, R. D. "Hidden Opportunities in the Prediction of College Grades for Different Subgroups." *Journal of Educational Measurement,* 1973, *10,* 205–210.

Goldman, R. D. "Grading Practices in Different Major Fields." *American Educational Research Journal,* 1974, *11,* 343–357.

Goldman, R. D., and Hewitt, B. N. "Adaptation Level as an Explanation for Differential Standards in College Grading." *Journal of Educational Measurement,* 1975, *12,* 149–161.

Goldman, R. D., Schmidt, D. E., Hewitt, B. N., and Fisher, R.

"Grading Practices in Different Major Fields." *American Education Research Journal*, 1974, *11*, 343–357.

Goldman, R. D., and Slaughter, R. E. "Why College Grade Point Average Is Difficult to Predict." *Journal of Educational Psychology*, 1976, *68*, 9–14.

Grose, R. "The Grading Game." *College and University*, 1975, 723–737.

Hadamard, J. *The Psychology of Invention in the Mathematical Field*. Princeton, N. J.: Princeton University Press, 1945.

Hargadon, F. A. "Responding to Charges of Test Misuse in Higher Education." In C. Daves (Ed.), *The Uses and Misuses of Tests: Examining Current Issues in Educational and Psychological Testing*. San Francisco: Jossey-Bass, 1984.

Hartog, P., and Rhodes, E. C. *An Examination of Examinations*. London: Macmillan, 1935. (See also Hartog, P., and Rhodes, E. C. *The Marks of Examiners*. London: Macmillan, 1936. Cited in Rowntree, D. *Assessing Students: How Shall We Know Them?* N. Y.: Harper & Row, 1977.)

Heidegger, M. *Being and Time*. N. Y.: Harper & Row, [1927] 1962.

Helson, H. "Adaptation Level as a Basis for a Quantitative Theory of Frame of Reference." *Psychological Review*, 1948, *55*, 297–313.

Helson, H. *Adaptation Level Theory*. N. Y.: Harper & Row, 1964.

Hewitt, R. *The Status of Pass-Fail Options at Twenty-Two Colleges and Universities*. Amherst: Office of Institutional Studies, University of Massachusetts, 1967.

Hinckley, E. D., and Rethlingshafer, D. "Value Judgment of Heights of Men by College Students." *Journal of Psychology*, 1951, *31*, 257–262.

Hobbs, J. "Grading versus Teaching." *Improving College and University Teaching*, 1974, *22* (4), 239–243.

Hofstadter, R. *Anti-Intellectualism in American Life*. N. Y.: Vantage, 1966.

Hoyt, D. *The Relationship Between College Grades and Adult Achievement*. Iowa City: American College Testing Program, 1965.

Huntley, J. "Academic Evaluation and Grading." *Harvard Educational Review*, 1976, *46*, 612–631.

Hutchins, R. M. *The Higher Learning in America.* New Haven: Yale University Press, 1936.

Ihde, D. *Experimental Phenomenology.* N. Y.: Putnam, 1977.

James, W. *The Principles of Psychology.* N. Y.: Dover, [1891] 1950.

Jedrey, C. M. "Grading and Evaluation." In M. M. Gullette (Ed.), *The Art and Craft of Teaching.* Cambridge: Harvard University Press, 1984.

Johnston, J., and Simon, S. "Grading: Past Practices and Future Possibilities." In L. Fraley and E. Vargas (Eds.), *Proceedings of the Third National Conference on Behavior and Technology in Higher Education.* Atlanta: Georgia State University, 1976.

Kirchbaum, H., Simon, S., and Napier, R. *Wad-ja-get?* N. Y.: Hart, 1971.

Kline, M. *Mathematics: The Loss of Certainty.* Oxford: Oxford University Press, 1980.

Klinger, E. "Modes of Normal Conscious Flow." In Pope, K., and Singer, J. L. (Eds.), *The Stream of Consciousness.* N. Y.: Plenum, 1978.

Koen, F., and Ericksen, S. *An Analysis of the Specific Features Which Characterize the More Successful Programs for the Recruitment and Training of College Teachers.* Final Report to the U. S. Office of Education, Project no. S-482. Ann Arbor: Center for Research on Learning and Teaching, University of Michigan, January, 1967.

Lavin, D. *The Prediction of Academic Performance.* N. Y.: Wiley, 1965.

Learning Research Center. "Teaching Assistants: A Beleaguered Lot." *Teaching-Learning Issues,* no. 10. Knoxville: University of Tennessee, 1969.

Levenson, H. "Differentiating Among Internality, Powerful Others, and Chance." In H. Lefcourt (Ed.), *Research with the Locus of Control Construct, I.* N. Y.: Academic Press, 1981.

Lindquist, V. R. *Northwestern Endicott Report, 1984.* Evanston, Ill.: The Placement Center, Northwestern University, 1983.

Lindquist, V. R. *Northwestern Endicott Report, 1985.* Evanston, Ill.: The Placement Center, Northwestern University, 1984.

Lunneborg, P. *College Grades: What Do Professors Intend to Communi-*

cate? Seattle: Assessment Center, University of Washington, 1977.

McBeth, Paul E., Jr., et al. v. Dr. Monty Elliott, et al. Circuit Court of Oregon for Jackson County, 1978.

McCall, W. *Measurement.* N. Y.: Macmillan, 1939.

McKeachie, W. "Students, Groups, and Teaching Methods." *American Psychologist,* 1958, *13,* 580–584.

McMillan, J. "Perceptions versus Potential of Multiple-Choice Tests." In Franz, R., Hopkins, R., and Toma, A. (Eds.), *Proceedings: Southern Marketing Association of 1979 Conference.* Lafayette: University of South West Louisiana Press, 1979.

Maxey, E. J., and Ormsby, V. J. *The Accuracy of Self-Report Information Collected on the ACT Test Battery.* Document no. 45. Iowa City: American College Testing Program, July, 1971.

Mentzer, T. "Response Biases in Multiple-Choice Tests." *Educational and Psychological Measurement,* 1982, *42,* 437–443.

Merleau-Ponty, M. *The Phenomenology of Perception.* London: Routledge & Kegan Paul, 1962.

Meyer, M. "The Grading of Students." *Science,* 1908, *28* (712), 243–250.

Miller, S. *Measure, Number, and Weight.* Berkeley: Select Committee on Education, University of California, 1966.

Milton, O. *Alternatives to the Traditional: How Professors Teach and How Students Learn.* San Francisco: Jossey-Bass, 1972.

Milton, O. *Will That Be on the Final?* Springfield, Ill: Charles C. Thomas, 1982a.

Milton, O. "Will That Be on the Final?" Paper presented at annual meeting of American Psychological Association, Washington, D. C., August, 1982b.

Milton, O., and Edgerly, J. *The Testing and Grading of Students.* New Rochelle: Change Publications, 1976.

Milton, O., and Eison, J. *Textbook Tests: Guidelines for Item Writing.* N. Y.: Harper & Row, 1983.

Myers, I. B. *The Myers-Briggs Type Indicator Manual.* Palo Alto: Consulting Psychologists Press, 1962.

National Center for Education Statistics. "High School Course Grade Standards." *NCES Bulletin.* Washington: U. S. Office of Education, November, 1984.

Nelson, A. *Undergraduate Academic Achievement in College as an Indicator of Occupational Success.* Washington, D. C.: Bureau of Policies and Standards, P.S. 75–5, United States Civil Service Commission, 1975.

Newman, F. *Higher Education and the American Resurgence.* Princeton: Carnegie Foundation for the Advancement of Teaching, 1985.

Odell, C. W. *Traditional Examinations and New Type Tests.* N. Y.: Century, 1928.

Oltman, P. K., and Hartnett, R. T. "The Role of Graduate Record Examinations in Graduate Admission." *Journal of Higher Education,* 1985, *56* (5), 523–537.

Osgood, C. E., Suci, G., and Tannenbaum, P. H. *The Measurement of Measure.* Urbana: University of Illinois Press, 1957.

Page, E. "Teacher Comments and Student Performance: A Seventy-Four Classroom Experiment in School Motivation." *Journal of Educational Psychology,* 1958, *49* (4), 173–181.

Penner, J. G. *Why Many College Teachers Cannot Lecture.* Springfield, Ill.: Charles C. Thomas, 1984.

Pollio, H. R. "Intuitive Thinking." In Underwood, G., and Stevens, R. (Eds.), *Aspects of Consciousness.* London: Academic Press, 1980.

Pollio, H. R. *Behavior and Existence.* Monterey, Calif.: Brooks/Cole, 1982.

Pollio, H. R., Eison, J. E., and Milton, O. "College Grades as an Adaptation Level Phenomenon." *American Journal of Psychology,* in press.

Pollio, H. R., and others. *Manual for the Coding of Student Self-Report Protocols.* Knoxville: Learning Research Center, University of Tennessee, 1984.

Polezynski, J., and Shirland, L. "Expectance Theory and Contract Grading Combined as an Effective Motivational Force for College Students." *Journal of Educational Research,* 1977, *70,* 238–241.

Quann, C. J. *Grades and Grading: Historical Perspectives and the 1982 AACRO Study.* Washington, D. C.: American Association of Collegiate Registrars and Admission Officers, 1984.

Riechmann, S., and Grasha, A. "A Rational Approach to Developing and Assessing the Construct Validity of a Student Learning Style Scales Instrument." *Journal of Psychology*, 1974, *87*, 213–223.

Sassenrath, J., and Garverick, C. "Effects of Differential Feedback from Examinations on Retention and Transfer." *Journal of Educational Psychology*, 1965, *56* (5), 259–263.

Saudergas, R., and Creed-Murrah, U. *State-Event Classroom Observation System*. Knoxville: Department of Psychology, University of Tennessee, 1980.

Semb, G., and Spencer, R. "Beyond the Level of Recall: An Analysis of Higher Order Educational Tasks." In L. Fraley and E. Vargas (Eds.), *Proceedings of the Third National Conference on Behavior and Technology in Higher Education*. Atlanta: Georgia State University, 1976.

Sherman, T. M. "Learning Improvement Programs: A Review of Controllable Influences." *Journal of Higher Education*, 1985, *56* (1), 85–100.

Smallwood, M. L. *An Historical Study of Examinations and Grading Systems in Early American Universities*. Cambridge: Harvard University Press, 1935.

Snyder, B. *The Hidden Curriculum*. N. Y.: Knopf, 1970.

Spencer, R. E., and Stallings, W. *The Improvement of College-Level Student Achievement Through Changes in Classroom Examination Procedures*. USOE Project no. 6-1174. Urbana: University of Illinois, 1970.

Stancato, F. A., and Eizler, C. F. "When a 'C' Is not a 'C': The Psychological Meaning of Grades in Educational Psychology." *Journal of Instructional Psychology*, 1983, *10*, 158–162.

Starch, D., and Elliott, E. C. "Reliability of Grading High School Work in English." *School Review*, 1912, *20*, 442–457.

Starch, D., and Elliott, E. C. "Reliability of Grading Work in Mathematics." *School Review*, 1913a, *21*, 254–259.

Starch, D., and Elliott, E. C. "Reliability of Grading Work in History." *School Review*, 1913b, *21*, 676–681.

Stimmel, B. "The Use of Pass/Fail Grades to Assess Academic Achievement and House Staff Performance." *Journal of Medical Education*, 1975, *50*, 657–661.

Strong, F. Dean of freshmen at California Institute of Technology, Pasadena. Personal correspondence to O. Milton, March 7, 1967.

Tennessee Higher Education Commission. *The Competent College Student*. Nashville: Tennessee Higher Education Commission, 1977.

Terry, P. W. "How Students Study for Three Types of Objective Tests." *Educational Research*, 1934, *27*, 333–343.

Thistlethwaite, D. *Effects of College upon Student Achievement*. Cooperative Research Project #D-098, USOE. Nashville: Vanderbilt University, 1965.

Thorndike, R. L., and Hagen, E. P. *Measurement and Evaluation in Psychology and Education*. N. Y.: Wiley, 1977.

Trani, E. *Helping Students Become More Sophisticated Consumers of Their Own Education*. FIPSE Project. Lincoln: University of Nebraska, June, 1979.

U.S. Department of Education. *Involvement in Learning: Realizing the Potential of American Higher Education*. Washington, D. C.: Study Groups on the Conditions of Excellence in American Higher Education, National Institute of Education, U. S. Department of Education, 1984.

Van Den Berg, D. *The Changing Nature of Man*. N. Y.: Dell, 1961.

Warren, J. *College Grading Practices: An Overview*. Washington, D. C.: ERIC, Report no. 9, 1971.

Wexley, K., and Thornton, C. "Effect of Verbal Feedback of Test Results upon Learning." *Journal of Educational Research*, 1972, *66* (3), 119–121.

Zimmerman, J. "What Motivates Students?" *Journal of Higher Education*, 1956, *27*, 449–543.

Index

A

"Academic bankruptcy," 10
"Academic forgiveness," 10
Achievement Anxiety Text, 127, 128
Adaptation Level Theory: academic discipline and, 41–42, 196; defined, 41, 178; examples demonstrating, 178–180; formula, 181; grade valuation and, 180–193; grade-point-average and, 186–187, 191–193; and interinstitutional grade valuation, 193–195; National Grade Survey and, 189–193; University of Tennessee survey and, 183–186
A-F system: origin of, 4; predominance of, 9
Aiken, L. R., 29, 271
Alpert, R., 127, 128, 134, 271
American Association of College Registrars and Admissions Officers (AACRAO), report by, 35
American Association of University Professors (AAUP), statement of, 222
American College Test (ACT) scores, and grade-point-average, 29–32, 113–116, 186–187, 191–193
American College Testing Program, survey by, 8, 271
Arreola, R. A., 33, 271
Assimilation, and grade meaning, 197–198

Association of American Colleges (AAC), statement of, 222
Astin, A., 271
Auditing courses, 66–67, 138–139
Averill, L., 222, 271

B

Bailey, D., 20, 274
Bakke, 16
Balch, J., 169, 271
Barton, K., 129, 272
Becker, H., 19, 125, 271
Berger, P. I., 157, 271
Birnbaum, R., 33, 271
Bob, M. L., 205, 271
Boulding, K., 13
Bowers, W. J., 271
Brazziel, W., 218, 272
Brown, W., 127, 128, 134, 272
Burwen, L. S., 29, 272
Business: complaints about student language skills, 82–83; implications of LOGO II results for, 147–148; responsibility of, in promoting learning, 147; studies relating grades to performance, 87. See also National Grade Survey, Personnel selection

C

Cattell, R., 127, 129, 134, 272
Characteristics, indicated by grades, 68–70
Cheating, 66, 138–139

281